Palgrave Studies in Ethics and Public Policy

Series Editor
Thom Brooks
Durham Law School
Durham University
Durham, UK

Palgrave Studies in Ethics and Public Policy offers an interdisciplinary platform for the highest quality scholarly research exploring the relation between ethics and public policy across a wide range of issues including abortion, climate change, drugs, euthanasia, health care, immigration and terrorism. It will provide an arena to help map the future of both theoretical and practical thinking across a wide range of interdisciplinary areas in Ethics and Public Policy.

More information about this series at
http://www.palgrave.com/gp/series/14631

Molly Gardner · Michael Weber
Editors

The Ethics of Policing and Imprisonment

palgrave
macmillan

Editors
Molly Gardner
Bowling Green State University
Bowling Green, OH, USA

Michael Weber
Bowling Green State University
Bowling Green, OH, USA

Palgrave Studies in Ethics and Public Policy
ISBN 978-3-030-07400-5 ISBN 978-3-319-97770-6 (eBook)
https://doi.org/10.1007/978-3-319-97770-6

This Palgrave Macmillan imprint is published by the registered company Springer Nature Switzerland AG
The registered company address is: Gewerbestrasse 11, 6330 Cham, Switzerland

Contents

Notes on Contributors

Thom Brooks is a Dean of Durham Law School and Chair in Law and Government at Durham University, UK. He is the author of *Punishment* (2012), *Hegel's Political Philosophy* (2013, 2d) and *Becoming British* (2016) and an advisor to the UK's Labour Party on immigration law and policy.

Christian Coons is an Associate Professor of Philosophy at Bowling Green State University. His research focuses on theory selection in normative ethics, moral epistemology, the nature of value, and the structural relationship between normative concepts. He has published work in each of the major sub-fields of moral philosophy: applied ethics, normative ethics, axiology, metaethics, political, and legal theory.

Stephen Darwall teaches philosophy at Yale University and writes about the foundations and history of ethics. His books include *The Second-Person Standpoint* (2006), *Welfare and Rational Care* (2002), *The British Moralists and the Internal 'Ought'* (1995), and *Impartial Reason* (1983). Recently, two collections of his essays have appeared: *Morality, Authority, and Law* (2013) and *Honor, History, and Relationship* (2013).

William Darwall is a doctoral student in Jurisprudence and Social Policy at the University of California, Berkeley Law School studying epistemology, social ontology, political economy, and democratization.

Amanda Gailey is an Associate Professor in the Department of English at the University of Nebraska-Lincoln. She teaches and writes on

American literature and digital humanities and is a gun control and academic freedom activist. She is the author of *Proofs of Genius: Collected Editions from the American Revolution to the Digital Age* (2015).

Molly Gardner is an Assistant Professor of Philosophy at Bowling Green State University. She has written about our duties to future generations, the rights of nonhuman animals, the non-identity problem, and the metaphysics of harming and benefiting.

Lori Gruen is the William Griffin Professor of Philosophy at Wesleyan University. She is the author and editor of ten books, one of which is *The Ethics of Captivity* (2014) that contains a chapter co-authored by Pierce, Meikle, and three other incarcerated men. Gruen has been teaching and learning from incarcerated students for over ten years.

Douglas Husak is Distinguished Professor of Philosophy and Law at Rutgers University. He is the author of over one hundred essays, book chapters, and monographs, including *Ignorance of Law* (2016), *Overcriminalization* (2008), and *Drugs and Rights* (1992). He is the former Editor-in-Chief of *Law and Philosophy* and the present Editor-in-Chief of *Criminal Law and Philosophy*. He is Co-Director of the Institute for Law and Philosophy at Rutgers University.

Mariam Kazanjian is a philosophy Ph.D. Student at Indiana University and a Dolores Zohrab Liebmann Fellow. Her dissertation research focuses on moral ignorance and moral responsibility and has won the Oscar R. Ewing Graduate Essay Award. She has been involved in prison teaching since 2015 and believes that her best work has been inspired by the stories of her friends and students at the Indiana Women's Prison.

Richard L. Lippke is a Professor in the Department of Criminal Justice at Indiana University. He is the author of four books and numerous articles on punishment theory, criminal law, criminal procedure, and sentencing. His most recent book was *Taming the Presumption of Innocence* (2016).

Clyde Meikle has been incarcerated in a maximum-security prison since 1994. He has been enrolled in college courses since 2009 and currently serves as a mentor to younger incarcerated men.

Julinna Oxley is a Professor of Philosophy at Coastal Carolina University. Her research and teaching interests are in applied ethics, feminist philosophy, political philosophy, and moral psychology. She is particularly interested in analyzing the ethical issues that are a result of oppression, the nature of social change, understanding how emotions change beliefs, and political virtue.

Andre Pierce has been incarcerated in a maximum-security men's prison since 1996. He has been studying philosophy and taking other college courses since 2009. He is the author of two other chapters as well as op-eds.

Steven Swartzer is a Teaching Assistant Professor of Philosophy at the University of North Carolina at Chapel Hill and outreach director for UNC-Chapel Hill's Parr Center for Ethics. He also serves on the Executive Committee of the National High School Ethics Bowl—an educational program that encourages teens to engage with each other in philosophically rigorous, collaborative discussions about controversial ethical issues.

Michael Weber is a Professor of Philosophy at Bowling Green State University. He has written about rational choice theory and the role of emotions in both ethical life and ethical theory. More recently he has been working on issues in egalitarian theory.

Introduction

Molly Gardner and Michael Weber

Two aspects of criminal justice have been at the forefront of American politics in the recent years. The first is police officers' use of deadly force, which came under increased public scrutiny as videos emerged, often taken by bystanders with smart phones, of people—primarily black men—being injured and killed by police officers under dubious circumstances. The second is the scope of the prison system. In the last 40 years, even as the crime rate has fallen, the rate of incarceration in the United States has increased by more than 500%,[1] with the result that the United States now incarcerates more people per capita than any other nation.[2] The number of people the United States detains before trial is, itself, greater than the number of people who are either detained or imprisoned in most other countries.[3] This problem of sheer numbers is compounded by a problem of race: a disproportionate number of those who are detained or imprisoned belong to a racial minority. And although racial inequalities in the prison system have started to diminish

M. Gardner (✉) · M. Weber
Bowling Green State University, Bowling Green, OH, USA
e-mail: mollyg@bgsu.edu

M. Weber
e-mail: meweber@bgsu.edu

M. Gardner and M. Weber (eds.), *The Ethics of Policing and Imprisonment*, Palgrave Studies in Ethics and Public Policy,
https://doi.org/10.1007/978-3-319-97770-6_1

over the past few years, black men, in particular, are still six times more likely to be imprisoned than white men.[4]

If we were asked to imagine a morally desirable system of criminal justice, we would not imagine the features sketched above. But what would a better system of criminal justice look like? The question might initially appear paradoxical because in an ideal society, everyone would behave justly, and we would not need a system of criminal justice. So to determine how we ought to reform our current institutions, we cannot compare them to a perfect ideal. But the alternative to a perfect ideal is not the real world, as it is. There is a whole continuum of ways our society could be better than it is now, but less than perfect. Part of the challenge, then, in evaluating our criminal justice system is to determine how far we should go in our idealization: to what less-than-perfect standard should we compare various features of the current system?[5]

In other work on the ethics of the criminal justice system, philosophers operate at a relatively high level of idealization. They do not suppose that everyone behaves justly, but they do suppose, for example, that wrongdoers act freely, or that agents of the state act impartially, or that the harms of punishment affect only those we mean to punish—that these harms do not have significant collateral consequences for families, communities, or whole systems of racial and socioeconomic oppression. This level of abstraction is appropriate insofar as the focus is on whether punishing wrongdoers can be justified in principle, and if so, whether that justification can be grounded in retributivism, consequentialism, or some other theory. But this level of abstraction is less helpful when it comes to assessing the criminal justice system, as it is. For that, we need to know, not only whether punishment by the state can be justified in principle, but also whether it has any unanticipated, morally significant consequences in practice. If so, how should those consequences be weighed against the case for punishment? We also need to attend to other features of the criminal justice system, such as policing tactics and pre-trial detention. These other parts of the system are theoretically distinct from punishment, but they can also have harmful effects that must be weighed against the case for the system they are part of.

In this volume, the contributors consider the ways in which non-ideal features of our actual circumstances—features such as the prevalence of guns in America, political pressures, considerations of race and gender, and the lived experiences of people in jails and prisons—impinge upon the conclusions we might have drawn from more idealized models of punishment and law enforcement. There are a number of common themes running throughout the chapters. One is the aforementioned contrast between ideal theorizing and the real circumstances we are in. Another is the attention to harmful consequences, not only of prisons themselves, but also to the events that often precede incarceration, including encounters with police and pre-trial detention. A third theme is the legacy of racism in the United States and the role that the criminal justice system plays in perpetuating racial oppression. In the remainder of this introduction, we will preview each chapter in relation to these themes.

The theme of real versus ideal theorizing is most prominent in Steven Swartzer's chapter, which uses disenfranchisement as a case study in non-ideal penal theory. Swartzer argues that in an ideal society free of racial oppression, suspending a convicted criminal's voting rights might well be a morally justified form of punishment. However, in some of the states where convicted criminals are disproportionately African American, this form of punishment has the effect of disenfranchising more than 20% of the adult African-American population. This, as Swartzer points out, is a consideration that tells very strongly against the moral permissibility of disenfranchisement as a punishment, even though such a consideration would be obscure from an ideal perspective.

The contrast between ideal theory and real circumstances is also apparent in Mariam Kazanjian's chapter, written in collaboration with six women in a prison college program, which attempts to reconcile ideal theories of punishment with the lived experience of these women. Kazanjian and her incarcerated students Lori Record, Anastazia Schmid, Cynthia Long, Jennifer Fleming, D'Antonette Burns, and Andrea Hubbell focus specifically on whether the philosophical literature on punishment accurately captures their sense of what rights they have lost and what rights they have retained. Although the students have some sympathy for both retributive and consequentialist theories of punishment, neither theory fully captures their sense that "despite their criminal histories, they retain both their dignity and their right to a second chance." Kazanjian concludes the chapter with an argument that her students' views are most closely aligned with the "mixed" theory of punishment advanced by John Locke.

The next four chapters are focused more directly on the harms associated with policing, jails, and prisons. Christian Coons draws our attention to the police shootings in the news and raises the question of whether the shootings we take to be unjustified are representative. He then suggests a formula we can use to estimate how many police shootings are justified and how many are "tragic mistakes"—i.e., shootings of individuals who posed no mortal threat. According to his formula, police officers would probably be justified in shooting approximately 80 people per year. However, the actual number of police shootings per year is many times higher than this. Coons concludes that "at least 830 people die unnecessarily at the hands of law enforcement each year, and 740 more than even a minimal standard of justice could accept."

In her contribution to this volume, Julinna Oxley argues that some of the problems with current policing practices can be traced to an inadequate conception of what the police are supposed to do. According to this "law and order" conception, the job of police officers is to stop and deter crime. Those who adhere to this conception are unduly susceptible to the norms of toxic masculinity. Adherence to the law and order model also perpetuates oppression and erodes social trust. In place of the law and order model, Oxley argues for a "community guardian" model of policing. Grounded in feminist care ethics, the community guardian model emphasizes the importance of community connections, effective communication, and transparency. Oxley argues that acceptance of such a model might help decrease violence and rebuild social trust.

Douglas Husak focuses on the police practice known as "stop, question and frisk" (SQF), which has been employed extensively in New York City. Many critics of the policy argued that police officers were using SQF disproportionately in neighborhoods that had higher percentages of minorities. In using SQF in this way, the officers were thought to be discriminating against people on the basis of their race; thus, critics argued that SQF should be abolished. Nevertheless, Husak cautions that there is a danger in taking racial discrimination to be a decisive objection to SQF. For even if SQF causes discriminatory harms, it may also have important benefits, many of which will go to the same groups that suffer the discriminatory harms. Husak concludes that we must take care to weigh the discriminatory harms of SQF against any benefits it also has.

In his contribution, Richard Lippke considers whether jails should be used at all, either to hold pre-trial detainees or to punish those who are convicted of relatively minor crimes. He notes that pre-trial detainees are legally presumed innocent, yet the conditions of the jails they are held in are determinately punitive. He also notes that many of the individuals convicted of relatively minor crimes are better served, not by punishment, but by rehabilitation. He concludes that we ought to do away with jails, at least as we currently know them.

Thom Brooks also argues for a reduction in punishment, but his focus is on restorative justice as an alternative to formal sentencing. According to Brooks, restorative justice is less costly than traditional forms of punishment, leads to less recidivism, and tends to help the victims of crime. Nevertheless, restorative justice is not always feasible. Brooks therefore argues for an intermediate option he calls "punitive restoration." Although traditional approaches to restorative justice forbid options like hard treatment, punitive restoration permits hard treatment even while it promotes the goal of reduced punishment overall.

The theme of racial inequalities runs through nearly every chapter in this volume, but is it most prominent in the final three chapters. In her contribution, Amanda Gailey draws a connection between police shootings, race, and the prevalence of guns in the United States. The number of guns in the United States heightens the risk that any negligent, reckless, or malevolent action will result in someone's death. However, Gailey argues that the United States' exceptionally lax gun policy is disproportionately harmful for black people, who are at an increased risk of being identified as criminal gun owners, who often receive prolonged prison sentences for nonviolent offenses committed in the presence of a gun, and who face an increased risk of being shot, either by other civilians or by the police. Drawing upon Michelle Alexander's argument that mass incarceration is the "New Jim Crow" (i.e., a new paradigm for enforcing unjust social hierarchies), Gailey argues that United States gun law is also "one of the ways through which the New Jim Crow operates."[6]

Gun violence—or violence, more generally—also forms the backdrop for the contribution by Lori Gruen, Clyde Meikle, and Andre Pierce. Meikle and Pierce are inmates in a maximum security prison, and in their co-authored contribution with Gruen, they recount some of their experiences growing up in poor, predominantly Black communities where violence was common. Although dominant white social norms tend to hold that violence is at odds with dignity, Gruen, Meikle, and Pierce argue that at least two forms of violence—retributive violence and pre-emptive violence—are often deployed to protect the dignity of people who live in what the authors call the "interstices." At the end of their piece, the authors consider alternative means to promote and protect dignity in black interstices.

In the final chapter of this volume, Stephen Darwall and William Darwall evaluate whether the American criminal justice system meets the standards of what Stephen Darwall has elsewhere called the "mutual accountability framework." According to that framework, our practices should be able to be justified from the standpoint of a representative moral authority. However, Darwall and Darwall argue that in light of its racially oppressive effects, the criminal justice system cannot be justified from such a standpoint. They conclude that "American carceral institutions clearly lack the authority to make and enforce the criminal law that they purport to have."

Notes

1. The Sentencing Project. 2017. Trends in U.S. corrections. https://sentencingproject.org/wp-content/uploads/2016/01/Trends-in-US-Corrections.pdf.
2. Ye Hee Lee, Michelle. 2015. Yes, U.S. locks up people at a higher rate than any other country. *Washington Post*, July 7, 2015.
3. Wagner, Peter, and Wendy Sawyer. 2018. Mass incarceration: The whole pie 2018. Prison Policy Initiative. https://www.prisonpolicy.org/reports/pie2018.html.
4. Hager, Eli. 2017. A mass incarceration mystery. *Washington Post*, December 15; The Sentencing Project, 2017. Trends in U.S. corrections. https://sentencingproject.org/wp-content/uploads/2016/01/Trends-in-US-Corrections.pdf.
5. This problem of reconciling idealism with realism is a recurring theme in other branches of ethics. For more work on the distinction between realism and idealism, see Michael Weber and Kevin Vallier, eds., 2017. *Political utopias: Contemporary debates*. Oxford: Oxford University Press.
6. Alexander, Michelle. 2010. *The New Jim Crow: Mass incarceration in the age of colorblindness*. New York: The New Press.

Punishment and Democratic Rights: A Case Study in Non-ideal Penal Theory

Steven Swartzer

Punishment, Idealizations, and Non-ideal Theory

In the United States, it is common for state governments to restrict the political rights of criminal offenders.[1] According to the most recent available estimates, more than 6 million US citizens are disqualified from voting because of a current or past criminal conviction.[2] Only Maine and Vermont do not suspend offenders' voting rights. Throughout the rest of the country, felons, and sometimes misdemeanants, cannot participate in elections during any term of incarceration.[3] Depending on their state of residence, many of these ineligible voters will regain the franchise after completing prison or jail sentences; others are prohibited from voting until they have completed additional years of probation or parole. Ex-felons residing in Florida, Iowa, and Kentucky are regularly denied access to the ballot box for life. Several states with the harshest criminal disenfranchisement policies disqualify more than 5% of their adult citizens; Florida disenfranchises more than 10%.[4] In contrast, nearly every

S. Swartzer (✉)
University of North Carolina, Chapel Hill, NC, USA

M. Gardner and M. Weber (eds.), *The Ethics of Policing and Imprisonment*, Palgrave Studies in Ethics and Public Policy,
https://doi.org/10.1007/978-3-319-97770-6_2

other liberal democratic nation guarantees voting rights for ex-convicts, and most allow (or even encourage) inmates to vote.

In this essay, I argue that limiting offenders' political rights is seriously unjust in societies as they are and are likely to be. Given the widespread use of this punishment in the United States, this is an important result. However, by identifying problematic assumptions common in philosophical and popular discussions of punishment, the central argument I offer against criminal disenfranchisement has broader philosophical implications, as well. To set the stage for this broader argument, the following remarks will be helpful.

According to John Rawls, criminal punishment is automatically beyond the scope of ideal theory—since punishment arises only because people sometimes fail to act justly, theory of punishment belongs to non-ideal, partial compliance theory.[5] Despite this, philosophical discussions of punishment in the analytic tradition are often highly idealized. Consider the challenge that has dominated penal theory. Punishment generally involves treating convicted offenders in ways that are *prima facie* objectionable: we forcibly confine offenders, take their money and property, suspend their rights, deny them easy access to loved ones, and cause various other forms of suffering. Given the *prima facie* injustice of such treatment, we require an account of why, when imposed as punishment, it is just. It is generally accepted that an appropriate justification, if there is one, will point to facts about what punishment is ideally for—to some ideal purpose or aim of punishment in generally just societies. If this idealized aim is itself just, and if the types of losses that we impose as punishments would be acceptable ways of pursuing that aim, most penal theorists would take the philosophical challenge to have been met.

Some philosophers are dissatisfied with this idealized discourse, urging that widespread social injustice might make ideal justifications of punishment inapplicable to more realistic societies.[6] Yet even many of these theorists pay insufficient attention to some of the most pressing concerns about contemporary American criminal justice—such as the significant racial disparities that are characteristic of the American penal system, or the various forms of injustice related to American policing. It may be that philosophers see these questions as sociological or legal, rather than philosophical; however, I believe that important philosophical and normative issues are likely to be missed if we pay inadequate attention to such concerns.

Penal theory falls out of the important question raised by non-compliance: What is a community to do about the fact that people sometimes act unjustly toward one another? What, for instance, is to be done about interpersonal violence? These are important questions, but they are easily interpreted too narrowly. It is easy to conceptualize punishment (or the threat thereof) as a natural or automatic response to the problem of non-compliance—in which case the central questions are about whether this natural response is the right response, or whether it adequately satisfies the relevant societal needs.

This is not the only possible understanding of punishment. Angela Davis's arguments for prison abolitionism rest on the view that contemporary American penal institutions and practices are best understood in terms of a prison industrial complex.[7] As Davis points out, this understanding requires "that punishment has to be conceptually severed from its seemingly indissoluble link with crime."[8] Instead, Davis theorizes about practices and institutions of punishment as "linked to the agendas of politicians, the profit drive of corporations, and media representations of crime [in conjunction with] the racialization of those most likely to be punished."[9]

As Davis's view illustrates, keeping in mind the gross injustices within the American penal system makes it easier to notice that there are other ways to understand the relationship between punishment and the important question of non-compliance. In particular, it becomes clearer that penal practices sometimes constitute or create the very injustices to which society must respond.

There is a pressing need within the philosophy of punishment for greater exploration of views, like Davis's, that do not start with the assumption that punishment exists primarily as a necessary response to injustice. Moreover, less idealized theorizing might serve as a corrective to distortions commonly introduced into philosophical and folk debates about punishment.[10] In doing so, it presents an alternative understanding of the important question raised by non-compliance. Consider, for example, that while partial compliance theory is predicated on the assumption that agents sometimes fail to act justly, debates about the justification of punishment regularly presuppose that the bad actors are those being punished, rather than those doing the punishing. Such presuppositions make it easy to forget or ignore that regarding the question of what counts as an offense, different standards are frequently imposed for different segments of the population. Such distortions make it easy to forget that many people have been and will be marked as criminals for refusing to mind their place. A more thoroughgoing non-ideal penal theory might instead start from the important truth that punishment is a political institution that often creates, reinforces, and replicates injustice—an institution that has regularly and widely been used as a tool of dominance and oppression.[11] In this way, such non-ideal theorizing supplements the dominant understanding of the question of how we, as an actual society, should respond to the fact of injustice.

This chapter uses the example of criminal disenfranchisement to demonstrate that non-ideal starting points can generate new insights into questions of penal justice in the real world—insights likely to be missed if we operate only within more idealized frameworks. The following section, "Criminal Disenfranchisement and Criminal Injustice" presents the main argument against restricting offenders' political rights. This argument begins with the well-documented racial and ethnic disparities in who is subjected to this punishment in the United States, and uses these disparities to tease out a deeper, more general challenge to this form of punishment. The sections entitled "Deterrence and Rehabilitation" and "Retributivism" tie the general argument to the more familiar philosophical discourse on punishment by drawing connections between this argument and the values that more idealized views use to justify punishment. Generally speaking, even idealized views have not been friendly to criminal disenfranchisement as a form of punishment. However, the arguments of these two sections go beyond the standard dialectic by showing how this dialectic, which incorporates problematic idealized assumptions, misses important ways that our penal practices and institutions might actively undermine punishment's apparent justificatory values. The final section briefly explores possible extensions of the main line of argument, and responds to a potential objection arising out of these extensions.

Criminal Disenfranchisement and Criminal Injustice

Social scientists frequently note that racial and ethnic minorities (primarily black men) are significantly more likely than white citizens to lose democratic rights through penal disenfranchisement.[12] Nine states disenfranchise more than 10% of their adult African American citizens, all at far higher rates than they disenfranchise non-African Americans (see Table 1). According to the most recent available estimates,

Table 1 Estimated disenfranchisement rates for African Americans and non-African Americans in select US states

	Non-African American disenfranchisement rate (%)	*African American disenfranchisement rate (%)*
Nevada	3.3	11.8
Arizona	3.9	11.9
Alabama	5.1	15.1
Mississippi	6.2	15.9
Wyoming	5.2	17.2
Tennessee	5.8	21.3
Florida	8.6	21.3
Virginia[a]	4.5	21.9
Kentucky	7.7	26.2

[a]These estimates do not take into account the more than 150,000 Virginia ex-felons who had their right to vote restored between 2016 and 2017 by then-Governor Terry McAuliffe—slightly more than 30% of Virginia's disenfranchised population
Source Uggen et al. (2016, 15–16)

more than 20% of African American adults in Florida, Kentucky, Tennessee, and Virginia are ineligible to vote due to state disenfranchisement policies.[13] Nationally, black citizens lose their civil rights at more than four times the rate of non-black citizens.[14]

Such disparities raise serious moral concerns about the practice of suspending criminals' democratic rights. But it is difficult to articulate these concerns within the confines of standard penological debates. Philosophers focusing on the abstract question of whether societies could (in principle) justifiably use this mode of punishment often see inequities in application and problems of comparative justice as irrelevant to their debate. According to many of these philosophers, what matters most fundamentally is the non-comparative question of whether it is (or would be) just for a given individual to receive a given punishment as a response for her criminal behavior, not whether it is just for her to receive this punishment while others do not.

According to this line of thinking, such disparities do not show disenfranchisement to be unjust *as a form of punishment*. Pointing out that some groups are more likely to lose their right to vote does not obviously help us address the non-comparative question of whether it is appropriate for them to receive that punishment when they do. To such philosophers, if the disproportionate impact on African Americans is problematic, the locus of the problem is to be found in whatever underlying factors explain why citizens of color receive this punishment more frequently than whites—or, why whites receive this punishment far less frequently than people of color—not in the punishment itself.[15] If racial disparities or other comparative injustices rendered a form of punishment unjustified, this would entail that imprisonment, probation, and even fines would all count as unjust forms of punishment.

This diagnosis misses an important point. Let us assume, as is plausible, that minority citizens face high rates of punishment because of structural racism and racial bias within the broader political, economic, and criminal justice systems.[16] Even if this is the ultimate source of the racial disparities in criminal disenfranchisement, this does not immunize disenfranchisement itself from criticism. Just the opposite. Disenfranchisement is objectionable in large part because of the morally significant risk it imposes of *reinforcing*, *perpetuating*, and *amplifying* patterns of racial subordination and bias. The reason is simple enough: when people of color lose political rights at disproportionately high rates, this erodes their power to fight racial injustice in its various forms. Simply put, inequality in the distribution of political rights contributes to further inequality and to further types of oppression. Disparities in application are directly relevant to whether a society can justifiably suspend offenders' political rights.

When racial and ethnic minorities are antecedently at greater risk of unjust treatment through the state's criminal justice system, forms of policing and punishment that diminish their collective political voice are likely to make matters worse. Characterized more generally, the problem is this: the practice of restricting offenders' political rights carries a morally significant risk that those most vulnerable to unjust treatment will be made even more vulnerable. The fact that a practice threatens to reproduce racial (and other forms of) injustice makes it at least *prima facie* wrong for racially (or otherwise) unjust societies to make use of it as a form of punishment.

It should be emphasized that the minority interests at stake are often of high moral importance. Of special salience today is the interest in ending abusive law enforcement practices. And we are not talking only about the interest in ending the *disparate* treatment that people of color receive through this system. Many of the interests involved include ending widespread practices, including, but not limited to, the repeated harassment of racial minorities by law enforcement and other forms of normalized police violence, that unjustly impose serious, concrete harms within African American communities.

Morally important interests like these are undermined when the right to political participation is tied to one's criminal record. When the power over the criminal law is itself used in subordinating or discriminatory ways, groups most vulnerable to unjust treatment are the very groups that are excluded from participation at disproportionately high rates. This form of punishment transforms the power to decide what, how, and who to punish into power over entry into the political process, thus threatening to remove political power from such groups in the very moment this power is most important. Moreover, the proponent of disenfranchisement cannot easily fall back on the idea that the individuals being punished in this way deserve to lose their political power, because this form of punishment does not only undermine the specific ***individuals*** who lose their political rights. By diminishing the political power of citizens of color as a class, disproportionate disenfranchisement makes all these citizens more vulnerable to racial injustice—including those who have never engaged in any serious wrongdoing. To take an obvious analogy, even wealthy and literate African Americans had legitimate personal complaints about poll taxes and literacy tests, because these policies barred many of their natural allies in the fight against racial oppression from the political process.

Given that domination of vulnerable groups often proceeds through the creation and enforcement of criminal laws, the practice of punishing lawbreakers by denying them basic political rights is especially likely to create a feedback loop that helps to reinforce, replicate, and amplify patterns of domination and subordination, when they occur. Insofar as all of this is a predicable consequence of disenfranchisement policies, this provides strong moral reasons against utilizing this form of punishment in any society that exemplifies a tendency toward such patterns of injustice.

It is worth pausing to flag two additional features of this general argument. First, this argument does not provide an in-principle objection to suspending offenders' democratic rights.[17] Instead, this argument focuses on a problem generated by this form of punishment in societies with systematic inequalities in their criminal justice institutions. Some (merely) possible idealized society might contain no such systematic injustice, and this argument does not speak to whether criminal disenfranchisement would be morally problematic in such a society. Yet even if not universal, this argument has wide applicability. For this argument criticizes disenfranchisement on the basis of its relation to social phenomena—such as the existence of domination and bias, and the tendency for criminal justice institutions and practices to reflect such biases when they occur—that are regular, non-accidental, and widespread. This argument thus presents a challenge to the use of this punishment in most (perhaps all) democratic societies as they exist today and are likely to exist indefinitely into the future.

Second, this argument goes beyond many of the prominent objections to disenfranchisement that focus on *ex*-convicts' civil rights. It is frequently argued that those released from prison have already "paid their debt to society," and that additional penalties continuing after this debt is repaid are unjust. It is also commonly argued that continuing disenfranchisement after release from prison interferes with ex-convicts' ability to successfully reintegrate into democratic society. If successful, such arguments would give us good reason to restore political rights upon release from prison. Yet these arguments do not go far enough. The argument I have offered suggests that we have strong moral reasons to enfranchise prisoners, as well as ex-convicts. Insofar as members of marginalized communities are frequently incarcerated at higher rates, and for longer terms, limiting inmates' democratic rights still threatens to erode the political influence of such marginalized groups. In fact, given that *prisoners* (and *convicted offenders*, more broadly) constitute a vulnerable and marginalized population in its own right, there is reason to think that this population's political power is significantly diminished by restrictions on prisoners' democratic rights. If this population faces a higher risk of unjust treatment at the hands of the state (which seems likely), prisoner disenfranchisement would exacerbate that threat.

Deterrence and Rehabilitation

The fact that suspending offenders' civil rights threatens to reproduce injustice makes it *prima facie* wrong for societies like ours, in which various forms of injustice are already pervasive, to employ this practice. The weightiness of this consideration depends on the strength of the prior tendency toward injustice, the strength of the potential feedback signal, and other factors. Yet it is unclear how these concerns are relevant to standard, idealized debates about justification. At a minimum, one might attempt to weigh these reasons alongside the reasons presented by the more idealized perspectives. On this accounting, since (as we will see shortly) standard penological theories offer no strong support for penal disenfranchisement, the argument of the previous section weighs decisively. But the non-ideal argument is also relevant in more interesting ways. In this section and the next, I use this argument to focus attention on ways that idealizations can obscure pressing concerns about criminal disenfranchisement that arise from the same values espoused by standard penological perspectives.

There is one further detail that should be addressed before continuing. I have assumed that criminal disenfranchisement is a form of *punishment*, rather than a non-punitive "collateral consequence" of criminal conviction. This is controversial. Disenfranchisement provisions are typically found not in the penal code, but in the parts of the civil code dealing with voter eligibility, alongside residency requirements and the like. Additionally, some philosophers defend felon disenfranchisement not as a punishment, but as a civil restriction justified (or at least permitted) on the basis of more general political principles.[18] For the purposes of the argument so far, it does not really matter whether or not disenfranchisement is punitive. What is important for that argument is that offender disenfranchisement is a practice that needlessly reinforces and reproduces injustice. However, the penal character of disenfranchisement may be more important in what follows. If disenfranchisement is ultimately non-punitive, it is unlikely to provide an excellent case study in the limitations of ideal penal theory.

Although I am not in a position to fully defend the punitive nature of disenfranchisement, this is a reasonable presumption. The practice of legally suspending an individual's civil rights as a response to a criminal offense fits well with most plausible philosophical definitions of legal punishment. Perhaps the most controversial issue is whether offender disenfranchisement satisfies an expressivist condition: that criminal punishment has a "reprobative or condemnatory character."[19] This condition is itself controversial, but even assuming that it is part of a full account of criminal punishment, there is good reason to hold that criminal disenfranchisement satisfies it. For a decision to disqualify citizens from voting for committing serious criminal infractions seems to have a very different character from decisions based on other grounds, such as a decision to disqualify minors, non-residents, or those swearing fealty to foreign kings. The difference is that the former seems to be condemnatory in a way that the latter are not. Moreover, it strikes me that even those who do not conceptualize disenfranchisement as punishment sometimes implicitly rely on this character when justifying or defending this practice. As a case in point, Altman argues that democratic societies have broad rights in defining their own political identities, and that limiting participatory rights of serious criminal offenders is a permissible way to do this. To illustrate his view, Altman considers an example of a society that includes someone guilty of genocide. According to Altman (2005: 265), disenfranchisement (in addition to penal sanctions) helps to "put the criminal at arm's length from the community, that is, to deem him as one who has failed to meet the minimal standards for remaining a full member of the community." Though Altman does not consider this act punitive, it is plausible that part of what is going on here is that the society is putting the offender at arm's length as a way of strongly *condemning* his actions.[20] Even if this dissociative act is part of how the society defines its own identity, it is nevertheless imbued with reprobation.

Though much more should be said on this matter, it is reasonable to assume that criminal disenfranchisement is properly understood as a form of punishment, and is thus in the need of a penal justification.

Standard Penological Criticisms of Disenfranchisement

Three putative justifications of punishment dominate penal theory: deterrence, rehabilitation, and retribution. In this section, I argue that restricting offenders' civil rights undermines the values that support both deterrence-based and rehabilitation-based rationales for punishment. (I address retribution in the section entitled, "Retributivism".)

It is already widely understood among critics of penal disenfranchisement that neither deterrence nor rehabilitation support the use of this punishment.[21]

First, there is no evidence that loss of political rights significantly deters criminal behavior. Indeed, there is reason to doubt its deterrent value. Effective deterrents are visible and predictable in a way that loss of democratic rights is not. Criminal disenfranchees blend into the crowd of citizens who do not vote because of other administrative hurdles or because they simply do not care to. Very few people understand their state's criminal disenfranchisement policies (or the policies of states in which they are likely to reside in the future). Moreover, most crime is committed by young and disaffected citizens, who are least likely to care about political participation in the first place, or least likely to see their participation as having any real impact.[22]

Second, there is little basis for endorsing this punishment on rehabilitative grounds: denying prisoners, probationers, or ex-felons civil rights does nothing to reform them, to prepare them to become more productive community members, or to help reintegrate them back into society. Restricting voting rights does not address any of the main impediments to successful reentry, such as addiction, lack of education, lack of meaningful social and economic opportunities, mental illness, or social alienation. In fact, some have argued that *encouraging* political participation would better promote rehabilitative goals by encouraging disillusioned citizens to take a more active civic role.[23] There is some evidence for this claim, but it is not decisive. Sociologists Jeff Manza and Christopher Uggen found a negative correlation between voting and subsequent criminal behavior[24]:

> Those who vote are less likely to be arrested and incarcerated, and are less likely to report committing a range of property and violent offenses. Moreover, this relationship cannot be solely attributed to criminal history; voting is negatively related to subsequent crime among those with and without a prior criminal history.[25]

Thus, voting might reduce recidivism. However, these authors caution that they were unable to demonstrate a causal link, and thus this conclusion is somewhat speculative.

One might reject this rehabilitationist objection to disenfranchisement as being too quick. Mary Sigler, for instance, contends that, given the important symbolic value of democratic rights, temporary (but not permanent) loss of such rights might help offenders become better citizens: "Despite the confident claims of disenfranchisement critics, it seems equally, if not more intuitive that temporary suspension of voting rights would promote reintegration by making salient the rights and responsibilities of citizenship."[26] Yet Sigler's argument fails to find empirical support. The stigma and disillusionment associated with losing civil rights often persist long after those rights are restored. Once again, not only are those who temporarily lose their political rights less likely to vote after restoration, but they also tend to see the government as less responsive to their communities' needs, and are more likely to avoid future political participation more generally.[27] Instead of helping offenders become better citizens, the evidence suggests that even temporary suspension of civil rights can drive one further away from civic engagement.

A Less-Idealized Perspective on Deterrence

The standard objections establish that disenfranchisement is not justified on the basis of either deterrence or rehabilitation. These objections are compelling, but they miss a further way that this mode of punishment runs afoul of the values embodied by these perspectives.

Begin with deterrence. This view is based on the assumption that, insofar as people respond to incentives, we can reduce crime by establishing the right disincentives. The folk psychological theories underwriting deterrence theory suggest that the principles guiding criminal activity apply to human behavior *writ large*. In responding to empirical criticisms of deterrence-based arguments for punishment, James Q. Wilson appeals to more general psychological principles:

> People are governed in their daily lives by rewards and penalties of every sort. We shop for bargain prices, praise our children for good behavior and scold them for bad [...] and conduct ourselves in public in ways that lead our friends and neighbors to form good opinions of us. To assert that "deterrence doesn't work" is tantamount to either denying the plainest facts of everyday life or claiming that would-be criminals are utterly different from the rest of us. They may be different to some degree [...] but these differences of degree do not make them indifferent to the risks and gains of crime.[28]

Given this underlying folk psychological picture, it should be surprising that deterrence theorists focus almost exclusively on the fact that criminal justice institutions deter would-be criminals from criminal activity. Such a focus misses other powerful incentives and disincentives associated with institutions and practices of punishment. In particular, this focus obscures the fact that penal institutions and practices are themselves shaped by broader systems of incentives and disincentives.

Some critics of American criminal justice who operate within less idealized perspectives have attempted to draw attention to these broader incentives. Davis's account of the prison industrial complex is one such view: once again, Davis argues that a convergence of racial, political, and economic incentives is largely responsible for America's current system of mass incarceration. In defense of a similar conclusion,

Michelle Alexander emphasizes that this system of mass incarceration was established, in large part, by incentivizing state and local law enforcement (and prosecutorial) participation in the war on drugs. According to Alexander, this analysis is based on the general principle that "Every system of control depends for its survival on the tangible and intangible benefits that are provided to those who are responsible for the system's maintenance and administration. This system [i.e., mass incarceration] is no exception."[29] Would-be criminals are not the only agents influenced by the incentives surrounding criminal justice.

A second point is also important. Idealized deterrence-based arguments frame the key question in terms of whether or not a form of punishment effectively deters *crime*. This cannot be the full story. There must be a more basic standard of bad behavior—some view as to what behaviors people should be discouraged from participating in—and we should not assume that this standard aligns neatly with the standards set by criminal law. This is especially important in the context of the present argument because some exercises of political and economic power, *including the establishment or perpetuation of certain punitive practices*, are themselves instances of bad behavior. One need not look far to find historical and contemporary examples of dominant groups using their political power in ways that undermine disfavored groups or that solidify prevailing power structures. Even if such exercises of power are never counted as crimes, they are nevertheless examples of people acting unjustly toward others, and are the kinds of behaviors that people should be discouraged from engaging in.

In the spirit of the less-idealized accounts of Davis and Alexander, the main argument above highlights the fact that penal disenfranchisement generates perverse incentives by conveying political advantage on those who use the criminal law (either intentionally or unintentionally) in biased ways. Consider Richard Lippke's contention that "democratic participation may be instrumental in securing other important rights, especially by making political officials wary of adopting policies that undermine or erode such rights."[30] This suggests that democratic officials will be less wary of eroding the rights of those lacking participatory rights. Unless those holding power and privilege are, in Wilson's terms, "utterly different from" everyone else, what is true of criminals should also be true of them: they too should be sensitive to "risks and gains" associated with various options, including the "risks and gains" associated with exercises of privilege and power. Given that suspension of offenders' democratic rights insulates decision-makers from criticisms by those who are punished, this punishment establishes costs and benefits that make public officials less sensitive to the weighty moral interests of marginalized groups that disproportionately bear the burden of unjust punishment.

Given that misuses of the power to punish are already both regular and serious, deterrence theorists should be greatly concerned about the creation of incentives encouraging such bad behavior. Society should discourage overt abuses of power, not reward them. Yet unjust patterns of punishment need not result from malicious intent to dominate, undermine, harass, or control disfavored groups; they are often the product of unconscious biases, fears, ignorance, inattention, group-think, and blindness to one's own privilege. By getting the incentives right, we can likely correct for these deeper, unconscious influences as well. Just as deterrence theorists think that we can discourage negligence and recklessness, we should also work to discourage the unintentional establishment of penal practices that further erode the position of marginalized groups. Other things being equal, if a type of behavior needlessly promotes genuine harms, we have reason to discourage people from engaging in it, even if those harms are unintentional. If criminal disenfranchisement undermines antecedently vulnerable communities, we have strong moral reasons to abandon this form of punishment.

A Less-Idealized Perspective on Rehabilitation

Rehabilitationist values are also of great importance to non-ideal penal theory. However, since criminal offenders are not the only actors who behave badly, they are not the only ones needing rehabilitation. The arguments so far highlight that the practice of suspending offenders' democratic rights undermines important forms of rehabilitation.

Consider, first, the case of unjust political institutions. The non-ideal perspective starts with the fact that injustice is a regular feature of real societies. Criminal disenfranchisement can interfere with reform of this injustice: by disproportionately excluding those with weighty interests in reforming unjust institutions, this punishment creates a feedback loop that threatens to reinforce, perpetuate, and amplify patterns of domination, rather than eliminate them.

Recall, once again, our guiding example. When more than 20% of African Americans in Virginia, Kentucky, Tennessee, and Florida are denied the vote, it is simply unbelievable that this has no real effect on their political power in those states, or their ability to effectively fight against other forms of racial injustice. Even small differences in voting eligibility and voter turnout can sometimes have large impacts on the composition of legislatures and executive branches, and on the policies those lawmakers ultimately enact. Moreover, in addition to the direct effects of criminal disenfranchisement on minority representation, this practice appears to have knock-on effects that depress turnout among eligible minority voters—especially those in the most disadvantaged communities. Political scientists Melanie Bowers and Robert R. Preuhs have found that strict disenfranchisement policies are also associated with lower voter turnout among black non-felons.[31] In similar fashion, Lerman and Weaver found that losing voting rights at one point in life makes one less likely to participate in the political process later in life, even after those rights are reinstated.[32] They also argue that losing one's voting rights can erode one's faith in the political system, and make one more likely to avoid other forms of political participation—such as contacting one's representatives or filing a grievance when one is the victim of official misconduct. Thus, penal disenfranchisement has a profound impact on the ability of marginalized communities to promote needed social reform.

Criminal disenfranchisement might also undermine the personal moral progress of many individual citizens. The right to democratic participation has often been thought to symbolize that a person is worthy of the respect and trust owed to all citizens. As Jeremy Waldron argues[33]:

> If A is [...] excluded from participation [...], A will feel slighted: he will feel that his own sense of justice is and that of people like him have been denigrated as inadequate to the task of deciding, not only something important, but something important in which he, A, has a stake as well as others. To feel this insult does not require him to think his vote—if he had it—would give him substantial and palpable power. [...] All he asks—so far as his participation is concerned—is that he and all others be treated as equals in matters affecting their interests, rights, and duties.

Extending Waldron's point, apart from the effects on their psyches, systematically stripping convicted offenders of democratic rights reinforces *other citizens'* perception of these offenders (and often those implicitly associated with them).[34] Given that the "untrustworthiness" of criminals is frequently offered as a leading reason for taking away their right to political participation,[35] disenfranchising these citizens would likely reinforce the view that they are unworthy of the same trust and respect given to other citizens, and that they are "inadequate to the task of deciding" matters of great importance.

When we do not respect or trust others, we are less likely to listen to them, to empathize with them, to imagine the world from their perspectives, and to learn things that they are well-positioned to understand. When directed at a particular group, this lack of trust makes us discount the probability that our own actions—and the social institutions we endorse—impose significant harms on them. It also makes us less sensitive to the possibility that such harms constitute serious injustices.[36] This is especially likely when those silenced through this process are already stigmatized and marginalized in other ways. Such individuals are likely to have their legitimate interests (including their weighty moral interests in ending their domination) further minimized or ignored by other citizens. What this implies regarding the possibility of reform is that the symbolic effects of disenfranchisement limit other citizens' ability to recognize their own or their society's wrongdoing toward marginalized citizens. Unless we can assume that we (and our social institutions) treat everyone else justly, we should be seriously concerned about such obstacles to personal and social reform.

If one operates within an overly idealized conception of punishment, in which there is a stipulated link between bad behavior, crime, and punishment, one is likely to miss the need for such reform. That is not to say that the standard rehabilitative conception of punishment is incapable of supporting criticisms of specific penal practices. The problem is that the criticisms offered by such an account are uniformly about the failure of certain practices to promote *offenders'* rehabilitation and moral reform. This presupposes that it is the criminal offender who needs reform, and questions about the rehabilitative effect (or lack thereof) of penal practices on non-criminals simply do not arise. But, given the fact of injustice within all actual societies, such questions cannot be ignored.

Retributivism

A similar challenge arises from within retributivist theories as well, although the conclusions are more uncertain. Standard varieties of retributivism hold that a punishment, *P*, is a justified response to an action-type, *A*, when (and because) people who *A* deserve to receive *P*, or when (and because) *P* is a fitting response to *A*-ing. Paradigmatically, those who maliciously harm others deserve to suffer in some way in return for the harms they have done. To retributivists, suspension of democratic rights is a justifiable punishment if those who commit crimes deserve to lose these rights, or if this loss is a fitting response to criminal wrongdoing.

Retributivists face a standard worry. Loss of civil rights is presumably not a fitting response for all illegal activities. It seems quite wrong to deprive people of voting rights for technical parole violations (such as failing a drug test, failing to secure employment, or missing a meeting with a parole officer),[37] stealing a pig or chicken,[38] or for selling sex toys.[39] Thus, retributivists need some relatively principled standard for which violations are deserving of this punishment and which are not. Yet there are few plausible principles available to justify specific penalties, and even fewer that are likely to justify suspending offenders' basic democratic rights.

According to the doctrine of *lex talionis*, punishments should "fit" the crime in a strong sense: punishment should be of the same type as the offense. Even setting aside obvious and well-known problems with this account,[40] *lex talionis* does not generally support the punishment in question. Since losing one's right to vote is not of a kind with assault, robbery, fraud, or murder, *lex talionis* cannot straightforwardly justify disenfranchisement as punishment for any of these offenses. At best, *lex talionis* applies to violations of some voting laws, such as directly interfering with someone else's ability to vote.

Defenders of disenfranchisement might contend that suspension of democratic rights is fitting not because of its relation to specific criminal offenses, but because criminal activity is itself a violation of the democratic order. Roger Clegg, for instance, argues that "It is not too much to demand that those who would make the law for others—who would participate in self-government—be willing to follow those laws themselves."[41] John Deigh likewise suggests that criminal acts "show that the citizen is unwilling to abide by the laws in the enactment of which he can participate" and therefore show that he is "unfit" to vote.[42] Similar ideas drive many of the social contract arguments for disenfranchisement.[43] According to this perspective, those who refuse to abide by the results of the democratic process fail to satisfy their responsibilities as democratic citizens, and thus do not deserve the same participatory rights as those who obey. It is unfair to expect others to accept democratically established rules, if one is not willing to abide by them oneself. For these reasons, loss of participatory rights is a fitting response to criminal misconduct.

While plausible-sounding, this argument has grossly unintuitive implications. Public urination, dodging sales taxes on online purchases, and speeding are also failures to comply with democratically determined laws. If violations of the democratic order make one deserving of disenfranchisement, this should be a justified punishment for any offense. This is clearly the wrong result.

Christopher Bennett advances a more compelling retributivist defense of disenfranchisement, based on the idea that punishment is an expressive or symbolic act that serves to censure or repudiate wrongdoing. According to Bennett, society must dissociate itself from wrongdoing, or else it effectively "condon[es] or accept[s] or becom[es] complicit in" such behavior.[44] Moreover, he argues, a natural way for a society to separate itself *as a political society* from a member's wrongdoing, is to suspend rights and privileges that normally flow from membership. Thus, the suspension of democratic rights (even if only temporarily) seems to be the right kind of symbolic act by which a state can effectively repudiate criminal behavior. However, even though Bennett accepts that society must denounce criminal acts in general, he does not insist that disenfranchisement is always an appropriate punishment. For, the symbolic act that society uses to dissociate itself from citizens' bad behavior must be proportional to the severity of the offense. Since suspending participatory rights is an especially dramatic act, Bennett argues, this punishment should be reserved only for "those most serious crimes that are in danger of undermining a person's status as a continuing member of the polity."[45] To take an analogy, someone could repudiate her friend's rude behavior by severing all contact, but that would usually be overkill.

While Bennett's expressive retributivism lends some support for disenfranchisement, his arguments incorporate the same problematic assumptions that our less idealized perspective seeks to correct. As was the case for deterrence and rehabilitation theories, our main argument against limiting political rights raises significant moral concerns about this practice that can be specified in terms of the value of retribution.

First, the arguments up to now strongly suggest that, even if the suspension of democratic rights is sometimes deserved or fitting, the use of penal disenfranchisement ultimately makes our political-legal system less reliable at meting out punishment in deserved or fitting ways. For, domination of disfavored groups often consists in their systematically facing undeserved and excessive punishment and in their facing violations for which perpetrators are routinely un(der)punished—if the main argument is correct, criminal disenfranchisement predictably leads to the perpetuation, replication, and amplification of such forms of injustice. To the extent that suspending offender's democratic rights predictably reproduces ill-fitting patterns punishment, it predictably undermines the reliability of the criminal justice system according to retributivist standards.

Limiting the use of disenfranchisement as a response to only the most serious crimes, as Bennett recommends, would certainly reduce the risk posed to marginalized communities. But these risks might nevertheless remain significant. After all, the believed seriousness of offenses, enforcement priorities, and the distribution of enforcement resources are all determined by the political process. These matters are subject to the same distortions as other uses of power, and are often tied to interests and biases of dominant groups. Thus, even if we endorse the principle of limiting disenfranchisement to serious crimes, we might nevertheless continue to disproportionately burden marginalized populations.

If disenfranchisement generates any significant risk for marginalized communities, the balance of retributivist considerations likely weighs against it. For even if loss of participatory rights is *a* fitting response to serious wrongdoing, it is not the *only* fitting response. By Bennett's own lights, there must be other symbols that societies can deploy—for states have a responsibility to denunciate bad behavior in general, not just those crimes sufficiently serious to warrant suspension of democratic rights. Some of the other available symbols could be utilized in serious cases, as well. Moreover, it is a reasonable hypothesis that some of the alternative penalties would not predictably undermine the retributive reliability of the broader political-legal system to the same degree that disenfranchisement does. Thus, by the retributivist's own lights, those other forms of punishment would better promote retributivist values.

Second, Bennett's defense of disenfranchisement treats the category of criminal behavior and the class of actions from which society should distance itself as co-extensive. This is, of course, misleading. The less idealized perspective takes it as a starting point that within actual societies, there is a significant amount of slippage between these two categories. When we start with this more accurate picture, expressive retributivism yields interesting implications. Bennett argues that if we structure our punitive practices in the wrong way, we effectively condone or become complicit in citizens' bad behavior. Given that disenfranchisement predictably leads to the reproduction of injustice when it occurs, communities that use this penalty cannot adequately denunciate either the original injustice or the further injustices that result. Instead of enabling a community to separate itself from injustices perpetrated against vulnerable communities, its penal institutions become entangled in these injustices, and bear partial responsibility for their perpetuation. The use of penal disenfranchisement thus sends the wrong message: that the polis is unconcerned with injustices that would predictably result from its penal choices. By conveying such a message, a society fails to honor the values that are central to expressive retributivism.

Finally, it bears emphasis that retributivists should be at least as concerned about people receiving more punishment than they deserve (or more punishment than is fitting) as they are about individuals going unpunished for their offenses. The arguments offered above contend that suspending offenders' political rights leaves marginalized groups more vulnerable to undeserved and excessive punishment. While we cannot predict the precise magnitude of this increased risk, we cannot simply assume that this risk is morally negligible. For history provides us repeated examples of cases in which this increased risk has manifested in significant abuse.

In fact, protecting vulnerable groups from abuses of state power is precisely the kind of consideration that has traditionally been considered weighty enough to override the need to dispense deserved punishments. Guaranteeing that offenders are punished to the full extent they deserve would require loosening procedural safeguards that make convictions more difficult to obtain. This is because an offender's deservingness is due to his guilt, not his conviction. Thus the more difficult it is to convict guilty parties, the worse we do at giving offenders everything they deserve. But many procedural guarantees—including the right to effective counsel, the right against unreasonable searches, the right against self-incrimination, the right to appeal, and the prohibition on double jeopardy, among many others—are justified because of risks posed by overzealous or abusive criminal justice officials. Such safeguards are justified precisely because the added protection from undeserved punishment (especially for those who are most vulnerable) is morally weightier than the additional deserved punishments that would otherwise be meted out. Thus we should not accept the retributivist argument for stripping offenders of their political rights unless it can be shown that the risks posed by the use of disenfranchisement are less weighty than the need to ensure that offenders receive *this specific* punishment. The importance of these competing values is likely to be missed if one does not pay adequate attention to the concerns driving non-ideal penal theory.

Concluding Remarks

I have argued against the common practice of suspending convicted offenders' basic political rights. A consistent theme in the forgoing discussion is that standard analyses of criminal disenfranchisement in terms of legitimate penal aims fail to appreciate broader ways in which penal practices frequently undermine these justifying aims. Moreover, these broader implications of penal disenfranchisement have been overlooked as a result of idealized assumptions and simplifications that are ubiquitous in ideal penal theory. Non-ideal theory, in contrast, acknowledges the importance of evaluating punishments in their social, political, and historical contexts. The fact that a given practice could, in principle, be part of a fully just penal system is insufficient to justify its use in the actual world.

When we take up a less idealized perspective, it becomes clearer that there may be some forms of punishment that should not be utilized by actual societies, regardless of whether these punishments could in principle be deployed justly. As the case of disenfranchisement illustrates, when a society treats some of its citizens unjustly, its choice of punishments can make matters worse. While this example makes the link between punishment and the reproduction of injustice especially vivid and straightforward, this will not be the only form of punishment that has such implications. Any penal practices that make society less responsive to the morally weighty concerns of vulnerable groups—those who are most likely to bear the burden of unjust punishment—are potentially open to this same challenge. For example, official or unofficial policies that restrict prison newspapers or prison writing programs, deny prisoners the right to organize or unionize, install onerous grievance procedures for addressing misconduct by criminal justice officials, or prevent ex-offenders from having meaningful economic and social opportunities are all likely to undermine political voices of marginalized communities.[46]

The concerns presented in this chapter should also encourage a more critical examination of incarceration itself, along with other aspects of American policing and punishment. If the main argument of this essay succeeds in identifying strong moral reasons for ceasing our practice of denying offenders their basic political rights, it might also shed light on similarly strong reasons to reform or abolish other familiar penal practices. Of course these reasons might sometimes be outweighed by important social needs that our familiar practices meet; but if we are concerned with ensuring that our social practices are morally defensible, this is not something we can assume without argument. Given how easily criminal laws can be used as tools of domination and oppression, it is important to acknowledge these reasons, and to incorporate them into one's ethical analysis. We are not justified in ignoring or downplaying the costs that real societies' penal choices impose—especially not when those costs are borne by those who are already vulnerable to injustice. These costs are real, they are significant, and they matter.

Acknowledgements I would like to thank audiences at the UNC-Chapel Hill's 2015 PPE/Value Theory Workshop, the 2016 Central Division meeting of the American Philosophical Association, and the 2016 meeting of Association for Practical and Professional Ethics. I would also like to thank Joshua Blanchard, Allison Fritz, Jennifer Kling, Clare LaFrance, John Lawless, Tim Loughrist, Garreth McMaster, Chris Melenovsky, Adam Thompson, Preston Werner, Mark White, Matt Whitt, Vida Yao, and anonymous referees for enlightening conversations about some of this paper's central ideas, or for feedback on previous drafts.

Notes

1. I focus on disenfranchisement in the US, but my main argument has broader applicability. I focus on the US simply because loss of offenders' political rights is much less common and less extreme in the rest of the world. Most other democracies allow ex-convicts to participate in the political process, and many even allow prisoners to vote. For an examination of the variations in criminal disenfranchisement policies throughout the world, see the essays in *Criminal Disenfranchisement in an International Perspective*, ed. Alec C. Ewald and Brandono Rottinghaus. Cambridge: Cambridge University Press, 2009.
2. Uggen, Christopher, Ryan Larson, and Sarah Shannon. 2016. *6 Million Lost Voters: State-Level Estimates of Felony Disenfranchisement, 2016.*

Washington, DC: The Sentencing Project. https://www.sentencingproject.org/publications/6-million-lost-votersstate-level-estimates-felonydisenfranchisement-2016/3.

3. The existing literature focuses on the disenfranchisement of felons and ex-felons. I prefer to frame the issue in terms of *criminal* disenfranchisement for two reasons. First, which offenses are categorized as felonies varies widely from state to state. Second, at least six US states suspend the voting rights of those serving prison or jail sentences for *any* crimes—including misdemeanors—at the time of an election. This includes Illinois (*Illinois State Constitution* Art. III, Section 2), Indiana (*Indiana Code* 3-7-13), Kentucky (*Kentucky Constitution*, Section 145), Michigan (*Michigan Election Code* 168, Section 758b), Missouri (*Missouri Revised Statutes*, Section 115.133.2), and South Carolina (*South Carolina Code of Laws*, Section 7-5-120(B)).
4. Uggen, Christopher, Ryan Larson, and Sarah Shannon. 2016.
5. Rawls, John. 1971. *A Theory of Justice*. Cambridge: Harvard University Press, 8–9, 240–241. For more on ideal and non-ideal theory, see Mills, Charles W. 2005. "Ideal Theory" as Ideology. *Hypatia* 20(3): 165–184; O'Neill, Onora. 1987. Abstraction, Idealization, and Ideology in Ethics. In *Moral Philosophy and Contemporary Problems*, ed. J.D.G. Evans, 55–69. Cambridge: Cambridge University Press; and Valentini, Laura. 2012. Ideal vs. Non-ideal Theory: A Conceptual Map. *Philosophy Compass* 7(9): 654–664.
6. See, e.g., Duff, R. A. 1998. Law, Language, and Community: Some Preconditions of Criminal Liability. *Oxford Journal of Legal Studies* 18(2): 189–206; Matravers, Matt. 2006. "Who's Still Standing?" A Comment on Antony Duff's Preconditions of Criminal Liability. *Journal of Moral Philosophy* 3(3): 320–330; Tadros, Victor. 2009. Poverty And Criminal Responsibility. *Journal of Value Inquiry* 43: 391–413; Holroyd, Jules. 2010. Punishment and Justice. *Social Theory and Practice* 36(1): 78–111; and Chau, Peter. 2012. Duff on the Legitimacy of Punishment of Socially Deprived Offenders. *Criminal Law and Philosophy* 6: 247–254, among others.
7. Davis, Angela. 2003. *Are Prisons Obsolete?* New York: Seven Stories Press.
8. Davis. 2003, 85.
9. Davis. 2003, 112.
10. For more on the potential distorting influences of ideal theory, see Mills. 2005.
11. See, e.g., Kennedy, Randall. 1997. *Race, Crime, and the Law*. New York: Random House; Eskridge, William N., Jr. 1999. *Gaylaw: Challenging the Apartheid of the Closet*. Cambridge: Harvard University Press; Davis, Angela. 2003; Wacquant, Loïc. 2009. *Punishing the Poor: The Neoliberal*

Government of Social Insecurity. Durham: Duke University Press; Mogul, Joey L., Andrea J. Ritchie, and Kay Whitlock. 2011. *Queer (In)Justice: The Criminalization of LGBT People in the United States*. Boston: Beacon Press; and Alexander, Michelle. 2012. *The New Jim Crow* (Revised Edition). New York: The New Press.

12. See, e.g., Harvey, Alice E. 1994. Ex-Felon Disenfranchisement and Its Influence on the Black Vote: The Need for a Second Look. *University of Pennsylvania Law Review* 142: 1145–1189; Fletcher, George P. 1999. Disenfranchisement as Punishment: Reflection on the Racial Uses of Infamia. *UCLA Law Review* 46: 1895–1907; Manza, Jeff, and Christopher Uggen. 2008. *Locked Out: Felon Disenfranchisement and American Democracy*. New York: Oxford University Press (Chapters 2–3); Uggen, Christopher, Sarah Shannon, and Jeff Manza. 2012. *State-Level Estimates of Felon Disenfranchisement in the United States, 2010*. Washington, DC: The Sentencing Project. http://sentencingproject.org/doc/publications/fd_State_Level_Estimates_of_Felon_Disen_2010.pdf; Uggen, Larson, and Shannon. 2016. Some critics argue that this disparate racial impact a guiding motivation for these policies—these critics argue that criminal disenfranchisement is part of a larger system of control that was built out of, and is now largely maintained by, bias against people of color. See, e.g., Ewald, Alec C. 2002. "Civil Death": The Ideological Paradox of Criminal Disenfranchisement Law in the United States. *Wisconsin Law Review*: 1045–1137; Dugree-Pearson, Tanya. 2002. Disenfranchisement—A Race Neutral Punishment for Felony Offenders or a Way to Diminish the Minority Vote? *Hamline Journal of Public Law and Policy* 23: 359–402; Behrens, Angela, Christopher Uggen, and Jeff Manza. 2003. Ballot Manipulation and the "Menace of Negro Domination": Racial Threat and Felon Disenfranchisement in the United States, 1850–2002. *The American Journal of Sociology* 109(3): 559–605; Behrens Behrens, Angela. 2004. Voting—Not Quite a Fundamental Right? A Look at Legal and Legislative Challenges to Felon Disenfranchisement Laws. *Minnesota Law Review* 89: 231–275, 244–247; Gordon, Lewis R. 2005. Philosophical Anthropology, Race, and the Political Economy of Disenfranchisement. *Columbia Human Rights Law Review* 36: 145–172; Holloway, Pippa. 2009. "A Chicken-Stealer Shall Lose His Vote": Disenfranchisement for Larceny in the South, 1874–1890. *The Journal of Southern History* 75(4): 931–962; and Alexander. 2012. For an opposing viewpoint, see Clegg, Roger, George T. Conway, III, and Kenneth K. Lee. 2008. The Case Against Felon Voting. *University of St. Thomas Journal of Law and Public Policy* 2(1).

13. Uggen, Larson, and Shannon. 2016, 16.
14. Uggen, Larson, and Shannon. 2016, 3.
15. For an argument along these lines, see Clegg, Roger. 2001. Who Should Vote? *Texas Review of Law & Politics* 6: 159–178. For a similar response to complaints about racial disparities in the use of capital punishment, see Van Den Haag, Ernest. 1985. Refuting Reiman and Nathanson. *Philosophy and Public Affairs* 14(2): 165–176.
16. See Kennedy, Randall. 1997; Mauer, Marc. 2006. *Race to Incarcerate* (2nd Edition). New York: The New Press; Wacquant, Loïc. 2009; Alexander, Michelle. 2012; and Lerman, Amy E., and Vesla M. Weaver. 2014. *Arresting Citizenship: The Democratic Consequences of American Crime Control*. Chicago: The University of Chicago Press, among many others.
17. That is not to say that such in-principle objections to disenfranchisement are doomed to fail. For my purposes here, I do not wish to take a stand on such matters.
18. See, e.g., Altman, Andrew. 2005. Democratic Self-Determination and the Disenfranchisement of Felons. *Journal of Applied Philosophy* 22(3): 263–273; and Sigler, Mary. 2014. Defensible Disenfranchisement. *Iowa Law Review* 99: 1725–1744. For a compelling response to these arguments from the perspective of democratic political theory, see Whitt, Matt. 2017. Felon Disenfranchisement and Democratic Legitimacy. *Social Theory and Practice* 43(2): 283–311.
19. Duff. 2013. See also Duff, R. A. 2001. *Punishment, Communication, and Community*. New York: Oxford University Press; and Bennett, Christopher. 2016. Penal Disenfranchisement. *Criminal Law and Philosophy* 10(3): 411–425.
20. As we will see, Bennett. 2016 explicitly endorses disenfranchisement *as a form of punishment* on such grounds.
21. See, e.g., Lippke, Richard L. 2001. The Disenfranchisement of Felons. *Law and Philosophy* 20: 553–580, 568–569; Cholbi, Michael J. 2002. A Felon's Right to Vote. *Law and Philosophy* 21: 543–565, 557–558; Brenner, Saul, and Nicholas J. Caste. 2003. Granting Suffrage to Felons in Prison. *Journal of Social Philosophy* 34(2): 228–243, 232–233; LaFollette, Hugh. 2005. Collateral Consequences of Punishment: Civil Penalties Accompanying Formal Punishment. *Journal of Applied Philosophy* 22(3): 241–261, 248–250; Uggen, Christopher, Angela Behrens, and Jeff Manza. 2005. Criminal Disenfranchisement. *Annual Review of Law and Social Science* 1: 307–322, 310–311; and Manza and Uggen. 2008, 35–36.
22. Whether or not offenders value the right to vote at the moment they are considering criminal behavior, interviews with convicted offenders

support the contention that many disenfranchisees care deeply about their inability to participate in political affairs. See Manza and Uggen. 2008, Chapter 6, and Lerman and Weaver. 2014.

23. See, e.g., Fletcher. 1999; Lippke. 2001, 574; Cholbi. 2002, 559; Brenner and Caste. 2003, 232–233; Austin, Regina. 2005. "The Shame of It All": Stigma and the Political Disenfranchisement of Formerly Convicted and Incarcerated Persons. *Columbia Human Rights Review* 36: 173–192; Kleinig, John, and Kevin Murtagh. 2005. Disenfranchising Felons. *Journal of Applied Philosophy* 22(3): 217–239, 230–231; and Bennett. 2016.
24. Manza and Uggen. 2008, Chapter 5–6.
25. Manza and Uggen. 2008, 133.
26. Sigler. 2014, 1738.
27. Lerman and Weaver. 2014, Chapter 8.
28. Wilson, James Q. 1985. *Thinking About Crime* (Revised Edition). New York: Vintage Books, 121.
29. Alexander. 2012, 72.
30. Lippke. 2001, 557.
31. Bowers, Melanie, and Robert R. Preuhs. 2009. Collateral Consequences of a Collateral Penalty: The Negative Effect of Felon Disenfranchisement Laws on the Political Participation of Nonfelons. *Social Science Quarterly* 90(3): 722–743.
32. Lerman and Weaver. 2014, Chapter 8.
33. Waldron, Jeremy. 1998. The Right of Rights. *Proceedings of the Aristotelian Society* 98: 307–337, 316. See also Lippke. 2001, 556 and Ewald. 2002.
34. See, e.g., Austin. 2005.
35. See Clegg. 2001; Clegg, Conway, and Lee. 2008; and Sigler. 2014. For response, see Fletcher. 1999; Cholbi. 2002; Ewald. 2002; Kleinig and Murtagh. 2005; LaFollette. 2005, 251–252; and Bennett. 2016.
36. This systematic lack of trust and the systematic failure to recognize certain members of society as being able to contribute to knowledge and understanding constitute a type of epistemic injustice. For a more detailed discussion of this type of injustice, see Fricker, Miranda. 1988. Rational Authority and Social Power: Towards a Truly Social Epistemology. *Proceedings of the Aristotelian Society* 98: 159–177.
37. The American parole system is a major driver of US prison populations:

> [I]n 1980, only 1% of all prison admissions were parole violators. Twenty years later, more than one third (35%) of prison admissions resulted from parole violations. To put the matter more starkly:

About as many people were returned to prison for parole violations in 2000 as were admitted to prison in 1980 for all reasons. Of all parole violators returned to prison in 2000, only one-third returned for new conviction; two-thirds were returned for a technical violation [...]. Alexander. 2012, 95 Given that most states that allow probationers to vote do not extend these rights to prisoners, parole violations are a major driver of American disenfranchisement.

38. For discussion of laws in several states punishing petty larceny—including theft of livestock—with disenfranchisement, see Holloway. 2009.
39. A handful of states currently prohibit the distribution of sex toys. Such laws can carry significant criminal penalties, including prison terms of up to three years and fines of up to $10,000; see Lindemann, Danielle J. 2006. Pathology Full Circle: A History of Anti-vibrator Legislation in the United States. *Columbia Journal of Gender and Law* 15: 326–346, 331–334. Felony convictions under Alabama's statute are considered crimes of "moral turpitude" and carry a *lifetime* disqualification from voting. The constitutionality of these statutes has not been completely resolved, as the federal courts have been divided on this issue. For discussion of the history and constitutional status of these laws, see Lindemann. 2006 and Glover, Richard. 2010. Can't Buy a Thrill: Substantive Due Process, Equal Protection, and Criminalizing Sex Toys. *The Journal of Criminal Law and Criminology* 100: 101–143.
40. For an excellent discussion of some of these problems, see Finkelstein, Claire. 2002. Death and Retribution. *Criminal Justice Ethics* 21(2): 12–21.
41. Clegg. 2001, 172.
42. Deigh, John. 1988. On Rights and Responsibilities. *Law and Philosophy* 7(2): 147–178, 158, although it should be noted that Deigh does not take disenfranchisement to be punitive.
43. For discussion of this, see Lippke. 2001, 561–568; Cholbi. 2002; Ewald. 2002; Brenner and Caste. 2003, 238–240; and Kleinig and Murtagh. 2005; and Bennett. 2016.
44. Bennett. 2016, 419.
45. Bennett. 2016, 423. For this reason, Bennett's form of retributivism could not plausibly be used to justify criminal disenfranchisement on the scale that it is practiced in the US.
46. For discussion of the anti-democratic impact of such practices, see Davis. 2003, Chapter 3 and Lerman and Weaver. 2014.

Bibliography

Alexander, Michelle. 2012. *The New Jim Crow* (Revised Edition). New York: The New Press.

Altman, Andrew. 2005. Democratic Self-Determination and the Disenfranchisement of Felons. *Journal of Applied Philosophy* 22(3): 263–273.

Austin, Regina. 2005. "The Shame of It All": Stigma and the Political Disenfranchisement of Formerly Convicted and Incarcerated Persons. *Columbia Human Rights Review* 36: 173–192.

Behrens, Angela. 2004. Voting—Not Quite a Fundamental Right? A Look at Legal and Legislative Challenges to Felon Disenfranchisement Laws. *Minnesota Law Review* 89: 231–275.

Behrens, Angela, Christopher Uggen, and Jeff Manza. 2003. Ballot Manipulation and the "Menace of Negro Domination": Racial Threat and Felon Disenfranchisement in the United States, 1850–2002. *The American Journal of Sociology* 109(3): 559–605.

Bennett, Christopher. 2016. Penal Disenfranchisement. *Criminal Law and Philosophy* 10(3): 411–425.

Bowers, Melanie, and Robert R. Preuhs. 2009. Collateral Consequences of a Collateral Penalty: The Negative Effect of Felon Disenfranchisement Laws on the Political Participation of Nonfelons. *Social Science Quarterly* 90(3): 722–743.

Brenner, Saul, and Nicholas J. Caste. 2003. Granting Suffrage to Felons in Prison. *Journal of Social Philosophy* 34(2): 228–243.

Calvani, Terry. 1971–72. Homosexuality and the Law—An Overview. *New York Law Forum* 17: 273–303.

Chau, Peter. 2012. Duff on the Legitimacy of Punishment of Socially Deprived Offenders. *Criminal Law and Philosophy* 6: 247–254.

Cholbi, Michael J. 2002. A Felon's Right to Vote. *Law and Philosophy* 21: 543–565.

Clegg, Roger. 2001. Who Should Vote? *Texas Review of Law & Politics* 6: 159–178.

Clegg, Roger, George T. Conway, III, and Kenneth K. Lee. 2008. The Case Against Felon Voting. *University of St. Thomas Journal of Law and Public Policy* 2(1): 1–19.

Davis, Angela. 2003. *Are Prisons Obsolete?* New York: Seven Stories Press.

Deign, John. 1988. On Rights and Responsibilities. *Law and Philosophy* 7(2): 147–178.

Duff, R. A. 1998. Law, Language, and Community: Some Preconditions of Criminal Liability. *Oxford Journal of Legal Studies* 18(2): 189–206.

Duff, R. A. 2001. *Punishment, Communication, and Community*. New York: Oxford University Press.

Duff, R. A. 2013. Legal Punishment. *Stanford Encyclopedia of Philosophy* (Summer 2013 Edition), Edward N. Zalta (ed.). http://plato.stanford.edu/archives/sum2013/entries/legal-punishment/.

Dugree-Pearson, Tanya. 2002. Disenfranchisement—A Race Neutral Punishment for Felony Offenders or a Way to Diminish the Minority Vote? *Hamline Journal of Public Law and Policy* 23: 359–402.

Eskridge, William N., Jr. 1999. *Gaylaw: Challenging the Apartheid of the Closet.* Cambridge: Harvard University Press.

Ewald, Alec C. 2002. "Civil Death": The Ideological Paradox of Criminal Disenfranchisement Law in the United States. *Wisconsin Law Review* 5(5): 1045–1137.

Ewald, Alec C., and Brandon Rottinghaus (eds.). 2009. *Criminal Disenfranchisement in an International Perspective.* Cambridge: Cambridge University Press.

Finkelstein, Claire. 2002. Death and Retribution. *Criminal Justice Ethics* 21(2): 12–21.

Fletcher, George P. 1999. Disenfranchisement as Punishment: Reflection on the Racial Uses of Infamia. *UCLA Law Review* 46: 1895–1907.

Fricker, Miranda. 1988. Rational Authority and Social Power: Towards a Truly Social Epistemology. *Proceedings of the Aristotelian Society* 98: 159–177.

Glover, Richard. Can't Buy a Thrill: Substantive Due Process, Equal Protection, and Criminalizing Sex Toys. *The Journal of Criminal Law and Criminology* 100: 101–143.

Gordon, Lewis R. 2005. Philosophical Anthropology, Race, and the Political Economy of Disenfranchisement. *Columbia Human Rights Law Review* 36: 145–172.

Harvey, Alice E. 1994. Ex-Felon Disenfranchisement and Its Influence on the Black Vote: The Need for a Second Look. *University of Pennsylvania Law Review* 142: 1145–1189.

Holloway, Pippa. 2009. "A Chicken-Stealer Shall Lose His Vote": Disenfranchisement for Larceny in the South, 1874–1890. *The Journal of Southern History* 75(4): 931–962.

Holroyd, Jules. 2010. Punishment and Justice. *Social Theory and Practice* 36(1): 78–111.

Kennedy, Randall. 1997. *Race, Crime, and the Law.* New York: Random House.

Kleinig, John, and Kevin Murtagh. 2005. Disenfranchising Felons. *Journal of Applied Philosophy* 22(3): 217–239.

LaFollette, Hugh. 2005. Collateral Consequences of Punishment: Civil Penalties Accompanying Formal Punishment. *Journal of Applied Philosophy* 22(3): 241–261.

Lerman, Amy E., and Vesla M. Weaver. 2014. *Arresting Citizenship: The Democratic Consequences of American Crime Control.* Chicago: The University of Chicago Press.

Lindemann, Danielle J. 2006. Pathology Full Circle: A History of Anti-vibrator Legislation in the United States. *Columbia Journal of Gender and Law* 15: 326–346.

Lippke, Richard L. 2001. The Disenfranchisement of Felons. *Law and Philosophy* 20: 553–580.

Manza, Jeff, and Christopher Uggen. 2008. *Locked Out: Felon Disenfranchisement and American Democracy.* New York: Oxford University Press.

Matravers, Matt. 2006. "Who's Still Standing?" A Comment on Antony Duff's Preconditions of Criminal Liability. *Journal of Moral Philosophy* 3(3): 320–330.

Mauer, Marc. 2006. *Race to Incarcerate* (2nd Edition). New York: The New Press.

Mogul, Joey L., Andrea J. Ritchie, and Kay Whitlock. 2011. *Queer (In)Justice: The Criminalization of LGBT People in the United States.* Boston: Beacon Press.

Mills, Charles W. 2005. "Ideal Theory" as Ideology. *Hypatia* 20(3): 165–184.

O'Neill, Onora. 1987. Abstraction, Idealization, and Ideology in Ethics. In *Moral Philosophy and Contemporary Problems,* edited by J. D. G. Evans, 55–69. Cambridge: Cambridge University Press.

Rawls, John. 1971. *A Theory of Justice.* Cambridge: Harvard University Press.

Sigler, Mary. 2014. Defensible Disenfranchisement. *Iowa Law Review* 99: 1725–1744.

Tadros, Victor. 2009. Poverty and Criminal Responsibility. *Journal of Value Inquiry* 43: 391–413.

Uggen, Christopher, Angela Behrens, and Jeff Manza. 2005. Criminal Disenfranchisement. *Annual Review of Law and Social Science* 1: 307–322.

Uggen, Christopher, Ryan Larson, and Sarah Shannon. 2016. *6 Million Lost Voters: State—Level Estimates of Felony Disenfranchisement, 2016.* Washington, DC: The Sentencing Project. https://www.sentencingproject.org/publications/6-million-lost-voters-state-level-estimates-felony-disenfranchisement-2016/.

Uggen, Christopher, Sarah Shannon, and Jeff Manza. 2012. *State-Level Estimates of Felon Disenfranchisement in the United States, 2010.* Washington, DC: The Sentencing Project. http://sentencingproject.org/doc/publications/fd_State_Level_Estimates_of_Felon_Disen_2010.pdf.

Valentini, Laura. 2012. Ideal vs. Non-ideal Theory: A Conceptual Map. *Philosophy Compass* 7(9): 654–664.

Van Den Haag, Ernest. 1985. Refuting Reiman and Nathanson. *Philosophy and Public Affairs* 14(2): 165–176.

Wacquant, Loïc. 2009. *Punishing the Poor: The Neoliberal Government of Social Insecurity*. Durham: Duke University Press.

Waldron, Jeremy. 1998. The Right of Rights. *Proceedings of the Aristotelian Society* 98: 307–337.

Whitt, Matt. 2017. Felon Disenfranchisement and Democratic Legitimacy. *Social Theory and Practice* 43(2): 283–311.

Wilson, James Q. 1985. *Thinking About Crime* (Revised Edition). New York: Vintage Books.

Philosophers in Prison: Students in the Indiana Women's Prison College Program Reflect on Philosophical Theories of Punishment

Mariam Kazanjian

While I cannot fully do justice to the richness of all of our conversations and that of each individual essay, this work is the result of a collaborative effort between myself and my students, and so authorial credit should also go to Lori Record, Anastazia Schmid, Cynthia Long, Jennifer Fleming, D'Antonette Burns, and Andrea Hubbell.

Since philosophy is a communal enterprise, it is a particular privilege to hold a philosophical conversation with people whose voices are too often excluded, like my students at the Indiana Women's Prison. These women taught me that Aristotelian virtue ethics might give us some insight into abusive relationships, and Plato's tripartite soul can express the intensity of drug addiction. When my class had the opportunity to present at Bowling Green's conference on the Ethics of Policing and Prisons, they

M. Kazanjian (✉)
Department of Philosophy, Indiana University Bloomington,
Bloomington, IN, USA

M. Gardner and M. Weber (eds.), *The Ethics of Policing and Imprisonment*, Palgrave Studies in Ethics and Public Policy,
https://doi.org/10.1007/978-3-319-97770-6_3

chose to speak about just punishment, and particularly about education behind bars. In this paper, I try to faithfully recreate some of their reasoning, convinced that the perspective of the punished adds something important to the wider conversation about punishment.

Our class studied theories of punishment as part of a broader survey of social and political philosophy. As is typical, the syllabus divided consequentialist and retributive theories of punishment into separate units. We began by studying retributive theories, whose authors agree that blameworthiness is a sufficient reason to punish an offender.[1] The philosophers in the texts we read think that people should get what they justly deserve in recompense for their crimes, without committing themselves on questions of method (although many seem to prefer some version of *lex talionis*). They also reject the notion that we can waive considerations of desert to better serve the offender or society. As Immanuel Kant says, "justice would cease to be justice if it were bartered away for any consideration whatever."[2]

Responding to these readings, that class agreed that even if retributive sentiments could justify a practice of punishment, they do not justify current penal practices in America. More than one in one hundred Americans are incarcerated, roughly 2.3 million inmates,[3] a sum larger than the total of all prisoners in the 36 largest prisons in Europe.[4] America also leads the world in the rate at which it imprisons its own citizens, 750 people per 100,000, a significantly higher percentage than that in countries that are known human rights violators: Iran, South Africa, and Russia.[5] However, my students noted that politicians often cite seemingly retributive, tough on crime agendas to justify the current state of mass incarceration.

Though the numbers are disturbing, the first-person accounts by the women in my class are more so. Jennifer Fleming wrote this haunting passage:

> 126871 that is how I am identified now. I have lost my children, my home, my car, and my freedom. My dad's ashes and my cat were barely saved from the garbage dump and the pound. I have been stripped, searched, judged, and degraded in every way. My children no longer have names; they have case numbers.

Fleming concludes by saying that she only wishes that "instead of focusing on how severely [she] should be punished" someone has taken the time to "actually see [her]"—the mother, Sunday-school teacher, daughter, and student.

In such a system, the women believe that there are many reasons blameworthy people should not be punished. As Douglas Husak says, "desert cannot hope to answer all the questions about the justifiability of the distribution of punishment."[6] Sometimes the legally available punishments seem grossly disproportionate to the crime, even when the offender admits, as Fleming does, that she is willing to "take full responsibility" for her poor choices. Whether the costs are too great will be determined on a case-by-case basis—but certainly in a country where a man served 50 years without parole for stealing videotapes it is reasonable to think that they often are.[7]

The students also noted that racial disparities in punishment in America make appeals to desert complicated. So that we could better understand the philosophical aspect of this question, my students read Ernest Van Den Haag, who firmly states: "Equality seems morally less important than justice. And justice is independent of distributional inequalities."[8]

The women question if, in practice, justice can really be independent of distributional inequalities. Student Andrea Hubbell points out that not only does unequal justice seem to undermine the deterrent effect of the law, but it also threatens our faith in its moral foundations. She quotes Martin Luther King Jr., writing: "Injustice anywhere is a threat to justice everywhere."

However, this concern with racial disparities in punishment revealed one important point of commonality between retributivist thinking and my students'. They are absolutely opposed to the punishment of the innocent for any reason whatsoever, and suspect that racism and class prejudice sweep innocent people into the penal system every day. Prisoners trade disturbing anecdotes about friends unjustly incarcerated for small infractions. Evidence suggests that these anecdotes are part of a larger pattern of aggressive and discriminatory policing, combined with prosecutorial pressure to accept plea-bargains, which often end up branding blameless individuals as felons before they ever see a judge.[9]

The women at IWP are more sympathetic to some central commitments of a consequentialist theory of punishment. When the course readings turned to consequentialists, they found many things they liked. They are drawn to the idea that, since punishment is itself a harm, it is only justified when the punishment will allow us to avoid a larger harm.

As Bentham puts it: "all punishment is itself evil…if it ought at all to be admitted, it ought only to be admitted in as far as it promised to exclude some greater evil."[10] The students agreed with consequentialists that legal punishment can have the net positive effect of deterring, incapacitating, or reforming criminals, and can be justified by reference to those things.[11]

However, they are quick to point out that punishment in America is focused primarily on incapacitation and deterrence, not rehabilitation. Prison in America is, as graduate student Anastazia Schmid writes, "one of the worst circumstances a human being could ever be brought to," and the women are left grasping "at any opportunity in the environment that [they can] find." The natural consequence is that after years lost and limited opportunities behind bars, returning citizens bearing the stigma of a felony conviction cannot obtain jobs or receive government aid. This state of affairs threatens to undermine the benefits of legal punishment, and greatly increase its costs.

Over half of newly released prisoners will be recommitted within three years of their release date.[12] The number of parolees who are arrested for a new crime is even higher, an alarming 68%.[13] Rehabilitative programs change this, particularly increased educational opportunities for prisoners, which have been shown to dramatically reduce recidivism rates and correlate with other positive outcomes, like better employment opportunities, increased earnings, and continued educational achievement.[14] This has cascading financial and social benefits for the community, and could eventually reduce state spending on corrections and other related expenditures, which reached 55 billion in 2014, and was projected to increase to 57.2 billion in 2015.[15]

Focusing on these sorts of statistics is very persuasive to certain audiences, something that the women, some of who have testified before the state legislature, recognize. Politicians often resist funding rehabilitative programs. One Republican congressman in New York scoffed that instead of saving for college he would "sit [his son] down and explain how to rob a bank" so that the young man could receive a free education in prison.[16] Yet, it makes sense, as student Cynthia Long says, for the community to care about rehabilitating offenders into "law-abiding men and women," who contribute to "economy while influencing others to follow the same positive path." As D'Antonette Burns adds with characteristic wit: "a released prisoner will be coming soon, to a neighborhood near you!"

Yet despite sympathizing with some key consequentialist arguments, and recognizing the winning power of the statistics, student Hubbell expresses a critical reservation about consequentialist reasoning:

> Even though these statistics are a wonderful thing and should, in my opinion, be taken into consideration, reducing recidivism is not the reason for implementing [rehabilitative] programs. Reducing recidivism is a byproduct, but we should practice restorative justice first of all because it is the right thing to do.

Rehabilitation might benefit society by lowering the costs of punishment and deterring future crimes more effectively than incarceration alone. Yet, even if it failed to benefit the community, Hubbell thinks this is something we owe to each other.

Over the course of all our discussions, it became clear that the women's views could not be fully explained by either retributive or consequentialist arguments. At times they focused on the corrective and beneficial aspects of justice, and at other times raised questions of permissibility and proportion. Along with all of this they consistently raised concerns about how offenders seem to have no voice and few rights once they have been convicted of a crime. These women want recognition and respect as members of the moral community. Schmid writes that what she needs most is for someone to see her "as a human being and not a DOC number," to "see beyond the khaki uniform and the badge…the crime I committed, and the label society put on me."

The view of punishment that the students expressed seems the closest to one of the classic "mixed" theories, which incorporates insights from both retributive and consequentialist thinkers. The most famous of these mixed views belong to H.L.A. Hart and John Rawls, but many philosophers agree on the need for a hybrid account of punishment.[17] One of the benefits of such views is that they can better respond to criticisms of either consequentialism or retributivism, sidestepping concerns about punishing the innocent for instrumental reasons, or mercilessly inflicting harsh punishments on blameworthy individuals.

The women's prime contention—that a theory of punishment should account for the moral claims of offenders—is most like one classic mixed theory of punishment, John Locke's rights-forfeiture view. Locke's unique focus on restitution and the rights of offenders makes the comparison an especially apt one. I do not have space for a defense of a rights-forfeiture theory of punishment, though it has been amply defended and criticized in other places.[18] However, since I think my students' have a consistent and compelling view, I will try to make clear some of the similarities and explain why the parallel is a productive one.

Locke believes that punishment, properly administered, will have good consequences for society and for the criminal. At one point in the *Second Treatise*, Locke analogizes punishment to the treatment of a sick body, saying that political power necessarily includes the authority to "tend to the preservation of the whole, by cutting off those parts, and those only, which are so corrupt that they threaten the sound and healthy."[19] The political body is thus preserved by punishment. Still, despite this gruesome metaphor, Locke is also concerned with the welfare of the offender. He thinks that through punishment the lawbreaker might "repent," and the punishment will "thereby deter him, and by his example others, from doing the like mischief" in the future.[20] Punishment in this sense is both socially useful and individually remedial, serving to protect society and correct the criminal.

From the above passages, it is clear that Locke often relies on consequentialist reasoning, using forward-looking concerns to justify punishment. Still, he adds some desert-based constraints onto the practice of punishment, making his theory a properly mixed one. First, the person punished must be responsible for his or her actions. He cannot be one who "comes not to such a degree of reason wherein he might be supposed capable of knowing the law, and so living within the rule of it."[21] Under this heading, Locke includes lunatics and children. Second, we ought to retribute to a wrongdoer only "what is proportionate to his transgression."[22] Once an offender has been apprehended, no one has "no absolute or arbitrary power to use a criminal…according to the passionate heats or boundless extravagancy of his own will."[23]

Third, the person punishing must have the proper authority to do so. In "A Second Letter Concerning Toleration," Locke writes, "though useless punishment be unlawful from any hand, yet useful punishment from every hand is not lawful."[24] Returning to the analogy of the sick man, Locke explains that "a man may have the stone, and it may be useful, more than indirectly" for him to "be cut."[25] However, "this usefulness will not justify the most skillful surgeon in the world, by force, to make him endure the pain and hazard of cutting" because the surgeon has "no right without the patient's own consent to do so."[26] Locke concludes emphatically that without the right to operate, considerations of use are no "good argument."[27]

Finally, Locke will consistently return to the idea that the loss of certain rights *does not abrogate all other rights* and that even a known criminal is entitled to certain protections. As he puts it, "though I may kill a thief that sets on me in the highway, yet I may not (which seems less) take away his money and let him go."[28] A man by putting himself in a state of war with society by some criminal act "forfeits his preservation and life together," but not all his rights, and not always permanently.[29] As with the highway robber, he loses only what he must lose to protect the state, like for instance his liberty, or to repay the person who has been wronged, by forfeiting an equitable portion of his property.

Locke is obviously deeply concerned with the rights of offenders, unsurprising given his historical circumstances. Like many of his contemporaries, Locke witnessed extremes of religious and political persecution and, because of this, provides a theory of punishment that limits the state's power to abuse citizen rights, even the rights of offenders. For this reason, Locke's rights-forfeiture theory of punishment provides a language of advocacy for my students. It most closely matches how they talk about the moral claims that they can make qua human beings. It also has uptake in a rights-conscious country like America, allowing the women to persuasively make those claims in political discourse.

Besides defending the rights of offenders, Locke also focuses on another topic that comes up often when these women discuss punishment: reparation. Like most rights-forfeiture theorists, Locke is particularly focused on reparation, or restoring what has been lost by the injured party. He says that the person "who has suffered the damage," he can require "from the offender so much as may make satisfaction for the harm he has suffered."[30] The victim's right to compensation cannot be abridged. Even though the magistrate, who can otherwise "remit the punishment of criminal offences" when it does not serve the common good, may not dispense with an individual's claim to reparation.[31] This the injured person "alone can remit."[32]

Although Locke is particularly focused on restoring property to injured parties, it is possible to use the same sort of reasoning in restorative justice practices by focusing on moral restitution.[33] As Fleming says, after her crushing battle with addiction all she wants is a space to "earn her name back." By focusing on reparation instead of taking primarily punitive actions, we both recognize these women as members of our moral community, and also give them a way to make things right. By offering options for this sort of restitution, like education programs in prisons with a sentence reduction attached for a completed degree, we give them, as student Lori Record puts it, "a way back into society," and for her in particular, "a way back into her family."

Because he strongly affirms offender's rights and the significance of reparation, I believe that Locke's theory can give the best and most coherent defense of my students' belief that, despite their criminal histories, they retain both their dignity and their right to a second chance. In closing I will add one additional thing that a rights forfeiture theory might suggest. When we respect someone's rights as a fellow human being, we are bound to value her opinion in matters that deeply concern her. I see no reason why offenders should have lost this right entirely, whichever other rights they may have lost. It matters what they think is the best rationale for punishment, because they live with the outcome of the debate in a way that most of us will not. These women belong in our conversations, academic and otherwise, about the practice of punishment.

Notes

1. See Moore, Michael S. 1987. The Moral Worth of Retribution. In Ferdinand Schoeman ed., *Responsibility, Character, and the Emotions: New Essays in Moral Psychology*. Cambridge: Cambridge University Press; Murphy, Jeffrie G. 1973. Marxism and Retribution. *Philosophy and Public Affairs* 2: 217–243; Morris, Herbert. 1968. Persons and Punishment. *The Monist* 52(4): 475–501; and Nozick, Robert. 1981. *Philosophical Explanations*. Cambridge, MA: Harvard University Press, 366–374.
2. Kant, Immanuel. 1887. *The Philosophy of Law: An Exposition of the Fundamental Principles of Jurisprudence as the Science of Right*. Trans. W. Hastie, B.D. Edinburgh: T & T Clark, at 196.
3. Pew Center on the States. 2008. *One in 100: Behind Bars in America 2008*. Washington, DC: Pew Research Center. http://www.pewtrusts.org/en/research-and-analysis/reports/2008/02/28/one-in-100-behind-bars-in-america-2008.
4. Kant. 1887, 5.
5. Kant. 1887, 5.
6. Husak, Douglas. 1992. Why Punish the Deserving? *Nous* 26(4): 447–464, at 449.
7. The case is *Lockyer v. Andrade*, in which the Supreme Court rejected eighth amendment challenges to California's controversial three-strikes law, which mandates 25 years to life for any third-time recidivist. Justice

Souter wrote a fiery dissent, saying "If Andrade's sentence [for stealing videotapes] is not grossly disproportionate, the principle has no meaning." For a further discussion of this and other similar cases see Alexander, Michelle. 2012. *The New Jim Crow* (Revised Edition). New York: The New Press.

8. Van Den Haag, Ernest. 1986. The Ultimate Punishment: A Defense of Capital Punishment. *The Harvard Law Review* 99: 1662–1669, at 250.
9. See Alexander, Michelle. 2012, Chapters 2 and 3.
10. Bentham, Jeremy. 1988. *An Introduction to the Principles of Morals and Legislation*. Amherst: Prometheus Books, Chapter 13.
11. See Pettit, Phillip. 1997. Republican Theory and Criminal Punishment. *Utilitas* 9(1): 59–79; Smart, J.J., and Bernard Williams. 1973. *Utilitarianism: For & Against*. Cambridge: Cambridge University Press; and Walker, Nigel. 1991. *Why Punish?* Oxford: Oxford University Press.
12. Pew Center on the States. 2008, 4.
13. Erisman, Wendy, and Jeanne Bayer Contardo. 2005. *Learning to Reduce Recidivism: A 50-State Analysis of Postsecondary Correction Education Policy*. Washington, DC: The Institute for Higher Education Policy.
14. Meyers, Stephen J. 2012. Establishing Successful Postsecondary Academic Programs: A Practical Guide. *The Journal of Correctional Education* 63(2): 6–26, at 7.
15. National Association of State Budget Officers (NASBO). 2015. *Examining Fiscal 2013–2015 State Spending*. Washington, DC.
16. Kaplan, Thomas. 2014. Cuomo Drops Plant to Use State Money to Pay for College Classes for Inmates. *New York Times*, April 2.
17. See Berman, Mitchell. 2008. Punishment and Justification. *Ethics* 118(2): 258–290; Garvey, Stephen P. 2004. Lifting the Veil on Punishment. *Cornell Law Faculty Publications*; and Husak, Douglas. 1992.
18. For a defense see Wellman, Christopher Heath. 2017. *Rights Forfeiture and Punishment*. New York: Oxford University Press. For criticism see Rosebury, Brian. 2015. The Theory of Offender's Forfeited Right. *Criminal Justice Ethics* 34(3): 259–283.
19. Locke, John. 2003. *Two Treatises of Government and a Letter Concerning Toleration*. Ian Shapiro ed., New Haven, CT: Yale University Press, at 177.
20. Locke. 2003, 103.
21. Locke. 2003, 125.
22. Locke. 2003, 103.
23. Locke. 2003, 103.
24. Locke, John. 1824. *The Works of John Locke in Nine Volumes*. London: Rivington, at 113.
25. Locke. 1824, 113.

26. Locke. 1824, 113.
27. Locke. 1824, 113.
28. Locke. 1824, 199.
29. Locke. 2003, 110.
30. Locke. 2003, 104.
31. Locke. 2003, 104.
32. Locke. 2003, 104.
33. Locke does have an account of capital punishment, about which there is a series of interpretive problems I will not cover here. Despite some misleadingly retributive language, it seems possible that Locke thinks that a murderer has forfeited his right to life, not because he must repay his crime in kind, but rather because he is dangerous. Locke also discusses penal servitude as an alternative to the death penalty, and generally agitates for more moderate punishments.

Bibliography

Bentham, Jeremy. *An Introduction to the Principles of Morals and Legislation.* Amherst: Prometheus Books, 1988.

Berman, Mitchell. "Punishment and Justification." *Ethics*, vol. 118, no. 2, pp. 258–290, 2008.

Erisman, Wendy, and Jeanne Bayer Contardo. *Learning to Reduce Recidivism: A 50-State Analysis of Postsecondary Correction Education Policy.* Washington, DC: The Institute for Higher Education Policy, 2005. Web. 19 Dec 2015. at ix.

Garvey, Stephen P. "Lifting the Veil on Punishment." 2004. https://scholarship.law.cornell.edu/facpub/276.

Husak, Douglas. "Why Punish the Deserving?" *Nous*, vol. 26, no. 4, pp. 447–464, 1992.

Kant, Immanuel. *The Philosophy of Law: An Exposition of the Fundamental Principles of Jurisprudence as the Science of Right.* Trans. W. Hastie, B.D. Edinburgh: T & T Clark, 1887.

Kaplan, Thomas. "Cuomo Drops Plant to Use State Money to Pay for College Classes for Inmates." *New York Times*, April 2, 2014.

Locke, John. *The Works of John Locke in Nine Volumes.* London: Rivington, 1824. Online. pg 113.

———. In Ian Shapiro (ed.), *Two Treatises of Government and a Letter Concerning Toleration.* New Haven, CT: Yale University Press, 2003.

Meyers, Stephen J. "Establishing Successful Postsecondary Academic Programs; A Practical Guide." *The Journal of Correctional Education*, vol. 63, no. 2, pp. 6–26, 2012.

Moore, Michael S. "The Moral Worth of Retribution." In Ferdinand Schoeman (ed.), *Responsibility, Character, and the Emotions: New Essays in Moral Psychology*. Cambridge: Cambridge University Press, 1987.

Morris, Herbert. "Persons and Punishment." *The Monist*, vol. 52, no. 4, pp. 475–501, 1968.

Murphy, Jeffrie G. "Marxism and Retribution." *Philosophy and Public Affairs*, vol. 2, pp. 217–243, 1973.

National Association of State Budget Officers (NASBO). *Examining Fiscal 2013–2015 State Spending*. Washington, DC: Author, 2015.

Nozick, Robert. *Philosophical Explanations*, pp. 366–374. Cambridge, MA: Harvard University Press, 1981.

Pettit, Phillip. "Republican Theory and Criminal Punishment." *Utilitas*, vol. 9, no. 1, pp. 59–79, 1997.

Pew Center on the States. *One in 100: Behind Bars in America 2008*. Washington, DC: Pew Research Center, 2008. Web. 21 Dec 2015. at 5.

Rosebury, Brian. "The Theory of Offender's Forfeited Right." *Criminal Justice Ethics*, vol. 34, no. 3, pp. 259–283, 2015.

Smart, J.J., and Bernard Williams. *Utilitarianism: For & Against*. Cambridge: Cambridge University Press, 1973.

Van Den Haag, Ernest. "The Ultimate Punishment: A Defense of Capital Punishment." *The Harvard Law Review*, vol. 99, pp. 1662–1669. Harvard: Harvard Law Review Association, 1986.

Walker, Nigel. *Why Punish?* Oxford: Oxford University Press, 1991.

Wellman, Christopher Heath. *Rights Forfeiture and Punishment*. New York: Oxford University Press, 2017.

How Many Police Shootings Are Tragic Mistakes? How Many Can We Tolerate?

Christian Coons

My father was a high school track coach. In 2011, one of his former runners, David Turner, was shot dead by a sheriff's deputy in Bakersfield, California. As in the famous Michael Brown case, eyewitness accounts varied wildly. Given the limited evidence, I did not know what to think, but tended to trust the sheriff's report. Why? Because the account already seemed so damning I could not believe it was white-washed. According to the report, deputies investigating reports of teenagers asking adults to buy alcohol at a convenience store approached the 56-year-old Turner as he left the convenience store with his 19-year-old son. The report indicated that Turner stopped and answered the officer's questions; but became annoyed and began to walk off. The deputies then struck him from behind with a baton. Turner, angered, turned and swung his plastic grocery bag, which held two 24-ounce cans of beer. Deputy Wesley Kraft drew his handgun and fired twice; Turner was killed. The shooting was quickly ruled justified—Kraft faced no criminal trial.

C. Coons (✉)
Bowling Green State University, Bowling Green, OH, USA
e-mail: clcoons@bgsu.edu

M. Gardner and M. Weber (eds.), *The Ethics of Policing and Imprisonment*, Palgrave Studies in Ethics and Public Policy,
https://doi.org/10.1007/978-3-319-97770-6_4

This sort of thing is common where I grew up.[1] Yet it sparked unusual public attention because Turner was a former NFL player. Local editorials and letters to the editor seemed to take one of two positions. On one hand were those who displayed no sympathy for Turner—he had a criminal record and had been involved with drugs, and "what did he expect would happen" if he attacked the officer—he had it coming. Public outrage, on the other hand, was focused on whether the events really occurred as the sheriff described. Conspiracy theories surfaced—there was 6-second gap in parking lot surveillance footage—a gap that would have contained the 5 seconds wherein Turner left, was struck, struck back, and was shot twice. But what upset me was what these conspiracy theories seemed to presuppose—that no deep injustice occurred if the sheriff's report were true. I have witnessed a few situations where a high school bully or crazed drunk at a party did something on a par with swinging a bag of groceries at someone—and, unlike Turner, did so unprovoked. Were I to have had a gun, could I have shot the bully or drunk dead? And without facing a criminal charge? No. So what is the difference between me and a sheriff's deputy? The deputy is trained and equipped to deal with such threats without using lethal force; I am not. The deputy is sworn to protect the public and expected to act with courage; I am not. So the most obvious differences suggest the deputy should be in *hotter* water than I should be.

Being a moral philosopher by trade, I started to sketch principles to guide and assess law enforcement's (hereafter "police" for brevity's sake) use of lethal force. My thought was that with a few notable exceptions, the rules for police should be the same as those that apply to the public. But as soon I started, I found I had been scooped. By whom? Law enforcement agencies themselves. Though codes vary somewhat, by in large there is no special set of rules for police; rather it seems there is simply a pervasive difference in how those rules are applied and enforced.[2] Or at least, that's what Turner's case clearly suggested to me. On the other hand, my brother-in-law is a police officer, indeed now he is the acting chief in a major American city. He once shot a suspect in self-defense and his case seemed justified. Maybe those alarmed about police shootings are dangerously drawing general conclusions from a handful of high-profile cases.

This is a big country. Many thousands of dangerous confrontations occur between police and civilians each year; decisions need to be made in a split second and under duress. We not only have an armed police force, but also an armed public. Tragic mistakes will happen. And beyond innocent mistakes we can surely foresee some mistakes that are not. In short, we should expect some serious injustices to occur, though we need not tolerate or condone them. Law enforcement officers and administration—like any every other profession—will have its share of "bad apples." And in investigating these cases we can, sadly, also predict that law enforcement will sometimes err on the side of protecting their own rather than doling out impartial justice.

Even so, many are convinced that we are facing a problem that is bigger than the expected "bad apples." But how could we know? Is there any way to support that conviction? How could we, when we cannot even draw shared conclusions about the individual cases? Finding abuses in a few cases tells us little about the situation at large—is this a "bad apple" or even just a bad department, or a symptom of a larger institutional problem? If the only way to answer this second question—whether there is a larger institutional problem—is by "building up" from the conflicting evidence we have in individual cases, then we may seem doomed to live with our pre-conceptions: Those who see injustice in the individual cases will find an institutional crisis; those who do not, will not. This paper introduces a novel method for determining how many police shooting victims are mistakes. I then apply commonsense standards about when a shooting is just to estimate how many shootings justice could tolerate, and how close we are from that threshold.

A Different Approach

I think we can approach the question in a different way. We might be able to approximate the extent of the problem, or discover that there is no problem, by looking at the proportions: i.e., how many citizens the police kill vs. police killed by citizens. Examining these proportions, we will see, actually gives us a way to estimate both how many times officers faced a potentially lethal threat during the year and how many times officers made a "tragic mistake"—killed though doing so was not necessary to protect themselves.

Specifically, if we can estimate just how lethal a real threat would be to an officer—that is, estimate the odds of officers surviving such threats, then given that we know how many officers are killed in these confrontations, we can calculate how many lethal threats they likely faced. To illustrate, suppose we somehow knew that when Lions and Hippos fight, typically the Lion dies about half the time, and the Hippo dies the other half of the time. If you then learn that Lions killed 40 Hippos last year, you can now estimate both, how many Hippos killed Lions: about 40, and, how many fights they had: about 80.

So intelligent guesses at police survival rates illuminate how many threats police actually face. This would put us in position to estimate how many tragic mistakes police make each year—i.e., how many people were killed that posed no mortal threat. For example, if police kill 50 in a year, but likely faced only 30 actual threats, we can infer that probably *at least* 20 people died tragically. I say "at least" because we'd need to also add any cases where killing a real threat was unnecessary—cases when the threat was real, but could have been thwarted *without* use of lethal force (e.g., with a Taser or beanbag gun, etc.).

Of course, there is a crucial difference between tragic mistakes and unjustifiable ones. An officer may kill justifiably even when no real threat is present—what matters is whether the officer had sufficient grounds to believe there was a real threat. For instance, when a citizen points an unloaded gun at an officer, surely the officer may shoot provided it is not known the gun is unloaded. And despite the dangers of labeling some killings as "suicide by cop" there are instances of the phenomenon—sometimes citizens intentionally pose as lethal threats.[3] It is too much to expect that police be certain a threat is real before acting. In short, even a perfectly just police force will make some tragic mistakes. However, if these mistakes are typical—if police shootings rarely involve real threats—we can agree that we have a serious institutional problem. Let us see where some preliminary estimates take us.

Estimating the Number of Real Threats

According to the FBI, from 2013–2017, an average of 37.6 police officers were killed per year in violent confrontations with civilians.[4] For simplicity, let us round up and assume there are about 40 such killings each year. Given 40 such killings, how many confrontations with real threats—i.e., citizens with the means and manifest intention to mortally harm—do police likely face each year? The answer depends on how lethal real threats are to the police—i.e., police survival rates. The higher the survival rate, the higher our estimate.

Initially, it might seem that police should have a *lower* survival rate than the real threats they face. After all, a real threat is not merely one who has the immediate means and state of mind to kill—it is one who has also already manifested these features. In short, real threats always get to "draw first"—the police must wait for at least some evidence of the threat. This huge and inherent police disadvantage—call it the "defender's disadvantage"—is one of the many reasons why police work can be considered heroic.

Though it is difficult to quantify the defender's disadvantage, it is surely significant. On the other hand, many other factors suggest police may have a *higher* survival rate in confrontations with real threats. For one, despite some studies that suggest otherwise, we can presumably expect that police have superior firearms training, both in accuracy and draw/firing speed.[5] We also need to take into account the police's widespread use of body armor. I will consider each in turn.

First, let us just charitably suppose that officers are so well-trained in drawing and firing speed that the aggressor's advantage is *fully nullified*. If we stopped there, we'd revert to a model where neither has an advantage in a mortal confrontation. On this model, 40 police deaths would allow us to estimate that police encountered 80 real threats—and so we could be reasonably certain that police would make a tragic mistake for each person they kill beyond 80.

But the actual number police kill is well over 80; in fact, it probably exceeds 1000 annually. Prior to 2015, estimates about the number of civilians killed by American law enforcement varied widely—ranging from 500 to 1500—the only consensus was that each estimate was unreliable.[6] Things changed in the wake of the infamous 2014 shooting of Michael Brown in Ferguson, Missouri. Beginning in 2015, a number of projects were launched that aimed to comprehensively track lethal encounters with law enforcement. Their estimates ranged from 995 to 1357 killed in 2015, from 963 to 1583 killed in 2016, and from 987 to 1751 in 2017.[7] The higher estimates came from studies that included all those killed by police or killed in police custody. The lower estimates, like the Washington Post's, focus exclusively on police *shootings*. While it is tempting to think it is ok to focus primarily on shootings, recall that some of the most notorious uses of force—the careless and likely malicious transport of Freddie Gray and the videotaped choking death of Eric Garner—were not shootings at all.[8] Even so, I too will focus on shootings and assume police kill 1000 civilians in self-defense each year. Doing so ensures our estimate is both round and conservative. Furthermore, there is a relevant difference between defensive shootings and cases like

Gray and Garner's. I want to focus on law enforcement's intentional use of lethal force—acts that foresee ably result in deaths. Non-shooting cases typically do not meet that threshold. Rather, these acts (e.g., an unnecessary chokehold or abusing a suspect) often place individuals in mere mortal danger but the officer will not expect death as an outcome.

If police do not have an advantage against real threats, things look really grim. We would expect for any 40 police deaths, the police would have faced roughly 80 real threats, and if police killed all of them the result would be 80 lethal shootings by police. In that case, given 1000 police shootings per year, we could estimate at least 920 unnecessary deaths annually: police would kill actual (and not merely apparent) threats only about 1/13th of the time. Justice, it seems safe to assume, is not consistent with a margin of error that large. Hopefully some refining will give us a less depressing result. So let us refine further, this time seeking comfort in body armor.

A Rand corporation study found that outfitting the 26% of field officers who do not have body armor with body armor would save about 8.5 lives a year.[9] The study carefully argued that these unprotected officers are just as likely to face a lethal threat as their protected peers. Thus, we can infer that among the 74% that do wear it, 25 are saved because of it. So without body armor, we would have observed around 65 deaths. So if we now use 130 to estimate the number of actual threats police face, we will have controlled for the benefit of police body armor. This still would entail that the police kill over 870 people who are not actual threats, and more importantly that they kill an actual threat only about 1/11th of the time.

But we need to make another major adjustment in the police's favor. Specifically, police do not just shoot to protect themselves, but sometimes to protect other citizens (e.g., sniper shoots hostage-taker). Obviously, these shootings should not count as tragic mistakes just because officers are not actually threatened. What proportion of shootings are of this type? To make an educated guess, one needs a database that also provides a summary of the circumstances of each killing. The Guardian's database provides a short summary while the NYPD's summaries are more detailed. I looked at the relevant proportions (officer vs. bystander defense) in departments with detailed public records. Among large departments, the NYPD's records are most complete. I looked at the last 6 available months of the Guardian's database, and the NYPD's reports over four years 2008–2012. In six months nationwide

(July–December 2016), 17 of 564 (3%) shootings appeared to be cases of bystander defense, and in 4 years of the NYPD's more detailed reports 1 in 45 (just over 2%) appeared to be cases of bystander defense.[10] Of course, some of these shootings may also be tragic mistakes; the threat to the bystander may be illusory or insufficient; for example, NYPD's lone case seemed dubious as it was a son threatening his mother with a pan. But for the sake of charity and simplicity, let us assume that *no* shootings of this type are tragic mistakes: All the threats were real, and the police had no means of dealing with it but by using lethal force. Accordingly, let us generously round up and remove a full 5% of our estimated 870 tragic deaths. With that adjustment police kill an estimated 830 people who are not actual threats, making a tragic mistake over 9 out of every 10 times they kill. If this is right then, in terms of annual death toll, the police threat to the non-threatening American public is still more than twice meningitis or tuberculosis and approaching influenza.[11]

Unfortunately, the major remaining factor to consider suggests things are even worse. So far, we have been only counting tragic deaths where there is no actual threat. But, of course, killing *actual* threats is also tragic when non-lethal means could have been used instead. I have no idea how often police could have used non-lethal means to thwart lethal threats. But even if David Turner's bag with two beers did pose a lethal threat, I imagine two highly trained and well-equipped officers would have some way of dealing with it without killing him. In short, it seems mistakes of this kind are made often.

Even so, adding this factor is problematic. First, doing so would be to assume, rather than independently support, the conclusion that some shootings are unnecessary. Second, it is a factor that is hard to estimate. Third, many may feel that these "tragic mistakes" are less tragic—as the citizens in question posed a real (and not merely apparent) threat to police or third parties. As such, let us again simply ignore this factor; as I think we are already in a position to conclude we may have a serious institutional problem: Justice presumably demands that police avoid tragic mistakes more than 4% of the time.

When Is Many, Too Many?

Ideally, law enforcement should use lethal force only when it is necessary—that is, when they are likely to be killed if they do not use lethal force—call this the "Probable Lethal Threat Standard" or "*Probable*" for short. If officers both (a) comply with *Probable* and (b) are not advantaged in confrontations with threats; then we could expect the number actual threats police face to be no more than two times the number of police slain. So, given 40 slain police, they would have most likely faced 80 lethal threats, and were they to have killed them all of them, they'd kill 80 civilians and the proportion of law enforcement deaths to civilian deaths would be 1:2. Any further killings beyond 80 would guarantee violations of *Probable*. But as noted above, though suspects enjoy the "aggressor's advantage," police have their own advantages: superior training and body armor. I have assumed that training cancels out the aggressor's advantage. The Rand study allowed us estimate that, all other things equal, if 40 police are killed annually, then—given body armor's efficacy and prevalence—police likely faced around 130 lethal threats. So, if police collectively comply with *Probable*, then we should expect no more than 130 lethal shootings by law enforcement. So, we know the number actually killed is far from what justice demands. Of course, maybe some deviation from this ideal rule is ok. After all, failures to comply with *Probable* can be consistent with an *intention* to comply: the officer might fail to comply only because they have made a mistake about whether someone constitutes a probable lethal threat. But this concession can only take us so far; if officers' judgments about who is a threat are not at all reliable, then they should not be using lethal force at all. Therefore, I submit that police shooting must be beyond any defensible deviation from *Probable* if *Probable* is violated most of the time. For us, this would mean we could be sure our practice is not even minimally just if over 260 people are shot and killed by police each year. This number represents what we could expect if (a) law enforcement complied with *Probable* only half of the time, and (b) we allow police to reason as if they were not wearing body armor when determining what constitutes a lethal treat. But instead police kill almost 4 times as many people as what this minimal standard requires.

One might complain that a *probable* threat doctrine is too burdensome; it puts the police at too great of a risk. But the statues and internal guidelines for lethal force already typically use "probable" or "likely" as the relevant threshold. Lowering the threshold—formally or informally—just shifts the very same threats onto the innocent public, a threat that is greater to them because the public is not wearing body armor. Think of it this way: If police surrounded a building known to contain 4 people—1 well-armed unidentified cop-killing maniac and

3 innocents—I presume they would not be entitled to shoot any figure that abruptly exits. A 25% threat rather than *probable* threat standard could permit one to shoot each person in the building either en masse or serially. Any standard less than probable threat not only unequally protects police, but also yields more *net* killings—such a standard values lives in general less, and treats civilian lives as mattering less. Compliance with a *probable* threat standard minimizes net killings while valuing police and civilian lives equally. Yes, it is true that almost all confrontations involve suspected criminals, but surely we should not legally enshrine the view that the lives of suspected criminals matter less.

In sum, if my preliminary model is correct, then it is not even debatable whether we have a serious problem. I hope relevant experts find the approach intriguing and improve the model, perhaps with less depressing results. But as it stands, it appears that at least 830 people die unnecessarily at the hands of law enforcement each year, and 740 more than even a minimal standard of justice could accept.

Notes

1. Swaine, Jon, and Oliver Laughland. 2015. The County: The Story of America's Deadliest Police. *The Guardian*, Dec 1. https://www.theguardian.com/us-news/2015/dec/01/the-county-kern-county-deadliest-police-killings.
2. NYPD Firearms Discharge Report, 2012. New York City Government, 8. http://www.nyc.gov/html/nypd/downloads/pdf/analysis_and_planning/nypd_annual_firearms_discharge_report_2012.pdf. For an overview on how few of these cases get prosecuted, see http://www.washingtonpost.com/sf/investigative/2015/04/11/thousands-dead-few-prosecuted/?utm_term=.6282c63a8845.
3. For concerns about this classification, see Anon. 2015. Forced to Fire: Are US Police Hiding Behind 'Suicide by Cop' Shootings. *The Guardian*, Oct 6. https://www.theguardian.com/us-news/2015/oct/06/suicide-by-cop-the-counted; Voorhees, Josh. 2014. The Problem with 'Suicide by Cop'. *Slate*, Aug 26. http://www.slate.com/articles/news_and_politics/politics/2014/08/suicide_by_cop_the_dangerous_term_that_stops_us_from_asking_hard_questions.html.
4. Federal Bureau of Investigation, LEOKA Annual Reports, 2013–2017. 2017. https://ucr.fbi.gov/leoka. Please note that the average number of police officers killed by civilians in those years was 45.8. My figure involves only violent confrontations: it *excludes* cases where police

were "ambushed" and murdered by citizens with pre-meditation. These crimes, though especially tragic and upsetting, don't belong in our calculations as we're trying to discern whether law enforcement tends to be too aggressive in using lethal force to protect themselves and other citizens. Planned ambushes and pre-meditated "cop-killings" are not contexts where the officer can effectively issue lethal defense.

5. For questions about the superiority of their training, see Lewinski, W. J., Ron Avery, Jennifer Dysterheft, Nathan D. Dicks, and Jacob Bushey. 2015. The Real Risks During Deadly Police Shootouts: Accuracy of the Naïve Shooter. *International Journal of Police Science & Management* 17: 117–127.
6. Fischer-Baum, Reuben. 2014. Nobody Knows How Many Americans the Police Kill Each Year. *Five Thirty Eight*, Aug 19. http://fivethirtyeight.com/features/how-many-americans-the-police-kill-each-year/. For the best pre-2015 attempt at a comprehensive accounting, see Fisher, J. 2013. Police-Involved Shooting Statistics: A National One-Year Summary. http://jimfishertruecrime.blogspot.com/2012/01/police-involved-shootings-2011-annual.html.
7. The Washington Post's Police Shooting Database. 2015. https://github.com/washingtonpost/data-police-shootings; The Counted: Police Killings Database. 2015. https://www.theguardian.com/us-news/ng-interactive/2015/jun/01/the-counted-police-killings-us-database; The *Fatal Encounters* database. http://www.fatalencounters.org/; Mapping Police Violence Project https://mappingpoliceviolence.org/aboutthedata/.
8. For and account of the Freddie Gray case, see Cox, John Woodrow, Lynh Bui, and DeNeen L. Brown. 2015. Who Was Frddy Gray and How Did His Death Lead to a Mistrial in Baltimore. *The Washington Post*, Dec 16. https://www.washingtonpost.com/local/who-was-freddie-gray-and-how-did-his-death-lead-to-a-mistrial-in-baltimore/2015/12/16/b08df7ce-a433-11e5-9c4e-be37f66848bb_story.html?utm_term=.2ab1f66c101e. For Eric Garner, see Baker, Al, David Goodman, and Benjamin Mueller. 2015. Beyond the Chokehold: The Path to Eric Garner's Death. *The New York Times*, June 13. https://www.nytimes.com/2015/06/14/nyregion/eric-garner-police-chokehold-staten-island.html.
9. LaTourrette, Tom. 2010. The Life-Saving Effectiveness of Body Armor for Police Officers. *Journal of Occupational & Environmental Hygiene* 7: 557–562.

10. NYCPD Firearm Discharge Reports, 2008–12. 2012. http://www1.nyc.gov/site/nypd/stats/reports-analysis/reports-landing.page, and The Counted: Police Killings Database.
11. Deaths: Final Data for 2011. 2015. National Vital Statistics Report. 2015. U.S. Department of Health and Human Services. http://www.cdc.gov/nchs/data/nvsr/nvsr63/nvsr63_03.pdf.

The Ethics of Policing: A Feminist Proposal

Julinna Oxley

The most prominent criticism of law enforcement is that police resort to excessive force when it is unjustified, such as when citizens encounter police for minor infractions (routine traffic stops and petty theft) and end up shot or beaten.[1] One powerful explanation for why this happens is because the officers are applying a type of "broken windows policing", which was introduced in 1982 by political scientists James Q. Wilson and George L. Kelling.[2] Broken windows policing focuses on maintaining order and cleaning up the streets in an effort to curb crime. Police stop low-level crimes (such as smoking pot in public, loitering, fare-hopping, and littering) so that communities appear to be cared for and orderly. The central rationale for this approach is that apprehending minor crimes prevents violent crime, because these petty crimes are an underlying symptom of violent crime. Once a community is not in order, things can quickly get out of control. So by focusing on minor crimes, major crimes can be prevented.

A second explanation is that America's police force has become increasingly militarized, thus changing the dynamic between citizens and law enforcement from that of equal community members to that

J. Oxley (✉)
Coastal Carolina University, Conway, SC, USA
e-mail: joxley@coastal.edu

M. Gardner and M. Weber (eds.), *The Ethics of Policing and Imprisonment*, Palgrave Studies in Ethics and Public Policy,
https://doi.org/10.1007/978-3-319-97770-6_5

of disinterested, overly powerful police officers.[3] No matter which theory is correct, I will argue here that current policing practices stultify the ends of policing, which is to ensure a peaceful community. Moreover, the problems facing law enforcement today are entrenched, for as Rachel Harmon points out, at the present time, there does not exist a process to reform police institutions.[4] The entire system of law enforcement is not set up in a way that makes it easy to revise laws regarding police activity; moreover, there are disincentives for doing so.[5] In practice, the only limitations and restrictions placed on policing come from the courts who adjudicate the Constitutional limits of policing private citizens (*Terry* stops, *Miranda* rights, etc.).[6] A far more effective solution, says Harmon, would be to regulate police via local, state, and federal institutions through law and public policy; and to do this, citizens must push for change via their legislators.

My goal in this chapter is to outline a new model of law enforcement rooted in feminist ethics, so that we can envision models of policing that will better serve the public, and ultimately advocate for change in police oversight via legislation. This chapter begins by identifying the major problems with policing today. These are (a) a decayed sense of trust in law enforcement, (b) the cultural influence of toxic masculinity, and (c) the perpetuation of social oppression through police activity. Next, I use feminist care ethics to develop the *community guardian* model of policing. My central thesis is that care ethics identifies care and concern for others as the most rational basis for law enforcement; on this revolutionary model, fruitful law enforcement must be grounded in care and goodwill toward others, not just rational self-interest. This is *caring justice*. Finally, I explain how this model can be used to address the problems I identify, ultimately improving communication, building soft power, and engendering trust between law enforcement and their communities.

The Problem with Current Policing Practices

The current issues facing law enforcement are rooted in practices that began years ago, when the method of broken windows policing was adopted by NYC mayor Rudy Giuliani in the early 1990s, and was later reintroduced under Mayor Bill de Blasio and his police commissioner, William Bratton, in 2014. After implementation, major crimes such as murder, rape, and theft rapidly went down over the course of several years, and research seemed to suggest that there was a correlation between the advent of broken windows policing and the decline of violent crime. But it turns out that crime dropped in *other* large cities across the United States in the same time frame, and these cities *had not* implemented broken windows policing. Scholars now agree that broken windows policing does not work, and, moreover, that there are problems with how people even perceive disorder in communities.[7]

Broken windows policing paved the way for "stop and frisk" policies, an even more aggressive form of policing whereby police do not even wait for the misdemeanor offense; anyone can be stopped and questioned because they look suspicious. And while the method of carrying out NYC's stop and frisk program was ruled to violate the US Constitution by a federal court (because it operated on the basis of racial profiling), such practices continue today outside of NYC, and in many cases, such practices also violate *Terry* laws.[8] (In fact, some reporters argued that the arrest and subsequent death of Eric Garner can be attributed to broken windows policing, since he was being arrested for allegedly selling loose cigarettes.[9]) This appears to be a trend. Several cities have passed "quality-of-life" standards in order to allow police broad latitude in making arrests for crimes that diminish citizens' enjoyment of their city; the city of Chicago went further, and allowed *police* to define permissible public behavior, instead of clearly defining specific offenses via legislation.[10] This led to rampant abuses of authority and arrests for petty crimes that previously did not put people in jail.

The main problem with broken windows policing is that it often leads officers to take actions that are merely symbolic: police may carefully patrol certain streets in an effort to make it appear that a community is cared for; this symbolism works, and leads potential offenders to believe a community is cared for, and they thus move criminal activities elsewhere. So while the careful patrolling helps that particular neighborhood, crime is merely displaced and the overall picture is unaffected; unlawful activity still takes place in parts of town that do not have the resources to pay the cost of law enforcement.

This approach to policing has led to a situation that is dissatisfactory for both police and citizens. It is characterized by three features: (a) lack of trust between citizens and law enforcement, (b) law enforcement dominated by a culture of toxic masculinity, and (c) a system that perpetuates race and class oppression. I describe this here, and in the following section, I sketch a feminist theory of policing as an antidote.

Trust and Mistrust

The current climate between citizens and police, and police and citizens, is characterized by mistrust, especially for minority populations.[11] Distrust is problematic because it leads to greater violence between police and citizens. When police officers do not trust citizens or neighborhoods to not harm them, they are hyper-vigilant and may use force when it is inappropriate. And when citizens do not trust law enforcement, they are less likely to call the police, cooperate with the police, and more likely to run from law enforcement (which also increases the chances that they will be hurt). Surveying the many ways in which we must trust law enforcement, it is evident that relying on this public service is different than relying on mail delivery service, the military, our teachers, firefighters, or any other public servant, because their role in social life is to protect the public good, and hold people accountable to established laws. While we may need to trust the mailman to not read our mail, and the firefighter to show up promptly to put out a fire, we also need to be able to trust the law enforcement officer to resolve conflict in a peaceful way. This requires significant personal discretion, and far more latitude in judgment than other public offices. When an officer sees a violation of a law (such as a moving violation), they must make many decisions: (a) whether to pull the person over, (b) whether to issue a warning, (c) whether to give a ticket, (d) whether to give a ticket for a separate infraction in place of or in addition to the primary violation, (e) how to engage, (f) whether to call for backup, and (g) whether to draw a weapon.

In her analysis of trust, Anette Baier argues that there is a distinction between trust and mere reliance; trust requires acting with good will toward another, whereas reliance involves merely acting on the basis of mutual self-interest. I can rely on another to perform certain actions that are in our mutual self-interest, but genuine trust involves more than self-interest, it involves acting out of care and concern for another, and that makes me vulnerable to her. If we fail to act with good will toward others, trust will be betrayed.[12] When we trust others, we allow things that are valuable to us be known and thus vulnerable to others. Baier says we do this because we need others to help us guard, nurture, or help the things we care about. Although the motive of self-interest can be compatible with goodwill toward others, it is also compatible with ill-will and selfishness. Thus, in order to distinguish trust from mere reliability, it must contain a different attitude, namely one of care and goodwill.[13] Interaction merely based on mutual self-interest models game theoretic reasoning, not interpersonal connection, and individuals who operate in this way may not play fair or play at all, as they are waiting to see the other player's move first.

Baier's analysis is insightful when applied to the police–citizen relationship. "Trust, on the analysis I have proposed, is letting other persons (natural or artificial, such as firms and nations) take care of something the truster cares about, where such 'caring for' involves some exercise of discretionary powers."[14] Applying this line of reasoning to law enforcement, citizens must not merely rely on police officers to keep the peace; they must *trust* police officers because they must let them have discretionary power over what citizens care about—their lives, their happiness, and their well-being (insofar as the job of law enforcement is to enable a peaceful law-abiding state). Since citizens must trust in this way, it is not enough for police to act on the basis of mutual rational self-interest; they should have the motive of goodwill toward citizens, or at least have citizens' best interests in mind. At the minimum, officers should be motivated by a concern for public safety, or a desire to protect individuals from harm; ideally, they should be motivated by genuine care about citizens. Moreover, if the public perceives police officers to have citizens' interests at heart, more citizens will trust law enforcement. This is extremely important for developing strong community relationships.

Toxic (Hegemonic) Masculinity

A second problem plaguing policing today is that it is rooted in problematic conceptions of masculinity that have helped escalate the militarization of the police. The field of masculinity studies identifies different conceptions of masculinity, each of which includes patterns, practices, and qualities generally associated with manhood.[15] Michael Kimmel illustrates the different cultural meanings of masculinity within American society, and shows that among these conceptions, there is a hierarchy of masculinities that struggle for dominance.[16] (These include black masculinity, gay masculinity, etc.) Most importantly, toxic (or hegemonic) masculinity is the normative conception of masculinity that serves as the ideal toward which all men are supposed to strive, but which is extreme in its characterization of manhood. Toxic masculinity includes four problematic qualities: (1) men's concern with the opinions of other men,

(2) insecurity and anxiety over whether one has proved one's manhood, (3) competitiveness reflected in a need to dominate other men, and (4) a desire to denigrate contrast figures, including the feminine.[17]

Frank Rudy Cooper applies this understanding of masculinity to policing and argues that toxic (hegemonic) police masculinity—the norms of masculinity that provide a narrative of what policing should be like, and the ideals toward which they should strive—is manifested in two social practices.[18] The first is *command presence*, whereby the police person must appear confident, decisive, and in charge. The goal of command presence is linked to aggressiveness, which is required on the part of women police officers as well. The second norm is *punishing disrespect.* Police officers enter situations demanding deference to the badge, and those who are disrespectful deserve to be punished; challenging a police officer's respect is challenging his manhood.[19] While disrespect to the police is a justification to use force, it is also used as a reason to escalate the situation between a police officer and a citizen.[20] Cooper argues that these features culminate in "masculinity contests" where police officers are concerned that they may not be in control of a situation, and quickly seek to establish dominance. "Since manhood is demonstrated for other men's approval and the overwhelming majority of both officers and suspects are male, officers may often view the police-civilian encounter as an opportunity to stage a masculinity contest."[21] Moreover, this dynamic is codified into law, since APO laws (assaulting a police officer) are broadly applied, so as to include touching a cop, resisting arrest by holding onto your steering wheel, or even holding your home's gate closed.[22] In this regard, toxic masculinity is reinforced by law and politics, for police are nearly invincible and rarely blameworthy under the law.

While these masculinity norms somewhat still apply to women who are in the police force, women do not engage in masculinity contests in the same way that men police officers do. So the norms of toxic masculinity apply far less to women officers. Studies show that women police officers engage in excessive use of force at rates far below their men counterparts, primarily because they are less authoritarian in their approach to policing. They defuse potentially violent confrontations *before* those encounters turn deadly, they rely less on physical force, and use compassion and negotiation to be more effective communicators.[23] But these are not necessarily thought to be valuable traits, since police must remain "in control" of situations; thus, standard prerequisites for the job tend to include physical attributes and the ability to dominate another person. The current normative model of policing does not encourage cultivating the soft skills of communication and negotiation, so officers sometimes resort to force more quickly than necessary.

Policing Practices Perpetuate Oppression

In recent years, feminists have recognized that evaluating power dynamics also involves examining the way that race, class, nationality, citizenship status, and other factors are relevant to understanding contemporary moral problems. This is due to the emergence of the concept of intersectionality, introduced by Kimberlé Crenshaw in the early 1990s, a notion that describes the methodological study of the intertwining of racial oppression, class oppression, sexist oppression, and other manifestations of oppression, such as ability and religion. The central idea of intersectionality is that there are overlapping vectors of oppression (not just sexist oppression) that function together so that different people experience oppression differently. For example, as Crenshaw argues, black women experience oppression differently than white women.[24] bell hooks explains that the poor and minorities are victims of "multiple jeopardy" and "interlocking systems of oppression," since racism, sexism, and classism may be separable in theory, but not in fact.[25] Because intersectionality is a way of examining oppression, it is a useful way of looking at how different populations of people are oppressed in different ways.

The way that policing is carried out today not only mirrors the dominant power structures of oppression present in society, but it also perpetuates them. For example, although black men make up only 6% of the US population, they account for 40% of the unarmed men shot to death by police in 2016. Moreover, police respond more aggressively to people of color than they do to white people. In the majority of cases in which police shot and killed a person who had attacked someone with a weapon or brandished a gun, the person who was shot was white. But 3 in 5 of those killed after exhibiting less threatening behavior were black or Hispanic.[26] The most plausible explanation for this and other facts is an intersectional analysis of how oppression is cumulative. Intersectional theorists such as Patricia Hill Collins would argue that black men are more heavily policed because they threaten both (a) white supremacy and (b) white masculinity. Ideologies of race and gender intersect and subject black men to stereotypes that categorize them as dangerous criminals or ne'er-do-well hooligans. Patricia Hill Collins further argues that the "feared black male body" is a result of the stereotype of physical dominance, and that this fear of black men motivated the stop and frisk policing method.[27] And insofar as profiling reflects the existing social hierarchy, black and brown men remain more threatening to the social order than any other demographic.[28] The reality of the raced nature of the operation of the carceral state has motivated significant academic attention on reforming the criminal justice system.[29] Innovative scholarship in criminology (such as Left Realism) is increasingly focused on large-scale social restructuring, dramatic changes to legal codes or law enforcement, and paradigm shifts in correctional ideology for the American carceral state.[30] At the practical level, concerns that black and brown men have been untreated fairly by law enforcement have motivated the Black Lives Matter movement[31] as well as the movement to end mass incarceration.[32]

Viewed in their totality, it is clear that the problems facing law enforcement today are substantive. In the following section, I provide an antidote to this situation.

The Solution: Feminist Care Ethics

Contemporary approaches to the nature and foundation of our political relationships are situated primarily in the social contract tradition of Rousseau, Locke, and Hobbes. (In fact, the seminal work in the philosophy of law enforcement, John Kleining's *Ethics of Policing*, is also rooted in the social contract tradition. I discuss this in the following section.) This was the dominant approach to moral and political philosophy in the twentieth century, until feminist and critical race theorist critiques of the social contract tradition emerged, and care ethics became a prominent account of feminist ethical thinking. In my view, the social contract model of law enforcement is incomplete, and my goal in this section is to sketch a model of policing rooted in feminist care ethics, whose aim is to secure communities of trust, mutual respect, and dignity, in addition to social peace.

In general, feminist ethical theories emphasize the importance of relationships and responsibility for others, rather than rational agreement to contracts as the locus of moral activity. The most influential feminist ethical theory is care ethics, and as I argue in this section, it has the resources for providing significant contributions to theories of policing. Although there are different versions of care ethical theories, in general, they claim that:

1. The language of care, care activity, and care work are central to our everyday lives.[33]
2. The concepts, metaphors, and images associated with the practice of caring (rather than contracting) best express the dynamics of the moral life and should thus be the basis of ethics.[34]
3. We should seek to nurture and preserve the concrete relationships we have with specific others.[35]

Since the ethics of care "values the ties we have with particular other persons and the actual relationships that partly constitute our identity," it emphasizes the relatedness of people to each other and the caring nature of the relationship.[36] This is not exclusive to personal relationships. Even though care ethical theories were initially modeled on (and applied to) familial relationships and friendship, a number of philosophers have expanded the application of care ethics to political issues, international relations, and social topics, none of which are traditionally conceived as "caring" relationships.[37]

Virginia Held argues that care is both a practice and a value, and not merely about emotional bonds between individuals. And it is in this sense that it is relevant to law enforcement. Even though most people have a distant relationship with police officers, when citizens do interact with police, they engage in an intense interpersonal relationship that requires mutual trust. That trust is fragile, and care is required in order to build and maintain relations of trust. Held's point is that even if liberal schemes of law and governance undergird our social fabric, this picture is not the whole of human life, and "we should not lose sight of the deeper reality of human interdependency and of the need for caring relations to undergird or surround such constructions."[38]

While there are different versions of care ethics, the view I develop here is rooted in *feminist* care ethical theories, which include a critical analysis of the social construction of gender, gender norms, and gender roles. While there is nothing inherently feminist about care ethics, and not all care ethical theories adopt feminist commitments,[39] many care ethical theories express feminist aims and goals.[40] Feminist care ethical theories aim to highlight the existence of sexist inequality, subordination, and other factors of daily life that impeded women's development. Feminist care ethical theories advocate for values and norms that motivate community connections and facilitate interdependence.

Evaluating policing from the perspective of feminist care ethics enables us to better understand the problems confronting law enforcement in the twenty-first century. My thesis is that we need different models to guide our thinking about ways to organize the enforcement of the law, and that the dominating, increasingly militarized, "law and order" approach to policing would be improved were it counterbalanced with insights from feminist ethics. Contractual approaches to policing emphasize "law and order" criminal justice, in that they focus primarily on apprehending people who break the law. But the care ethical approach would argue that we should treat citizens, even those who break the law, as people who have families, children, jobs, and valued projects. As an illustration, suppose a policeperson perceives a citizen to be disrespectful. The "law and order" approach would see this disrespect as an opportunity to punish the individual, teach them a lesson, and suppress disrespect. But a care ethicist would argue that the officer should give the benefit of the doubt and educate the individual on how to be respectful to authority.

While care ethics may initially seem to be a wholly impractical way to approach law enforcement, it is a revolutionary approach that requires us to view citizens as part and parcel of the solution, not just subjects of law enforcement. Feminist care ethics can be used to ground a normative conception of policing that is rooted in communal relationships, responsibility toward others, and the educative nature of the law, rather than force and violence. In what follows, I show how the core concepts of feminist care ethics can be used to create a new model of law enforcement.[41]

The model I propose here is the *community guardian* model of policing, because it emphasizes that the job of the police is not just to protect the social environment, but that it is to protect a *specific* social environment, namely, the community in which one lives, and acknowledges that one polices one's neighbors. A guardian does not just maintain peace by stopping and deterring crime, but fosters a sense of trust, by showing care and concern for those he is charged with patrolling. Police have a significant responsibility to citizens not just to make sure that they follow the law, but to also treat them respectfully as members of the same community. The community guardian enacts *caring justice* and is first of all committed to nonviolence as the primary method for resolving disputes and responding to criminal activity. It requires police to treat citizens as neighbors, and approach them with equanimity. This model emphasizes the social and interpersonal activities of law enforcement, in addition to the physical aspects of the job.

The *community guardian* model of policing is unique in that it emphasizes that (a) the police person is a member of a community, and that (b) the police person's job is to defend against all acts of nonviolence, and not use violence. By approaching law enforcement as a way of meting out caring justice, officers model the type of behavior that they expect from citizens, especially by integrating norms that are rooted in care ethics: care, mutual respect, interpersonal dialogue and careful verbal communication, problem-solving, social harmony, and community-building. This should be done not at the price of controlling criminals, since surveillance will likely remain a feature of law enforcement, but these overall goals should be achieved by using respect as a norm to interpret a situation and care to guide interpersonal interaction.

This model of policing contrasts with those described by Kleinig.[42] He proposes several normative models of policing based on the type of work that police do; he notes that each model is insufficient in that, taken to an extreme, they are inadequate for describing the work that police do.

a. the crimefighter: the army of individuals that are needed to protect society from the "bad guys."
b. the emergency operator: individuals who authoritatively engage in peacekeeping and the provision of social services, offering emergency assistance to people in need.
c. the social enforcer: individuals who use coercive force to control social situations, such as demonstrations or accidents, to ensure crowd control.[43]

Kleining argues that the problem with these models is that citizens complain that the police are intimidating, and resort to force when mediation would be more appropriate. In addition, Kleinig acknowledges that police culture reinforces this by emphasizing the importance of physique and strength, and masculinizing police officers, even women officers.[44] He proposes the *social peacekeeper* model as the best model of policing, which encourages deescalating the use of nonnegotiable force, which police have at their disposal. He argues that the primary role of police is to ensure or restore peaceful order. Kleining argues that police "may engage in forms of social assistance that actually enhance the quality of social life, not only deterring crime and disorder and dissipating fear, but actually fostering social trust and cooperation."[45]

From the perspective of care ethics, police officers are members of the community that are in an interdependent relationship with other members of the community, in that they help the members of the community to flourish by maintaining peace, stability, and harmony; they stop members of the community from victimizing other members of the community. While police are not to show partiality for members of the community in the sense that they show favoritism toward others, they are to handle each situation uniquely, based on the situation at hand. They are to show care for members of the community, because their goal is to create a community that flourishes by enforcing the norms that govern it. As it stands now, law enforcement *appears* to care about communities and citizens, but individuals are treated as if they are already guilty of a crime, not as individuals who need the protection the law has to offer. Thus, officers' motives matter, because they inform how individual officers will respond to the citizens that they interact with. Care ethicists would view the moral duties of law enforcement in the following way: it is not virtuous or morally desirable for a police officer to perform his or her duties simply out of concern for (universal) principles of justice, for the sake of following the letter of the law, or merely because of personal benefit or even mutual advantage. Rather, officers should genuinely care for citizens and acknowledge their interdependent relationship with other citizens. Had Eric Garner—who died in a prohibited chokehold, after resisting arrest for selling loose cigarettes—been approached as a valuable citizen and father who lived in the community, rather than a lowlife criminal, he would not have died at the hands of the NYC police.

Application of the Care Ethical Model to Policing

How can this model be used to address the three social problems I identified at the outset? Let us first turn to the problem of mistrust. Kleining is right to emphasize the importance of social trust and cooperation, but they require a more robust grounding and elaboration to be effective. Nel Noddings argues that care is the foundation of moral interaction, even with strangers (to whom we have different, less stringent, obligations). On her view, our positive emotional engagement with others is critical to living the good life. This is for personal, familial relationships, as well as the proximate stranger.[46] Given Noddings' emphasis on the importance of emotional education (which she rightly insists starts "at home" where the origins of care have their roots), this insight can be implemented into police work, by recognizing that police persons play an educative role, in their interactions with citizens. Police can play a critical role in defusing tense situations and alleviating stress in an inherently stressful encounter, thus serving an important role in modeling desirable social interaction. Police who are adept at emotional management and intelligence can informally model appropriate emotional responses to conflict, by using good conflict resolution skills. The virtues of patience and compassion, as well as strength, would enable the exercise of power that involves the soft skills of diplomacy rather than dominance. Policing might then be a bit like parenting: modeling bad behavior just leads to more bad behavior on the part of the child. The way to generate better outcomes is by being a better role model.

Feminist policing recommends revising mandatory protocols and behavior to reflect trust, cooperation, and social harmony. How can this be done? First, police need to be trained how to deal with those with mental illness. The earlier cited Washington Post essay states that officers fatally shot at least 243 people with mental health problems: 75 who were explicitly suicidal and 168 for whom police or family members confirmed a history of mental illness. The analysis found that about 9 in 10 of the mentally troubled people were armed, usually with guns but also with knives or other sharp objects. This is not to say that police are always required to respond passively to people with mental health concerns, but that they should at least be trained to deal with the mentally ill, since the analysis also found that most died because police officers had not been trained to deal with the mentally ill.[47]

As long as inappropriate techniques are used against vulnerable populations such as children, elderly persons, pregnant women, people with physical and mental disabilities, limited English proficiency, and others, police will be perceived as uncaring, and this in turn will undermine public trust. As the President's Task Force on twenty-first century Policing (commissioned under President Obama) recommends, law enforcement agencies should have clear and comprehensive policies on the use of force (including de-escalation training), mass demonstrations (including the appropriate use of equipment), consent before searches, gender identification, and racial profiling.[48] In addition, the more officers know their constituents, and whether they have mental illness, then they can learn how to deal with them when conflict arises. This is an important aspect of "community policing" which encourages community input, and personal relationships.

Second, emphasizing caring justice can combat toxic masculinity. Although I have recommended that care should be a practice and a value among police officers, let me clearly state that I am not recommending that police adopt traditionally "feminine" qualities. Rather, I am arguing that there are certain desirable social skills and attitudes that are desirable and virtuous in *all* people, no matter the gender. The ability to communicate effectively, listen, use soft power, and negotiate with citizens, will relieve the stress of an encounter with the police. Currently, there is a presumption of guilt when police interact with citizens, and criminals are looked down upon; there is certainly no care shown toward people who are apprehended by police. Being apprehended by police is emotionally upsetting for most people, and some may have a flight or fight response to this interaction, knowing the substantial costs that come with arrest: financial (incurring a fine, ticket, or bond money), loss of time (time is now spent interacting with police instead of doing what they were doing before), and a criminal record which marks one as a "person of interest" for other crimes and additional surveillance.[49] Using reason, equanimity, negotiation, and communication can enable citizens to communicate better and feel more confident in the interaction.

An associated problem is that existing police culture does not incentivize effective communication and negotiation. It rewards the wrong kinds of actions. Low-pay scales do not attract high-quality applicants. Again, the skills typically valued by police departments are strength and the ability to assert authority, whereas police need to be trained in more sophisticated skills such as communication and negotiation. If the right skills are not emphasized in the hiring process, then the masculine culture which currently pervades police departments will not change. Since the statistics on women police officer's use of force shows a fraction of the violence used by men officers, one might think that hiring more women who are generally more socialized to deal with conflict using communication rather than physical dominance (and who are largely underrepresented in the force), would be an easy solution. But this is not so. While hiring more women police officers would help, agencies must revise what they take to be desirable skills on the part of their officers.

It seems clear that personal characteristics, such as emotional equanimity, and softer skills, such as good communication and negotiation rather than physical strength, should be used in the selection and hiring criteria. Eighty to ninety-five percent of police work involves nonviolent, service-related activities, and interactions with people in the community to solve problems anyway, so the tasks do not require physical strength so much as good they do good communication skills. With more diversity—including race, gender, language, life experience, and cultural background—policing in all communities would improve.

Finally, the community guardian model could combat the perpetuation of oppressive policing practices. In addition to teaching emotional regulation by modeling it, police officers using the community guardian model of policing could also reframe their approach to policing by engaging in the practice of meting out *caring justice* rather than maintaining "law and order." Virginia Held argues that care is a value in the same way that justice is a value; it is both an aspirational concept, and a practice. And in this regard, care is meant to be practiced and taken to be a relevant goal in every interaction. In fact, Held argues that even though the maintenance of justice is among the highest priorities for law enforcement, there is still room for care activities: as law enforcement "becomes more caring it can often accomplish more through educating and responding to needs, building trust between police and policed, and thus preventing violations of law than it can through traditional 'law enforcement' after prevention has failed."[50] Held's point is that care should play a central role in enforcing the law.

This method of reasoning about the nature of the interaction, and how to show caring justice to citizens, is distinct from proportionality-style reasoning, which has been used to successfully reduce officers' deadly shootings. In 2009, the Las Vegas PD adopted a use-of-force policy requiring officers to put the highest premium on "the sanctity of human life," and some other departments followed suit. Four years after, the city's officer-involved shootings had fallen by nearly half. Presumably this is because the officers viewed citizens as valuable people rather than potential threats. Chuck Wexler, executive director of the Police Executive Research Forum, a Washington police think tank, states: "The guiding principle has to be proportionality: Is my action proportional to the act being committed? We've recommended that the policy has to be ironclad, because if you say 'except if the officer fears for his life,' inevitably they will say they fear for their life."[51] While I agree that this is a good rule of thumb, it does not offer a method or justification for the attitudinal adjustments that I am arguing are necessary for policing today.

The promising approach is to establish a culture of transparency and accountability by engaging in community policing, which involves gathering input from different points of view, and hearing many perspectives, which is consistent with feminist methods and desired outcomes. Although some have argued that law enforcement agencies should track and monitor data on crime and trust, and to gather significant amounts of information to better understand how police departments operate, it would be a better use of resources to make information regarding policing public. To embrace a culture of transparency, law enforcement agencies should make all department policies available for public review and regularly post on the department's website information about stops, summonses, arrests, reported crime, and other law enforcement data aggregated by demographics.

Conclusion

I have argued here that the time for a feminist approach to law enforcement is now. The advantage of feminist ethical theories is that they resist hierarchical structures and seek to empower those who are disempowered, not by *overpowering* but by fostering mutual dependence. The normative conception of feminist policing I have sketched does this by emphasizing (a) community connections, (b) effective communication, and (c) transparency between law enforcement and the public. This can be applied to hiring practices, protocols, and community relations, by fostering community dialogue, rather than increasing surveillance, as a core responsibility of law enforcement. No doubt, structural changes to the criminal justice system at large—such as defunding the war on drugs—are also required to change America's law enforcement system.[52] But reforming the justice system alone (sentencing, the case load of public defenders, funding of private prisons) is insufficient, as it is the philosophy of policing communities that is foundational to the criminal justice system at large. I have argued here that feminist care ethics is a revolutionary approach to the practice of policing, and can play a significant role in creating a social order in which citizens and law enforcement alike can trust each other to care for their lives.

Notes

1. See Stamper, Norm. 2016. *To Protect and Serve: How to Fix America's Police*. New York, NY: Nation Books.
2. James Q. Wilson and George Kelling. 1982. Broken Windows. *The Atlantic*, March. https://www.theatlantic.com/magazine/archive/1982/03/broken-windows/304465/.
3. Balko, Radley. 2013. *Rise of the Warrior Cop: The Militarization of America's Police Forces*. New York, NY: PublicAffairs.
4. Harmon argues that the problem of regulating the police is the lack of institutional jurisdiction over policing practices. See Harmon, Rachel A. 2012. The Problem of Policing. *Michigan Law Review* 110: 761–817.
5. Police unions are perhaps the biggest obstacle, as they have blocked substantial reforms over the last several decades (Harmon, 2012, 765).
6. Police practice is disconnected from important nonjudicial institutions—such as schools, churches, and civic organizations that could serve as a support network of community-building between police and private citizens.
7. Sampson, Robert J. and Stephen W. Raudenbush. 2004. Seeing Disorder: Neighborhood Stigma and the Social Construction of "Broken Windows". *Social Psychology Quarterly* 67: 319–342.
8. Fagan, Jeffrey and Garth Davies. 2000. Street Stops and Broken Windows: Terry, Race, and Disorder in New York City. *Fordham Urban Law Journal*: 457–504.
9. Bowman, Quinn. 2014. NYC Congressman says outdated 'broken windows' policing a factor in Eric Garner death. PBS Newshour, December 4. http://www.pbs.org/newshour/rundown/nyc-congressman-says-outdated-broken-windows-policing-factor-eric-garner-death/.
10. Roberts, Dorothy E. 1999. Race, Vagueness, and the Social Meaning of Order-Maintenance Policing. *Journal of Criminal Law and Criminology* 89: 775–836.
11. See for example Duck, Waverly. 2017. The Complex Dynamics of Trust and Legitimacy: Understanding Interactions between the Police and Poor Black Neighborhood Residents. *Annals of the American Academy of Political & Social Science* 673: 132–149. This article shows how forms of surveillance can lead to coping strategies that are corrosive of trust and legitimacy between black neighborhood residents and law enforcement in particular.
12. Baier, Annette. 1986. Trust and Antitrust. *Ethics* 96: 231–260.
13. Baier. 1986, 234–235.
14. Baier. 1986, 240.

15. This is an interdisciplinary field, but has been heavily influenced by sociology. It examines the ways that different ideologies about manhood develop, change, are contested, and given the status of "truth" about what a man is. Assumptions about the meaning of manhood justify particular actions and social institutions.
16. Kimmel, Michael. 2012. *Manhood in America: A Cultural History.* Oxford: Oxford University Press. For example, there's working-class white masculinity, black masculinity, upper-class gay masculinity, and other versions in between.
17. Kimmel. 2012, 30–33
18. Cooper, Frank Rudy. 2009. "Who's the Man?": Masculinities Studies, Terry Stops, and Police Training. *Columbia Journal of Gender and Law* 18: 676–677.
19. Moreover, these practices are reinforced by law and politics: most states have laws prohibiting people from touching a police officer, which are interpreted widely. Even someone resisting arrest can count as assaulting a police officer in some states.
20. Myisha Cherry argues that officer Darren Wilson's account of the shooting of Michael Brown was entrenched in masculinity discourse: "Although both men were 6'4, Wilson said that Michael Brown made him feel like a 5-year-old boy. 'That's just how big he felt and how small I felt just from grasping his arm.' *TRANSLATION: I did not feel like a man! He was bigger and stronger than me. I was a little boy not a man. But I must be a man at all times!* Michael Brown allegedly said to Darren Wilson, 'You're too much of a f*cking p*ssy to shoot me.' *TRANSLATION: He thought I wasn't man enough to shoot him. I had to show him I was.*" Cherry, Myisha. 2014. The Police and Their Masculinity Problem. *The Huffington Post*, November, 26. http://www.huffingtonpost.com/myisha-cherry/the-police-and-their-masc_b_6225834.html.
21. Cooper. 2009, 299. In particular, he identifies stop and frisks as typical ways of enacting masculinity contests. When officers feel disrespected, they face a masculinity challenge.
22. *Coghill vs. United States, 982 A.2d 802 (D.C. 2009).*
23. The National Center for Women & Policing. 2002. Men, Women, and Police Excessive Force: A Tale of Two Genders. http://womenandpolicing.com/PDF/2002_Excessive_Force.pdf.
24. Crenshaw, Kimberlé. 1991. Mapping the Margins: Intersectionality, Identity Politics, and Violence Against Women of Color. *Stanford Law Review* 43: 1241–1299. See also Whose Story Is It Anyway? Feminist and Anti-racist Appropriations of Anita Hill. 1992. In *Race-ing Justice, Engendering Power*, ed. Toni Morrison, 402–441. New York: Pantheon.

25. hooks, bell. 1999. *Yearning: Race, Gender, and Cultural Politics*. Boston: South End Press, 59.
26. Kindy, Kimberly, Marc Fisher, Julie Tate, and Jennifer Jenkins. 2015. A Year of Reckoning: Police Fatally Shoot Nearly 1000. *Washington Post*, December 26.
27. Collins, Patricia Hill and Sirma Bilge. 2016. *Intersectionality*. New York: Wiley, 136. See also Collins, Patricia Hill. 2006. A Telling Difference: Dominance, Strength, and Black Masculinities. In *Progressive Black Masculinities*, ed. Athena Mutua. Abingdon: Taylor and Francis.
28. Collins, Patricia Hill, and Sirma Bilge. 2016, 158. Collins argues that the solution to repressive state action on the part of law enforcement is actually listening to the needs of the people they police.
29. See for example the work of legal scholar Jonathan Simon, particularly Simon, Jonathan. 2017. Racing Abnormality, Normalizing Race: The Origins of America's Peculiar Carceral State and Its Prospects for Democratic Transformation Today. *Northwestern University Law Review* 111: 1626–1654. Here he shows that the patterns of over-incarceration and police violence for people of color have actually gotten worse, even as progress in establishing stronger rights for individuals in the early stages of the criminal process has been made. Thus, we cannot ignore the significance of race in the American criminal justice system.
30. Madfis, Eric and Cohen, Jeffrey. 2016. Critical Criminologies of the Present and Future: Left Realism, Left Idealism, and What's Left in Between. *Social Justice* 43: 1–21.
31. For elaboration of this point, see Lebron, Christopher. 2017. *The Making of Black Lives Matter: A Brief History of an Idea*. Oxford: Oxford University Press.
32. Davis, Angela. 2003. *Are Prisons Obsolete?* New York: Seven Stories Press.
33. Carol Gilligan's early research suggests that men and women discuss morality using two different "voices:" The voice of justice and the voice of care. For Gilligan loyalty would be an expression of care to particular individuals in concrete relationships. (See Gilligan, Carol. 1982. *In A Different Voice*. Cambridge, MA: Harvard University Press.)
34. See especially Virginia Held, who argues that the concepts, metaphors, and images associated with the care involved in parenting/mothering best express the dynamics of the moral life. (See Held, Virginia. 2006. *The Ethics of Care: Personal, Political, and Global*. Oxford: Oxford University Press.) Nel Noddings argues that we all exist in a web of relationships, and that in these relationships of care, one should be both a care-er and a cared-for. We should seek to preserve and nurture the concrete and valuable relationships we have with specific persons. (See especially Chapters 2 and 3 of Noddings, Nel. 1984. *Caring: A*

Feminine Approach to Ethics and Moral Education. Berkeley: University of California Press.)

35. The obligations that flow from our caring relationships vary from one care theorist to another. For example, according to Gilligan, we should exercise special care for those we are concretely in relation to by attending to their particular needs, values, desires. Eva Feder Kittay, on the other hand, argues that we have an obligation to exercise special care toward those particular persons with whom we have valuable close relationships, particularly where the relationship is not one of mutual dependence but in a relationship of 'dependency' such as that of a child on a parent. (Kittay, Eva Feder. 1999. *Love's Labor: Essays on Women, Equality, and Dependence*. New York: Routledge.)
36. Held, Virginia. 2006.
37. Robinson, Fiona. 1999. *Globalizing Care: Ethics, Feminist Theory, and International Relations*. Boulder, CO: Westview Press; Held, Virginia. 2006.
38. Held, Virginia. 2006, 43.
39. Michael Slote's version of care ethics (Slote, Michael. 2007. *The Ethics of Care and Empathy*. New York: Routledge) is an example of a care ethical theory that is not feminist.
40. In fact, initially, care ethical theories were elaborated as an alternative to and as a response to perceived "male" moral theory, which emphasized individual autonomy, impartiality, universality, rights, and rationality. And so care ethical theories were keen to emphasize the importance of culturally feminine traits like interdependence, community, the emotions, and our connectedness to others.
41. Feminists in other fields—criminology, law, criminal justice, and gender studies—have already sketched out the important ways in which feminism and gender are relevant to evaluating the actions and activities of police officers. But this has not been done in the field of philosophy.
42. Kleinig, John. 1996. *The Ethics of Policing*. Cambridge: Cambridge University Press, 24–26.
43. Kleinig, John. 1996, 24–26.
44. Kleinig, John. 1996, 27.
45. Kleinig, John. 1996, 28.
46. Noddings, Nel. 1984, 30.
47. Kindy, Kimberly, Marc Fisher, Julie Tate, and Jennifer Jenkins. 2015.
48. *Final Report of the President's Task Force on 21st Century Policing*. 2015. Washington, DC: Office of Community Oriented Policing Services. http://files.policemag.com/documents/21stcpolicingtaskforce-finalreport.pdf.

49. Walter Scott is an example—he fled his car after being pulled over for a broken taillight, because he was on probation, and ended up getting killed. https://www.nytimes.com/2017/05/02/us/michael-slager-walter-scott-north-charleston-shooting.html.
50. Held, Virginia. 2006, 39.
51. Kindy, Kimberly, Marc Fisher, Julie Tate, and Jennifer Jenkins. 2015.
52. Feminist approaches to reforming the criminal justice system already exist, including care ethical approaches. One critique is that the care ethical approach unwittingly supports and maintains an unjust criminal justice system, and will not end mass incarceration. See Heiner, Brady and Sarah Tyson. 2017. Feminism and the Carceral State: Gender-Responsive Justice, Community Accountability, and the Epistemology of Antiviolence. *Feminist Philosophy Quarterly* 3: 1–36. My proposal is consistent with the movement to end mass incarceration, as it suggests that implementing care ethics will significantly reduce the numbers of people ultimately caught up in the criminal justice system in the first place.

Bibliography

Alexander, Michelle. *The New Jim Crow: Mass Incarceration in the Age of Colorblindness*, The New Press, New York, NY, 2010.

Baier, Annette. "Trust and Antitrust," *Ethics*, Vol. 96, No. 2 (Jan, 1986), pp. 231–260.

Balko, Radley. *Rise of the Warrior Cop: The Militarization of America's Police Forces*, PublicAffairs, New York, NY, 2013.

Cherry, Myisha. "The Police and Their Masculinity Problem," *The Huffington Post,* November, 26, 2014.

Collins, Patricia Hill. *Black Feminist Thought: Knowledge, Consciousness and the Politics of Empowerment*, Routledge, London and New York, 2000.

Collins, Patricia Hill, and Bilge, Sirma. *Intersectionality*, Polity Press, Cambridge, 2016.

Cooper, Frank Rudy. "Against Bipolar Black Masculinity: Intersectionality, Assimilation, Identity Performance, and Hierarchy," *UC Davis Law Review*, Vol. 39 (2006), p. 853.

———. "'Who's the Man?': Masculinities Studies, Terry Stops, and Police Training," *Columbia Journal of Gender and Law*, Vol. 18, No. 3 (2009), pp. 671–742.

Crenshaw, Kimberlé. "Mapping the Margins: Intersectionality, Identity Politics, and Violence Against Women of Color," *Stanford Law Review*, Vol. 43, No. 6 (1991), pp. 1241–1299.

———. "Whose Story is it Anyway? Feminist and Anti-racist Appropriations of Anita Hill", in Toni Morrison (ed.), *Race-ing Justice, Engendering Power*, Pantheon, New York, pp. 402–441, 1992.

———. *On Intersectionality: The Essential Writings of Kimberlé Crenshaw*, The New Press, New York, NY, 2015.

Davis, Angela. *Are Prisons Obsolete?* Seven Stories Press, New York, 2003.

Duck, Waverly. "The Complex Dynamics of Trust and Legitimacy: Understanding Interactions between the Police and Poor Black Neighborhood Residents," *Annals of the American Academy of Political & Social Science*, Vol. 673, No. 1 (Sept 2017), pp. 132–149.

Engster, Daniel. *The Heart of Justice: Care Ethics and Political Theory*, Oxford University Press, Oxford, 2007.

Enloe, Cynthia. "Masculinities, Policing, Women and International Politics of Sexual Harassment," *International Feminist Journal of Politics*, Vol. 15, No. 1 (2013), pp. 77–81.

Fagan, Jeffrey and Davies, Garth. "Street Stops and Broken Windows: Terry, Race, and Disorder in New York City, *Fordham Urban Law Journal*, Vol. 23, No. 2 (2000), pp. 457–504.

Fan, Mary D. "Panopticism for Police: Structural Reform Bargaining and Police Regulation by Data-Driven Surveillance," *Washington Law Review*, Vol. 87 (2012), pp. 93ff.

Gale, Mary Ellen. "Calling in the Girl Scouts: Feminist Legal Theory and Police Misconduct," *Loyola of Los Angeles Law Review*, Vol. 24 (January 2001), pp. 691ff.

Gilligan, Carol. *In A Different Voice,* Harvard University Press, Cambridge, MA, 1982.

Harmon, Rachel A. "When Is Police Violence Justified?" *Northwestern University Law Review*, Vol. 102, No. 3 (2008), p. 1119.

———. "The Problem of Policing," *Michigan Law Review*, Vol. 110 (March 2012), pp. 761ff.

______. "Why Arrest?" *Michigan Law Review*, Vol. 115 (December 2016), pp. 307ff.

Heiner, Brady T., and Tyson, Sarah K. "Feminism and the Carceral State: Gender-Responsive Justice, Community Accountability, and the Epistemology of Antiviolence" *Feminist Philosophy Quarterly*, Vol. 3, No. 1 (2017), Article 3, pp. 1–37.

Held, Virginia. "Feminist Transformations of Moral Theory," *Philosophy and Phenomenological Research*, Vol. 50, Supplement (Autumn, 1990), pp. 321–344.

———. *Feminist Morality: Transforming Culture, Society, and Politics*, University of Chicago Press, Chicago, 1993.

_____. *The Ethics of Care: Personal, Political, and Global.* Oxford University Press, Oxford, 2006.

hooks, bell. *Yearning: Race, Gender, and Cultural Politics*, South End Press, Boston, p. 59, 1999.

Jaggar, Alison. "Feminist Ethics: Projects, Problems, Prospects". In C. Card (ed.), *Feminist Ethics*, University Press of Kansas, Lawrence, KS, 1991.

———. "Feminist Ethics". In L. Becker and C. Becker (eds.), *Encyclopedia of Ethics*, Garland Press, New York, pp. 363–364, 1992.

Kimmel, Michael. *Manhood in America: A Cultural History*, Oxford University Press, Oxford, 2012.

Kittay, Eva Feder. *Love's Labor: Essays on Women, Equality, and Dependence*, Routledge, New York, NY, 1999.

Kingshott, Brian F. "Women in Policing: Changing the Organizational Culture by Adopting a Feminist Perspective on Leadership," *Criminal Justice Studies*, Vol. 22, No. 1 (March 2009), pp. 49–72.

_____. "Revisiting Gender Issues: Continuing Police Reform," *Criminal Justice Studies*, Vol. 26, No. 3, (2013), pp. 366–392.

Kleinig, John. *The Ethics of Policing*, Cambridge University Press, Cambridge, 1996.

———. "Legitimate and Illegitimate Uses of Police Force," *Criminal Justice Ethics*, Vol. 33, No. 2 (2014), pp. 83–103.

Lebron, Christopher. *The Making of Black Lives Matter: A Brief History of an Idea*, Oxford University Press, Oxford, 2017.

Lerman, Amy E., and Weaver, Vesla M. *Arresting Citizenship: The Democratic Consequences of American Crime Control.* University of Chicago Press, Chicago, 2014.

Madfis, Eric, and Cohen, Jeffrey. "Critical Criminologies of the Present and Future: Left Realism, Left Idealism, and What's Left In Between," *Social Justice*, Vol. 43, No. 4 (2016), pp. 1–21.

Miller, Eric J. "Role-Based Policing: Restraining Police Conduct Outside the Legitimate Investigative Sphere" *California Law Review*, Vol. 94, No. 3 (May 2006), pp. 617ff.

———. "Challenging Police Discretion," *Howard Law Journal*, Vol. 58 (2015), p. 521.

Noddings, Nel. *Caring: A Feminine Approach to Ethics and Moral Education*, University of California Press, Berkeley, 1984.

President's Task Force on 21st Century Policing. *Final Report of the President's Task Force on 21st Century Policing.* Office of Community Oriented Policing Services, Washington, DC, 2015.

Rich, Camille Gear. "Angela Harris and the Racial Politics of Masculinity: Trayvon Martin, George Zimmerman, and the Dilemmas of Desiring Whiteness," *California Law Review*, Vol. 102, No. 4, (2014), pp. 1027ff.

Roberts, Dorothy E. "Race, Vagueness, and the Social Meaning of Order-Maintenance Policing," *Journal of Criminal Law and Criminology*, Vol. 89, No. 3 (Spring 1999), pp. 775–836.

Robinson, Fiona. *Globalizing Care: Ethics, Feminist Theory, and International Relations*, Westview Press, Boulder, 1999.

Sampson, Robert J., and Raudenbush, Stephen W. "Seeing Disorder: Neighborhood Stigma and the Social Construction of 'Broken Windows'," *Social Psychology Quarterly*, Vol. 67, No. 4 (2004), pp. 319–342.

Simon, Jonathan. "Racing Abnormality, Normalizing Race: The Origins of America's Peculiar Carceral State and Its Prospects for Democratic Transformation Today." *Northwestern University Law Review*, Vol. 111, No. 6 (2017), pp. 1626–1654.

Slote, Michael. *The Ethics of Care and Empathy*, Routledge, London and New York, 2007.

Snow, David A., Soule, Sara A., and Kriesi, Hanspeter. *The Blackwell Companion to Social Movements*, Malden, MA, 2004.

Stamper, Norm. *To Protect and Serve: How to Fix America's Police*, Nation Books, New York, NY, 2016.

Stuntz, William J. *The Collapse of American Criminal Justice*. Harvard University Press, Cambridge, MA, 2011.

Tronto, Joan. *Moral Boundaries: A Political Argument for an Ethic of Care*. Routledge, New York and London, 1993.

Wilson, James Q., and Kelling, George. "Broken Windows," *The Atlantic*, March 1982.

Young, Iris Marion. *Inclusion and Democracy*, Oxford University Press, Oxford, 2000.

Policing and Racial Discrimination: Throwing Out the Baby with the Bath Water

Douglas Husak

Virtually all of the current commentary about policing in America places the issue of race at center stage. As a result of this narrow focus, many of the most fundamental questions are bypassed. For example, it is crucial to decide what powers the police should possess in a modern democratic society. But this basic issue is rarely addressed unless it is filtered through the lens of race. I do not pretend to be clueless about why the topic of race is so frequently raised when policing is scrutinized. The rash of highly publicized video shootings of unarmed minorities by zealous law enforcement officials is the most important factor in elevating the issue to its present stature. Although it is perilous to construct meaningful generalizations across each of the many autonomous and diverse departments throughout the United States, all reasonable persons concede that policing needs to be improved in light of its uncontested disparate

D. Husak (✉)
Rutgers University, New Brunswick, NJ, USA
e-mail: husak@philosophy.rutgers.edu

M. Gardner and M. Weber (eds.), *The Ethics of Policing and Imprisonment*, Palgrave Studies in Ethics and Public Policy,
https://doi.org/10.1007/978-3-319-97770-6_6

impact on minorities. I do not contest that the greater attention to racial dynamics is welcome and overdue.[1]

At the same time, however, I urge caution about the drift much of this scholarship has taken. Caution is advised in light of the relative lack of "viewpoint diversity" that characterizes much of the contemporary criminological literature in the United States. David Garland correctly observes that "the dominant current of thought in punishment and society scholarship is without doubt, progressive or left-liberal in its political orientation. There are few conservative voices in the field."[2] I should disclose that I too roughly share the political orientation Garland describes as dominant, and I would be appalled to be characterized as conservative. More precisely, however, I tend to think of myself as relatively non-ideological. Nonetheless, the dangers of group-think are well-known across a range of domains. When dissenting opinions are not represented, scholars are unchallenged and their reasoning is more likely to contain unwarranted inferences. In my judgment, quite a bit of the recent commentary about policing is vulnerable to this problem. As Garland warns, the absence of dissent among criminologists has "theoretical consequences."[3] In what follows, I aspire to provide a corrective to what I regard as an example of the phenomenon Garland has in mind. Because of its narrow focus on how policing affects minorities, I fear that some of the current scholarship goes too far in recommending that some valuable police powers should be withdrawn. In my judgment, it risks throwing out the baby with the bath water.

To support my point, I begin with a brief (and oversimplified) description of some recent legal and political history. Pursuant to *Terry v. Ohio*,[4] police have the constitutional power to briefly detain a person they have "reasonable suspicion" to believe is involved in criminal activity, even when they lack "probable cause" to arrest. The exercise of this power led to the practice of "stop, question and frisk" (henceforth SQF).[5] The widespread use of SQF became associated with a "broken-windows" theory of crime-control and eventually emerged as controversial because of growing evidence that it was used disproportionately in "high-crime" neighborhoods against minorities. Nowhere was this controversy greater than in New York City. In 2011 and 2012, for example, blacks and Hispanics comprised 87% of all persons stopped there, even though they represented only half of the population. In *Floyd v. City of New York*,[6] one of a set of class action suits was brought against the City of New York, its Police Commissioner (Ray Kelly), its

Mayor (Michael Bloomberg), and unnamed police officers. The plaintiffs alleged that the City employed a policy that unlawfully discriminated against persons on the basis of their race and/or national origin in violation of the Fourteenth Amendment and Civil Rights Act of 1964. In other words, the practice of SQF was said to be a thinly disguised subterfuge for "racial profiling." Attorneys for the defendants responded that SQF was instrumental in stopping crime, and people of color were disproportionately targeted solely because they were more likely to be criminals. In 2013, Judge Shira Scheindlin issued a sweeping ruling in favor of the plaintiffs. City officials were irate, and immediately announced their intention to appeal her decision—as they had every right to do.

Even before Judge Scheindlin's judgment was rendered, however, the controversy over SQF had assumed major political importance within the electorate. When Bill de Blasio ran for mayor in 2013, he promised to be "the only candidate to end the Stop-and-Frisk era that targets minorities."[7] This promise resonated strongly with liberal voters throughout the five boroughs, who elected (and subsequently re-elected) de Blasio as the mayor. Among his first actions in office was to announce that the City would *not* appeal the ruling in *Floyd* after all. Although the practice of SQF has not *ended* in his administration, it would be churlish to accuse de Blasio of breaking his promise. 685,000 people had been stopped in 2011; that total had plummeted to 12,400 in 2016.[8] As the numbers have fallen, the percentage of stopped persons who were determined to be "totally innocent" has dropped as well. Eighty-eight percent of those subjected to SQF were "totally innocent" in 2011; that percentage has fallen to 66% in 2017.[9] Although the police are required by law to complete a form recording the details of their confrontation, skeptics worry that more stops are now unreported. Nonetheless, no one doubts that the incidence of SQF has declined dramatically and turned up a higher rate of criminal behavior as a result of the policies initiated by the police department under Mayor de Blasio.

Those officials who favored a more aggressive use of SQF predicted disaster. According to Ray Kelly, the ousted Police Commissioner in New York City, the results would be awful. Although Kelly concedes that "it's hard to prove a negative," he claims that "in conjunction with a variety of other methods and strategies [SQF] has helped to drive crime down in New York City and to make the streets safer for everyone."[10] No one disputes the enormous crime drop throughout New York City in the past several years.[11] What *is* disputed, however, is the role that SQF has played in causing this impressive drop. When police engage in SQF, general crime deterrence was said to be their primary objective.[12] Former Mayor Michael Bloomberg has stated publicly that "by making it 'too hot to carry,' the N.Y.P.D. is preventing guns from being carried on our streets."[13] He complained that civil rights organizations just "don't get it." The low hit rates of SQF to detect weapons, he argued, were evidence that order maintenance policing was working: "Stops are a deterrent. It's the same reason we set up DWI stop points."[14] The legality of this strategy depends (inter alia) on the existence of an offense the police have reason to suspect may be underway. Police can allege only so often that they stop persons for engaging in "furtive movements"—the most popular basis for SQF. Drug proscriptions and other "quality of life" offenses give police the rationale they need.[15] Without SQF or the enforcement of the offenses that trigger it, Kelly's verdict is dire. As a result of the initiatives of the de Blasio administration, he predicted that "people will lose their lives."[16] Needless to say, the current mayor disagrees.

Whose prediction is correct? It is probably too early to tell, and we may never be certain. Clearly, the spectacular crime drop is a monumental achievement that has made life better and safer. But who deserves credit for the enormous progress that has been achieved? Although the answer is hotly debated among criminologists, almost everyone concurs that *some* of our success has been caused by more effective law enforcement.[17] Crime has fallen even though our country has made little progress addressing what most believe to be the "root causes" of crime. Socioeconomic inequality has actually increased and poverty has remained relatively constant throughout much of the time that crime has fallen. No criminologist predicted this combination of events would happen, and they disagree about why it is happening now. It is plausible to suppose that improved methods of law enforcement are among the many important factors causing the massive crime drop.

Despite this uncertainty, the early returns on de Blasio's initiatives provide no cause for alarm. For the most part, violent crime has continued to fall in New York City since the policy changes have been implemented. Although no empirical result can be taken as *proof*, the latest data have not confirmed Kelly's fears that aggressive uses of SQF are needed to keep offense rates low. Even though street stops have decreased by 93%,[18] rates of violent and nonviolent crime continue to plummet. 2017 has proven to be the safest year in the modern history of

New York City, with crime falling in all felony categories[19] (even while these rates have begun to tick upward in several other cities).[20] In addition, these gains in safety have been achieved without resorting to high rates of incarceration; New York City imprisons fewer and fewer of its citizens. What are we to make of these data? I do not pretend to have answers, and generalizations are perilous. The decline of SQF by 90% may have been wise, but a further drop to 100% may not. Perhaps the use of SQF was an effective tactic in the short run, but has proved to be counterproductive over the long term. When police regularly target a relatively high proportion of innocent citizens, it becomes more difficult to secure cooperation that allows crime to be detected or prevented in subsequent interactions.[21] What helped to reduce crime may not be necessary to sustain these results once a drop to tolerable levels has been achieved. In any event, the evaluation of any crime-prevention strategy, including SQF, must be sensitive to crime trends. Initiatives that might make sense when rates of violence are high would become indefensible when these rates fall.

Despite the empirical controversy that surrounds this issue, a fair amount of academic commentary alleges that the new policies governing SQF have not gone far enough. In my judgment, their recommendations are extreme. I will use some of the research of L. Song Richardson to illustrate the point of view that concerns me. Richardson draws from the voluminous literature on implicit bias compiled by social scientists to contend that "officers will be more likely to judge the ambiguous behaviors of Blacks as suspicious while ignoring or not even noticing the identical ambiguous behaviors of Whites. As a result, Blacks are more likely than Whites to be stopped by the police." Racial anxieties will then create "racial disparities in whether a frisk will occur or force will be used."[22] Obviously, police officers are not immune from these biases. Richardson amasses a wealth of evidence to show that "officers who work in urban, majority-minority neighborhoods are more influenced by implicit racial biases than officers who do not work in these neighborhoods."[23] Moreover, the nearly ineradicable nature of implicit bias and racial anxiety ensures that "it is highly unlikely if not impossible for stops and frisks to be conducted in a manner that does not result in unjustified racial disparities."[24] No wonder "black individuals bear the brunt of stops and frisks and other similar investigatory proactive policing practices."[25]

Although Richardson's own resistance to SQF depends on her views about implicit bias, it is arguable that it need not have done so. Even when *Terry* was first decided and the Court held that SQF was permitted under the Constitution, the Court noted that the practice "was a major source of friction between the police and minority groups."[26] Thus, Richardson's latest research re-enforces the problem recognized long ago. But if the data on which she relies are even roughly accurate, what are we to do? One might have expected her to propose a balancing: any advantages of the practice of SQF, one would think, must be weighed against the disadvantages of allowing some amount of racial discrimination in policing. Admittedly, performing this balancing will be difficult. To weigh the plusses against the minuses requires us to specify what the plusses *are*. As far as I can tell, however, Richardson makes no serious effort to do so. Instead, she draws a different and far stronger conclusion, and here is where I believe the unwarranted leap can be found: We should not merely exhort "officers to treat individuals with courtesy and respect during stops and frisks, although this should be encouraged so long as stops and frisks continue. Rather, repairing the broken police-public relationship will require abandoning the practice [of stop, question and-frisk]."[27]

This conclusion involves an enormous and wholly unsupported leap. Several problems are unresolved in her train of thought that are best identified by trying to reconstruct her opposition to SQF in a deductive form. Consider the following argument:

1. Almost all persons, including the police, are subject to implicit racial bias.
2. Eradicating this implicit bias is practically impossible.
3. This bias increases the probability that minorities will be subject to SQF.
4. The increased probability that minorities will be subject to SQF is discriminatory on racial and ethnic grounds.
5. Discrimination on racial and ethnic grounds is virtually intolerable. Thus,
6. SQF is virtually intolerable.
7. SQF has no social advantages that can show it to be desirable overall. Thus,
8. SQF should be abolished.

If philosophers of law are not to succumb to the group-think tendencies against which Garland warns, quite a few of these premises should be subject to challenge.

In the first place, much of the data on which Richardson relies has been contested. The tests of implicit bias used by social scientists do not always translate into discernable discriminatory practices by individuals.[28] Moreover, whatever biases are found may be eradicable. Training might lessen and even remove this bias altogether. Since persons differ markedly in the extent to which they exhibit racial biases, applicants might be chosen to serve as officers partly on whether their bias is minimal. Important though these reservations may be, I am sure Richardson is aware of them, so I will not press them further. In other words, I will not dispute (1) through (3). Instead, I will suggest that Richardson's conclusion goes too far even if each of these premises is correct. Unless something like (7) can be supported—and none of the social gains of SQF can show it to be desirable overall—we cannot derive (8) and conclude that SQF should be abolished *even if* it is inevitably used to support a practice that has a discriminatory impact on persons on racial and ethnic grounds. My focus, then, centers on whether SQF produces advantages that are capable of offsetting the disadvantages of its racially discriminatory character.

Before proceeding, I emphasize that my argumentative strategy in what follows should not be construed merely as a response to Richardson herself. Instead, I hope it will become clear that I intend my misgivings to apply to the position of *any* commentator who rejects a social policy simply by pointing out its negative characteristics, such as its racially discriminatory character.[29] Is such a criticism simply a powerful but only a *pro tanto* moral objection to it? Or does this powerful criticism suffice to show that the policy must be abolished *all-things-considered*? My reflections are pertinent to this latter issue, and thus are significant beyond Richardson's argument, which I use mainly for purposes of illustration.

Is (7) true? *Does* SQF produce significant social benefits? If so, we must decide whether these benefits are sufficiently great to offset any injustice of its racially discriminatory character. The first of these questions cannot be answered a priori. Instead, its resolution requires a specialization in criminology that virtually no academic philosopher (and certainly not me) is likely to possess. Even criminologists are divided on this empirical matter. What assistance, then, might a *philosopher* hope to offer? Since no legal theorist should pretend to *settle* this issue, my main contribution is to show that the case against SQF requires it to be considered. Without data from criminologists, the argument for abolishing SQF that begins with the inevitability of a racial bias is necessarily incomplete. As I will contend, the ultimate case against SQF remains incomplete *even if* these data are provided. Normative arguments about police powers are needed to make use of these data in shaping social policy.

It is patently obvious that the total abolition of SQF would have *some* detrimental effect on public safety. In fact, this effect is likely to be considerable. If so, the case against it depends on the outcome of the very balancing its opponents seem unwilling to undertake. I adapt an example from Ray Kelly's recent autobiography to illustrate the costs of abandoning this practice altogether.[30] Kelly asks his readers to imagine a scenario in which a bystander observes a person walking up and down the street attempting to open car doors. He proceeds from one parked vehicle to another, determining if any is unlocked. The bystander calls 911 to summon the police. Surely Kelly is correct that this conduct qualifies as "suspicious behavior" and that crime would be reduced if the police retain the power to stop and question this individual—regardless of his race or ethnicity. Of course, anyone can direct a question to anyone; the police, no less than private citizens, are protected by the First Amendment. But if the power of SQF were withdrawn, as Richardson recommends, the suspect Kelly describes is equally permitted to ignore the question and proceed on his way. If the power of SQF is retained, however, as current law allows, the police can demand an answer that satisfies them that the individual is not preparing to break the law.

A second related issue must be addressed in order to identify the real-world consequences of prohibiting SQF. All philosophers understand that it is far easier to critique than to defend a policy. If the police lose the power to stop and question, what procedures are likely to replace it? In other words, how can we be confident that whatever *alternatives* to SQF that would emerge would be *preferable* to it? It is hard to believe that police can or should do nothing in a scenario such as that described by Kelly. Criminologists have long cautioned about a *net-widening effect* when a relatively unobtrusive option is removed from the table. If SQF were unavailable, one would anticipate that police would respond to suspicious behavior by making greater use of their power to *arrest*. If so, the above individual would have to explain to a prosecutor or judge rather than to a policeman that his behavior is innocent. Why would this change be worrisome? When persons are arrested, they acquire an *arrest record*. An arrest is the most serious consequence that many persons experience as a result of their interaction with the criminal justice system. For better or worse, arrest records typically confer a lifetime of disadvantage—a problem to which I will return.[31] When a suspect is made only to answer questions to the satisfaction of the police, however, no such record is compiled. I doubt the opponents of SQF would be happy if more minorities were arrested because police lack the power to exercise a less intrusive option. Those who demand the abandonment of SQF should be careful what they wish for.

As I hope is clear, no one can definitively decide whether it is sensible to abandon SQF without an answer to the fundamental question with which I began, viz., what powers should the police possess in an advanced democratic society? My own judgment, which I am relatively confident is widely shared, is that police *should* have the power to subject the individual Kelly describes to SQF. I make this judgment *even if* Richardson is correct to conclude that this power will inevitably be employed in a manner that involves discrimination against racial and ethnic minorities. The evaluation of almost any social policy invariably requires careful trade-offs between winners and losers. SQF is no exception. Or is it? In a variety of contexts, moral and political philosophers *resist* assessing social policies within a cost–benefit framework. When an action is subject to a *deontological constraint*, all but the most committed consequentialists would not allow it to be performed, even when it maximizes the good. I readily concur that the evaluation of many rules and doctrines in criminal justice are properly governed by one or more deontological constraints. To cite just one of many examples, the hallowed rule against convicting defendants in the absence of *proof beyond a reasonable doubt* cannot plausibly be thought to achieve the best consequences overall.[32] Might SQF be subject to such a limitation as well? What deontological constraint plausibly applies to it?

Doubtless many of its opponents believe the discriminatory character of SQF brings it squarely within a deontological constraint and suffices to disqualify it. Recall that premise (5) alleges "Discrimination on racial and ethnic grounds is virtually intolerable." But I am skeptical; premise (4) conceals an ambiguity that opens (5) to doubt. Premise (4) states "The increased probability that minorities will be subject to SQF is discriminatory on racial and ethnic grounds." The sum of given cases of SQF, however, might well involve a racially discriminatory *impact* without involving a racist *intent*. That is, the unquestionable discriminatory character of SQF need not betray a racist *motivation*—which clearly would trigger a deontological constraint and support (5). Instead, SQF may involve only a racially disparate *impact*, which I take to be less objectionable than a racist intent.[33] Why construe the data Richardson cites about implicit bias to show that police are racially motivated whenever they employ SQF? Suppose most or all of the individuals described in Kelly's scenario turned out to be white. Would we then allow the police to stop them? Alternatively, suppose most or all of the individuals described in Kelly's scenario turned out to be minorities. Should we then prohibit the police from stopping them? As far as I can see, we can and should decide whether police should be granted the power to subject this individual to SQF even in the absence of any information about his race. If a practice should be precluded merely because of its disparate racial *impact*, the entire criminal justice system and a great many other public and private institutions would have to be dismantled. In other words, the problem Richardson describes cannot be confined solely to the practice of SQF. After all, the implicit biases that plague police also infect prosecutors, judges, juries, and anyone else in criminal justice—or, indeed, anyone who participates in any legal or non-legal institution whatever. When so extended, the general argument Richardson mounts against SQF amounts to a *reductio* against *all* such practices. Why single out one practice when all others are equally vulnerable? Thus it would be helpful to attempt to find a deontological constraint that applies to each instance of SQF *without* appealing simply to its racially disparate impact.

Arguably, then, the case against SQF ultimately depends on *additional* considerations that show its gains cannot offset its costs. Legal philosophers are better positioned than criminologists to weigh in on this matter. In the remainder of this chapter, I will explore *two* related but distinct deontological constraints that might be invoked for this purpose. First, SQF might violate one or more *rights* that function something like *trumps* to obviate appeals to cost–benefit calculations. Second, SQF might violate the Kantian *means principle* and impermissibly *use* persons as a mere means to a greater good. These two constraints pertain not only to policies that disproportionately harm minorities, but also apply across-the-board to *all* policies. I will conclude that neither of these two constraints should preclude the use of SQF altogether. But my position is somewhat tentative. First, I do not pretend to have conclusive arguments to establish the compatibility between SQF and the deontological constraints I will consider. Second, additional constraints I do not examine might disqualify SQF. Nonetheless, I hope my arguments support a plausible basis for believing that the ultimate fate of SQF depends on how its advantages are balanced against its disadvantages.

I begin my discussion of the *first* basis for denying that SQF should be accessed through consequentialist reasoning by asking: Who should decide whether these tradeoffs are worth making? In a democracy, one might suppose the decision must invariably be entrusted to the electorate.[34] Police are granted the power to use SQF in a free society because the public wants them to have it. In a liberal city such as New York, this power is severely limited, as is indicated by the strong majority that led to de Blasio's victory. In high-crime jurisdictions which have a stronger law-and-order mentality, however, the preferences of the electorate might well be otherwise. If we follow this approach and defer to democratic processes, it would be no easier to decide whether a trade-off is worth making than to specify an optimal level of municipal taxation. But should this question really be resolved through democratic channels? Or should the fate of SQF be no more entrusted to the electorate than that of Freedom of Speech or Freedom of Religion—which clearly involve rights?

It is no mean feat, however, to identify a right that SQF violates—other than an alleged right that depends on its racially disparate impact. The right to privacy may seem like a viable candidate; it underlies the Fourth Amendment protection against unreasonable searches. But the Court in *Terry* held that this right was *not* violated when police have a reasonable suspicion to make a stop. Presumably, the right to dignity is violated whenever police conduct SQF in an especially humiliating way—as in a strip search, for example. Apart from such intrusive frisks, however, it is doubtful that an ordinary *stopping* or *questioning* qualifies as humiliating or undignified. Unless *Terry* was wrongly decided, then, some *other* right would need to be identified when SQF is performed routinely. No familiar right comes to mind.

Suppose, however, that one or more rights *are* violated by each instance of SQF. This determination would not be dispositive to the case against SQF unless its advantages were "merely" utilitarian and therefore eligible to be "trumped." But no such trumping could occur if rights exist on *both* sides of the issue. Might this be so? To begin to answer this crucial question, it is important to note that the main beneficiaries of the spectacular crime drop I mentioned are the very persons who otherwise would have been victimized. Obviously, any of us could become a casualty at any time. Yet rates of victimization are distributed very unevenly throughout the population.[35] Since whites were less likely to have been victimized in the first place, little progress could have been made in decreasing crime by reducing their incidence of victimization. But blacks, always disproportionately affected by crime in the United States, have benefitted disproportionately from the crime drop.[36] Since violent crime violates rights, the very groups of persons whose rights would otherwise have been violated have been spared. Of course, these individuals remain nameless; it is impossible to identify the specific persons who *would have* been victimized had crime rates remained near their peak levels. But why should the fact that prospective victims cannot be named entail that they lack rights? At any rate, we can say with a relatively high level of confidence that minorities have benefited disproportionately from whatever role the police have played in causing crime rates to fall. Some commentators allege that "the drop in homicides is probably the most important development in the health of black men in the past several decades."[37] Arguably, then, the gains of the crime drop are not "merely utilitarian"; the rights of racial and ethnic minorities are at stake in *both* sides of the balancing equation.[38] As an aside, I mention that these considerations help to make our system of criminal justice look a good deal less racist than its harshest critics allege. Despite its popularity, the racist explanation for the persistence of SQF has never been wholly satisfying. As racism generally recedes elsewhere, it is hard to explain why it is so widely believed to survive intact within the criminal justice system in particular.[39]

I will say no more about rights in moving to the consideration of a *second* deontological constraint that might jeopardize SQF. In order to evaluate this practice further, it might be helpful to situate it within theories of *preventive harming*. SQF is one of a number of practices that target persons who may or may not turn out to be innocent in order to help reduce crime. Practices of preventive harming are morally controversial because they seemingly violate the Kantian *means principle*. Exactly how this principle should be formulated is a deep matter that has spawned a huge literature I will not discuss here.[40] I will simply assume that most moral philosophers acknowledge the difficulty of using one person as a mere means to benefit another. Legal theorists have said a great deal about preventive harming in other contexts (primarily those involving terrorism), and some of their insights might be adapted to gain a better normative perspective on SQF.[41]

A philosophical examination of the compatibility between SQF and the means principle might begin by calling attention to the pervasiveness of practices that appear to implicate this principle (or at least some versions of it).[42] My point of departure is that such practices are far more pervasive than moral, political and legal philosophers have tended to admit. Many everyday behaviors harm one person today to minimize harm to another person tomorrow, and the realization that these practices are routine may help to shine a new light on the topic at hand. Some of the examples I will mention are so mundane and familiar that they can easily escape our notice. Several of the social and legal practices I describe probably *cannot* and presumably *should* not be altered or reformed easily. If harms are justified for preventive purposes in the contexts I will mention, we should ask whether or for what reason we might regard them as especially controversial when caused by the police in the form of SQF.

Most of these practices and policies I have in mind are typically called *collateral consequences*.[43] In what follows, I understand a collateral consequence broadly, encompassing any harm suffered by a person caused by her interaction with the criminal justice system (beyond whatever constitutes her official punishment). Notice that this (admittedly imprecise) definition does not require that anyone is ever actually *punished*. *Any* interaction, including being subjected to SQF, can suffice. The important point is that a vast array of harms, especially in employment and housing, are due to a person's interaction with a system of criminal justice in the United States, and, when these harms are designed to prevent future harms, they form the topic of my examination because they implicate the same means principle that seemingly leads to anxiety about SQF.[44]

Quite a few of the measures that harm offenders for preventive purposes take place *after* the defendant's "official punishment" has ended. As I have indicated, however, a number of worrisome and far-reaching collateral consequences require a mere *arrest*—which is permitted when the police have *probable cause* to believe a person is engaged in criminal activity. The total impact of these collateral consequences dwarfs those predicated on conviction or punishment. Deprivations that require a mere arrest affect astounding numbers of people; approximately 25% of the adult population of the United States have an arrest record for actual or alleged conduct not involving a traffic offense, and easily-accessed criminal intelligence databases are filled with information about people who may be monitored because of the risk they are thought to pose. Thus, some seventy million Americans are potentially affected by collateral consequences due to their interaction with the criminal justice system. For perhaps the majority of such persons, the most worrisome feature of their arrest is not punishment but their resulting criminal record, as it triggers any number of practices of preventive harming. These collateral consequences are both formal (de jure) and informal (de facto). In his seminal book on criminal records, James Jacobs alleges that the need to balance the goal of preventing crime with the civil liberties of persons who interact with the criminal justice system is "one of the greatest law enforcement challenges of our time."[45]

Collateral consequences have a bad reputation among legal theorists—probably even worse than SQF itself. For a number of reasons, a few of the reformers who are appalled by SQF have also called for an end to most or all of the collateral consequences that result from arrest. Some have gone so far as to recommend the enactment of laws to outlaw discrimination against arrestees—much as we ban discrimination on grounds of race or religion.[46] As I have suggested, fully a quarter of the adult population of the United States is subject to the harms that can result from a mere arrest, and no one seriously disputes that persons with an arrest record are treated more harshly than those without such a record at every stage of the criminal justice process.[47] Perhaps more significantly, private parties respond similarly in discriminating against arrestees. Ninety-two percent of employers who replied to a survey say they require a background check for some or all jobs[48] and admit to drawing an unfavorable inference from a negative finding.[49] To add insult to injury, it is equally apparent that these practices place an especially heavy burden on minorities, thereby raising the ire of liberals and prioritarians.[50] From a procedural point of view, it also seems outrageous that a single police officer has the de facto power to place an individual at a lifelong disability in employment and housing.[51] For these reasons alone, it is surprising that many of those philosophers who are worried about the justifiability of preventive harming generally have tended to overlook the significance of the collateral consequences that follow from an arrest.

Despite legitimate concerns, it would be hard to categorically reject the justifiability of a great many of the collateral consequences I have described. Inasmuch as three-year recidivism rates are as high as 68%, no one should be too quick to fault persons for treating a criminal record as predictive of future criminality.[52] As John Monahan observes, "It has long been axiomatic in the field of risk assessment that past crime is the best predictor of future crime. All actuarial risk assessment instruments reflect this empirical truism."[53] The California Static Risk Assessment Instrument, for example, contains 22 risk factors for criminal recidivism, fully 20 of which—all but gender and age—are indices of past crime.[54] In short, past crime is the least controversial risk factor used to predict future criminality. In addition, it is hard to see how anyone could realistically hope to *preclude* anyone from drawing negative inferences, even from an arrest. What mechanism could possibly be put into place to dissuade individuals from doing so? More importantly, are we really so certain that these inferences should *not* be drawn? Should state or private elementary schools be barred from refusing to hire a teacher who had been arrested for child abuse? Would we be paranoid to discharge a housekeeper we learned had been arrested for stealing from her former employer? Moreover, job seekers with a spotless record might have a valid complaint against a government policy requiring private employers to treat a criminal record as irrelevant.[55] The rationale that underlies the foregoing examples of preventive harming is deeply imbedded in our social life.

Even so, one might challenge my suggestion that any of the social and economic practices I have mentioned above are permissible. If they are objectionable, they cannot form the basis of an analogy to reduce opposition to SQF. It may be tempting to condemn these practices because, in quite a few instances, the harm to be prevented would not have taken place; its occurrence is simply a matter of fallible prediction. But *all* practices that depend on future contingencies are vulnerable to the same worry; persons who use deadly force in self-defense or in war cannot be certain their victims would have made good on their threats. Obviously, anyone would prefer to have more accurate data than a mere arrest to identify those persons who pose elevated risks of future criminality.[56] In the absence of better data, however, it seems sensible to act on the best evidence available.[57] Surely certainty cannot be required for *subjective permissibility*—that part of moral philosophy that governs how rational persons are allowed to behave on the basis of the evidence available to them. Even if we were able to do so, a prospective employer should not be made to treat arrestees as "innocent until proven guilty" or cease to discriminate in the absence of "proof beyond a reasonable doubt" of future misbehavior. I mention these demanding legal standards of proof simply to point out that we require nothing comparable when we assess the social and economic practices I have discussed.

If I am correct that a host of familiar social and economic practices implicate the means principle, I believe we should be less inclined to invoke this principle as a formidable obstacle to SQF. That is, measures that harm one person to reduce the risk of harm to others are not quite as worrisome on moral grounds as many moral and legal philosophers have supposed. Again, I will not attempt to undertake the difficult task of showing what might be correct or incorrect about the means principle, or how it could be reformulated to provide a plausible barrier to morally problematic social practices.[58] My goal is more modest. I conclude only that this deontological constraint should not simply be trotted out as though it constitutes a fatal objection to given measures such as SQF.

If we concede that rights are implicated on both sides of the equation and that the means principle may not be an insuperable obstacle to SQF, we should be more prepared to make trade-offs in assessing it. A small sampling of the difficult questions to be confronted would include the following: Should we really renounce an entire practice and allow the suspect in Kelly's example to proceed without being made to answer questions because we have no way to prevent racially discrimination enforcement in *other* cases? Can the state at least reduce the racially disparate impact of SQF to less worrisome levels? How important *is* it to eliminate the effects of racial bias in policing altogether? Will the very communities in which these effects occur suffer more than they will gain? What negatives *other* than the possible failure to prevent crime are caused by SQF?[59] Are serious psychological maladies, for example, produced in persons in "high crime" communities as a result of their frequent interactions with police? How will these psychological consequences affect the quality of democratic institutions?[60] To what extent will minorities lack confidence and be reluctant to cooperate with law enforcement if relations are not improved? If their lack of cooperation is nontrivial, will police succeed in further curtailing rates of victimization in minority communities? And how can we possibly hope to *quantify* the foregoing variables? We lack a metric to express these diverse factors by a common denominator—which would be necessary to perform a proper weighing. They seem *incommensurable*. If I am correct, no one should fault a legal theorist such as Richardson for failing to provide the missing balancing.

But she should at least recognize that these questions are *crucial* and *must* be addressed if her conclusion (8) against SQF is to follow from her premises. She needs to refute (7) for her argument to be sound. My conjecture is that Richardson does not appreciate the need to refute (7) because no one has pressed her on this matter, and no one has pressed her on this matter because of the lack of "viewpoint diversity" Garland described in the second paragraph of this chapter.

Where, then, are we left? I see no persuasive reason provided either by legal theorists or moral philosophers to deny that the fate of SQF should be decided by weighing its advantages against its disadvantages. Neither of the two deontological constraints I have discussed provides a clear basis for drawing a contrary conclusion. Unfortunately, as I have admitted, I have no recommendation about how to perform the necessary balancing. I am prepared to concede that the weight of the factors used in this calculation should be tilted or skewed because of the racially discriminatory impact of SQF. In principle, however, this enormous negative can be outweighed by whatever crime-reduction effects SQF may succeed in achieving. The final verdict on SQF, then, depends as much on criminological data as on the musings of moral philosophers or the protests of commentators who are committed to the eradication of racial injustice. But what should be done in the meantime, when these various factors are not quantified and commentators lack a consensus? Perhaps the best solution is to allow the outcome of this and most other policing practices to be rendered through democratic procedures after all. In case the opponents of SQF find this judgment too unpalatable, it is important remind them that it does not give a green light to the unfettered use of SQF. As we have seen, the incidence of this practice was drastically curtailed in New York City, largely as a result of an effective political campaign mounted against it. Other jurisdictions, however, may decide to be more permissive. In any event, commentators move too quickly if they would abolish a police practice such as SQF altogether by citing its disproportionate impact on minorities.

Notes

1. For example, see Bell, M. C. 2017. Police Reform and the Dismantling of Legal Estrangement. *Yale Law Journal* 126: 2054–2150.
2. Garland, D. 2017. Theoretical Advances and Problems in the Sociology of Punishment. *Punishment & Society* 20: 8–33.

3. Garland, D. 2017.
4. 392 U.S. 1 (1968).
5. Critics and supporters alike frequently omit the "question" part of the "stop, question and frisk" formula. This omission is curious, as it leaves out a power that is just as important as those it includes.
6. 959 F. Supp. 2d 540 (2013).
7. See Taibbi, M. 2017. *I Can't Breathe: Killing on Bay Street*. New York: Spiegel & Grau, 143.
8. New York Civil Liberties Union: Stop and Frisk Data. 2017. https://www.nyclu.org/en/stop-and-frisk-data.
9. New York Civil Liberties Union: Stop and Frisk Data. 2017.
10. Kelly, R. 2015. *Vigilance*. New York: Hachette Books, 274.
11. Zimring, F. E. 2012. *The City That Became Safe: New York's Lessons for Urban Crime and Its Control*. Oxford: Oxford University Press.
12. Friedman, Matthew. 2015. The Role of Race in Police Interdictions: Evidence from the New York's Police Department's Use of *Stop, Question, and Frisk* Policing. http://poseidon01.ssrn.com/delivery.php?ID=201095112122097000018010112080095086040043066035030023010101080110083021091107085089018000021043022098116011006106122121122001047027049064068072112112027073127015029069028007126088024083008122125006064107003099125099016126016003116028100027123005098127&EXT=pdf.
13. Buettner, Russ. 2012. Judge Bars Testimony by Expert in Frisk Suit. *The New York Times*, August 17, A16.
14. Bloomberg, Michael. 2012. Stop-and-Frisk Works as 'Deterrent. WNYC NEWS, May 10. http://www.wnyc.org/story/208256-blog-bloomberg-stop-and-frisks-work-deterrent/.
15. See Husak, Douglas. 2017. Drug Proscriptions as Proxy Crimes. *Law and Philosophy* 36: 345–366.
16. Kelly, R. 2015, 294.
17. See Koper, Christopher S., and Evan Mayo-Wilson. 2006. Police Crackdown on Illegal Gun Carrying: A Systematic Review of Their Impact on Gun Crime. *Journal of Experimental Criminology* 2: 227–261.
18. Travis, Jeremy, et al. 2015. Tracking Enforcement Rates in New York City, 2003–2014. http://www.jjay.cuny.edu/sites/default/files/News/Enforcement_Rate_Report.pdf.
19. See Southall, Ashley. 2017. Killings in New York Fall to a Record Low as Crime Rates Dive Overall. *The New York Times*, December 27.
20. See Williams, Timothy. 2017. Violent Crime in U.S. Rises for Second Consecutive Year. *The New York Times*, December 28.

21. See Friedman, Barry, and Maria Ponomarenko. 2015. Democratic Policing. *New York University Law Review* 90: 1827–1907.
22. Richardson, L. Song. 2017. Implicit Racial Bias and Racial Anxiety: Implications for Stops and Frisks. *Ohio State Journal of Criminal Law* 15: 73–88.
23. Correll, Joshua, et al. 2007. Across the Thin Blue Line: Police Officers and Racial Bias in the Decision to Shoot. *Journal of Personality and Social Psychology* 92: 1006–1023.
24. Richardson, L. Song. 2017, 88.
25. Richardson, L. Song. 2017, 87.
26. 392 U.S. 1 (1968), 14n11.
27. Richardson, L. Song. 2017, 88.
28. See Forscher, Patrick S, et al. 2017. A Meta-analysis of Change in Implicit Bias. psyarxiv.com/dv8tupsyarxiv.com/dv8tu. 2017; Singal, Jessie. 2017. Psychology's Favorite Tool for Measuring Racism Isn't Up to the Job; *The Cut*, January 11, 2017. https://www.thecut.com/2017/01/psychologys-racism-measuring-tool-isnt-up-to-the-job.html.
29. For another example of what I believe begins as a sensible criticism but quickly goes too far, see Vitale, Alex. 2017. *The End of Policing*. New York: Verso Books.
30. Kelly, R. 2015, 272.
31. Jacobs, James B. 2015. *The Eternal Criminal Record*. Cambridge: Harvard University Press.
32. On this ground, some consequentialists *reject* the presumption of innocence as traditionally construed. For example, see Laudan, Larry. 2016. *The Law's Flaws: Rethinking Trial and Errors?* College Publications.
33. For some nice discussions of whether the contrast between impact and intent is morally relevant, see the contributions in *Foundations of Indirect Discrimination Law*, ed. Hugh Collins and Tarunabh Khaitan. 2018. Oxford: Hart Pub. Co.
34. See Friedman and Ponomarenko. 2015.
35. See Peterson, Ruth D., and Lauren J. Krivo. 2010. *Divergent Social Worlds: Neighborhood Crime and the Racial-Spatial Divide*. New York: Russell Sage Foundation.
36. Bureau of Justice Statistics. 2018. http://www.bjs.gov/index.cfm?ty=tp&tid=922.
37. See Sharkey, Patrick. 2018a. Two Lessons of the Urban Crime Decline. *New York Times*, January 13. See also his 2018b. *Uneasy Peace: The Great Crime Decline, The Renewal of City Life, and the Next War on Violence*. New York: W. W. Norton.
38. For an apparent disagreement, see Dworkin, Ronald. 1977. *Taking Rights Seriously*. Cambridge: Harvard University Press, esp. 12–13.

39. For caution about whether the recent and widely publicized instances of police misconduct are best explained by racism, see Sekhon, Nirei. 2017. Blue on Black: An Empirical Assessment of Police Shootings. http://papers.ssrn.com/sol3/papers.cfm?abstract_id=2700724.
40. See, for example, the diverse perspectives presented in the special issue on *the means principle* in 2016 *Criminal Law and Philosophy*, 10.
41. I have waded into this morass myself. See Husak, Douglas. 2013. Preventive Detention as Punishment? Some Possible Reservations. In *Prevention and the Limits of the Criminal Law Andrew*, ed. Zedner, Lucia and Patrick Tomlin, 178. Oxford: Oxford University Press and 2011. Lifting the Cloak: Preventive Detention as Punishment. *San Diego Law Review* 48: 1173–1196.
42. Many of the thoughts in this part of my paper are drawn from Husak, Douglas. *The Vast Scope of Preventive Harming* (forthcoming).
43. See Hoskins, Zachary. 2018 (forthcoming). *Beyond Punishment.*
44. See Logan, Wayne A. 2013. *Review* 88: 1103–1118.
45. Jacobs, James. 2015, 30.
46. See some of the discussion cited in Chin, Gabriel L. 2018 (forthcoming). Collateral Consequences of Criminal Conviction. In *Academy for Justice, A Report on Scholarship and Criminal Justice Reform,* ed. Eric Luna.
47. Jacobs, James. 2015, 227.
48. Jacobs, James. 2015, 277.
49. Jacobs, James. 2015, 291.
50. See Temkin, Larry. 2016. Equality as Comparative Fairness. *Journal of Applied Philosophy* 34: 43–60.
51. Jacobs, James. 2015, 291.
52. Jacobs, James. 2015, 298.
53. Monahan, John. 2018 (forthcoming). Risk Assessment in Sentencing. In *Academy for Justice, A Report on Scholarship and Criminal Justice Reform*, ed. Eric Luna.
54. Turner, Susan, James Hess, and Jesse Jannetta. 2009. *Development of the California Static Risk Assessment Instrument (CSRA).* UCI Center for Evidence-Based Corrections. http://ucicorrections.seweb.uci.edu/files/2009/11/CSRA-Working-Paper.pdf.
55. Jacobs, James. 2015, 282.
56. Some theorists despair that the data could *ever* be good enough. See Cooke, David J., and Christine Michie. 2010. Limitations of Diagnostic Precision and Predictive Utility in the Individual Case: A Challenge for Forensic Practice. *Law and Human Behavior* 34: 259–274.
57. I do not mean to imply that the discriminatory practices conducted by employers correspond to those supported by the best empirical evidence about the risks of future harms. See Denver, Megan, Garima Siwach,

and Shawn D. Bushway. 2017. A New Look at the Employment and Recidivism Relationship through the Lens of a criminal Background Check. *Criminology* 55: 174–204.

58. My sympathies tend to lie with Guerrero, Alex. 2016. Appropriately Using People Merely as a Means. *Criminal Law and Philosophy* 10: 777–794.
59. See Lerman, Amy E., and Vesla M. Weaver. 2014. *Arresting Citizenship: The Democratic Consequences of American Crime Control.* Chicago: University of Chicago Press.
60. See Atiba Goff, Phillip. 2018. On Stop and Fisk, We Can't Celebrate Just Yet. *New York Times*, January 7.

The Case Against Jails

Richard L. Lippke

In recent years, the jail population in the United States has hovered around three-quarters of a million people.[1] This constitutes about one-third of all persons held in custody, with state and federal prisons holding the rest. The distinction between jails and prisons is significant, although one suspects it is unappreciated by many casual observers of the US criminal justice system. Prisons are operated, or at least overseen, by the state and federal governments. They contain only persons who have been convicted and sentenced for their crimes. Jails, by contrast, are owned and operated by municipalities or counties, with the funds supporting them coming from the local jurisdictions in which they exist. Importantly, these municipal and county jails contain many persons who have not been convicted or sentenced. On most estimates, more than 60% of jail inhabitants are pre-trial detainees, individuals who have either been denied bail or who simply cannot afford to pay it.[2] Somewhat surprisingly, there is little effort by local and regional governments to distinguish the living conditions of pre-trial detainees, who are "presumed innocent," and their convicted counterparts. Also, most jail inmates who

R. L. Lippke (✉)
Department of Criminal Justice, Indiana University, Bloomington, IN, USA
e-mail: rllippke@indiana.edu

M. Gardner and M. Weber (eds.), *The Ethics of Policing and Imprisonment*, Palgrave Studies in Ethics and Public Policy,
https://doi.org/10.1007/978-3-319-97770-6_7

have been convicted have committed misdemeanors or low-level felonies and so are facing less than a year's confinement.[3]

The academic literature on jails is sparse, at least compared with the academic literature on prisons, which is substantial.[4] The literature on jails that does exist uniformly paints a depressing picture of them: Jails are invariably described as squalid facilities that are poorly monitored for violence against or exploitation of inmates by other inmates, lacking in the means to maintain adequate hygiene, and offering poor diets, little privacy, and almost no programming of any kind.[5] The denizens of jails are mostly poor, disproportionately black or Hispanic, under-educated, have been sporadically employed, and sometimes have been homeless. They also suffer high rates of mental illness or drug and alcohol abuse.[6] In short, our jails are refuges, of sorts, for socially marginal individuals who have run afoul of the law, though usually not in terribly serious ways.

In the academic literature on imprisonment, there has been, for some time, an abolitionist fringe, though it is perhaps more than a fringe in parts of Europe.[7] Much of that literature laments the organization and aims of many contemporary prisons, urges less use of them, and urges significantly shorter sentences in them. None of this requires the abolition of prisons, of course, and I concur with prison abolitionists on all of this. The abolitionist case is weakest, arguably, when we contemplate violent recidivists, and indeed many abolitionists seem to reluctantly admit that a few offenders might have to remain confined.

What I want to explore, in this essay, is the case for abolishing jails. I believe that the case for abolishing jails is stronger than the case for abolishing prisons. Jails contain many persons who have not yet been convicted. The grounds for confining them appear to be deeply suspect. Also, those jail inhabitants who have been convicted have likely not been shown to be very dangerous individuals; they have mostly engaged in minor forms of offending or else they would have been sent to prisons. Jail confinement is not only expensive, but it also systematically erodes the prospects of individuals for achieving more normal, productive lives. We should concentrate on helping the under-educated, mentally ill, addicted, homeless, and unemployed, rather than on harming them further. Also, in the academic literature on prisons, it is widely accepted that persons about to be released from prison need help in finding their way in civil society, or else they are apt to quickly recidivate.[8] Yet by the nature of the crimes of which they have been convicted or charged, many of the inhabitants of jails are on the cusp of re-entry. Facilitating their successful re-entry should, it seems, be our overriding aim.

The discussion that follows is divided into three parts. In the first, I take up the topic of pre-trial detention and the enormous number of jail inhabitants held in it. The case for substantially reducing the use of pre-trial detention is strong. The risks of releasing many persons charged with crimes are often exaggerated, especially given the availability of other, less drastic means of keeping track of them. The practice of requiring money bail is deeply problematic and has well-known negative consequences. Finally, even if some persons charged with crimes must be detained, there seems little justification for keeping them in "punishment-like" conditions.

In the second part, my focus is on jail inmates who have actually been convicted. Though censure and hard treatment are arguably essential features of legal punishment, the fact is that those convicted of misdemeanors or low-level felonies have not been shown to be guilty of crimes that merit much censure and hard treatment. In fact, some of them will have been convicted of offenses about which scholars have raised substantial doubts. More than a few of them will have been arrested and convicted because their poverty made them easy targets of police and prosecutorial monitoring and law enforcement. Further, although some of those who will be sent to jail are guilty of offenses that should be punished and might be punished in unbiased fashion, jail confinement worsens their lives in predictable ways, making many of them more susceptible to further offending. I argue that we should instead provide such offenders with welfare services of various kinds, to coax them back toward productive, law-abiding lives. Punishing them, albeit briefly, might make us feel good, but it hardly constitutes an intelligent response to the problems raised by their offending.

In the third section, I address the strength of the case that I have made for abolishing jails. The chief difficulty is that many of the persons convicted of relatively minor crimes and confined in jails live such disorganized and hapless lives that they will not take advantage of the services that we might offer them in lieu of hard treatment. Some of them will refuse to appear or participate meaningfully in education or job training programs, drug or alcohol abuse treatment, or programs designed to help them cope with their mental illness. What then? Worse than this, some will reoffend and their doing so will be directly traceable to their refusals to take advantage of the help we have proffered.

Why should such individuals not then be confined in jails because they deserve it or because we need to make clear to them and others who might be tempted to behave like them that we mean business? I concede that there will be some individuals who will refuse our best efforts to help them. For one thing, even more enlightened approaches to punishment cannot fix forms of dysfunctionality in persons engendered by poverty, social exclusion, and (at times) their own biological or psychological make-ups. We might have to confine some minor offenders. But there is scant justification for confining them in the types of facilities of which our jails consist, even if our exasperation with them might tempt us to do so.

Jail and Pre-trial Detention

As I have already indicated, more than 60% of those held in jail at any given time are individuals who have been charged with crimes though not yet convicted of them. Such individuals are held in what certainly appear to be punishment facilities though they have not been shown, by the authorities, to be eligible for or deserving of legal punishment. Some of them are deemed by state authorities to be too dangerous to be released back into civil society, even with measures designed to keep track of them. Others are thought to be likely to abscond and thus not reappear to face the charges against them. Some are confined because they are too poor to post bail. Importantly, the inability to post bail might show little about the risks persons pose to others in the community. Bail is required of persons charged with crimes in order to satisfy a different aim of the criminal justice system—namely, to provide some assurance that the accused will appear for further legal proceedings concerning their cases. Those who post bail and abscond stand to lose the money or property they put down as collateral.

Numerous legal scholars who have examined pre-trial detention (or perhaps better, "pre-adjudication detention," since the vast majority of charges are resolved through plea bargaining) have urged drastic reductions in its use, if not its complete elimination.[9] Some contend that such detention is inconsistent with accused persons enjoying a presumption of innocence. Others argue that the state is not very good at predicting which of the persons it deems to be dangerous really do pose risks to the community.[10] Also, pre-trial detention puts pressure on persons accused of minor offenses to plead guilty so that they can get out of jail, even if some of those who enter guilty pleas are innocent or not provably guilty.[11]

Oddly, less attention is paid by critics of pre-trial detention to what is, to my way of thinking, its most confounding feature—namely, that pre-trial detainees are treated, for all intents and purposes, just like persons who have been convicted. In order to address that feature of pre-trial detention, it will not do to dramatically curtail our use of it. Instead, we will have to modify pre-trail detention facilities so that they are not like punishment facilities. We could take steps toward doing this by significantly improving the material conditions of pre-trial detention and easing some of the jail-like restrictions that are imposed on pre-trial detainees.[12] For instance, we could confine pre-trail detainees in facilities that are more like decent hotels, with private, comfortable rooms. We could also permit their spouses and other family members to have ready and easy access to them. Further, we could compensate pre-trial detainees for their lost liberty, since they will probably be unable to work and provide for their families. We are unlikely to do any of these things, of course, but that does not come anywhere close to showing that we should not do them. If we are to clearly and decisively distinguish the not-proven-guilty (or as some would say, the "presumed innocent") from the convicted, then these are among the things that we surely should do.[13] And if we did them, then our jails would have many fewer inhabitants.

Such a partial emptying of the jails might seem to involve some sleight of hand. Sure, three-fifths of current jail inmates would no longer be held in them. But they would be held in different kinds of confinement facilities, albeit ones with considerably improved amenities. It is worth noting that those improved amenities would likely have potent symbolic meaning. Pre-trial detainees would surely notice the differences between their treatment and the treatment of those still confined to local or regional jails. So would the public, which would have to foot the bill. Yet we should not rest content with better pre-trial detention facilities. There are persuasive arguments that we overuse pre-trial detention and against the employment of bail to determine who is kept in it and who is not.

Start with the practice of requiring bail of persons charged with crimes when the courts deem them to be unworthy of being released on their own recognizance. Surprisingly, some critics of pre-trial detention generally do not regard the payment of bail as a precondition of pre-trial release to be problematic. Antony Duff, for one, contends that having to pay bail is defensible, as it can be seen as a way for accused persons to offer the community assurance that they will appear to answer to the charges against them.[14] I set to one side the seeming tension in Duff's claims that accused persons owe the community such assurance and that they are to be presumed innocent. The more important point, for my purposes, is that many persons accused of crimes are indigent and cannot afford to pay even modest amounts of bail; neither can they find others (e.g., family members) who are able or willing to pay it for them. Hence, such persons will be remanded to custody because of their poverty, not because they have refused to provide the community assurance that they will appear to face the charges against them.

Again, bail requirements have little to do with protecting the public from the risk of further pre-trial crime by accused persons. Yet we should scrutinize the practice of depriving persons of their liberty pre-trial simply because they cannot put down money or property to, it seems, shore up their resolve to appear for later court proceedings. First, many of the charges for which the indigent might wind up held on remand are simply not serious enough to warrant so intrusive an interference with their basic rights. Eighty per cent of the cases processed by the criminal justice system in the United States involve misdemeanors.[15] Admittedly, some of these cases will involve alleged criminal misconduct that is serious enough that we should attempt to make sure that accused persons appear to answer for it. But most cases will not involve such misconduct, and confinement as a means to ensure their appearance at subsequent court hearings seems excessive. This might even be true in some cases in which individuals are charged with low-level felonies. Second, absconding is a crime for which persons can be re-arrested and charged. Granted, it is inefficient and costly to have to capture absconders, but it is not clear why the costs of doing so should not be borne by societies that, like our own, place a high value on individual liberty. It might be easier and less costly to confine those who cannot afford bail pre-trial, although that proposition is less than obviously true, given the costs of jail confinement. Yet efficiency and lower costs are not usually thought of as values that outweigh the disvalue of significant liberty-deprivation. Third, making bail is obviously no guarantee that accused persons will appear for further court proceedings. Some people do skip bail; that much is clear.[16] Does paying it make persons less likely to abscond? It is very hard to tell, since we have no way of comparing the percentage who pay it and fail to appear with the percentage who cannot pay it and fail to appear, for the latter are never given the chance to "not appear." It is assumed that the percentage of the second group would be significantly higher than the percentage of the former group, but I doubt that we have any hard evidence for that assumption. Fourth, there exist other ways, besides remanding them, to encourage accused persons who are indigent to appear for subsequent court hearings. They could be released but required to report their whereabouts on a regular basis, or required to wear electronic monitoring devices. These alternatives are used in some jurisdictions, albeit more often to keep track of accused persons who are deemed dangerous. But they could and should be used in place of pre-trial confinement of accused persons who are too poor to pay bail. They could also be used on accused persons who we have reason to believe might fail to appear because they have histories of absconding.

Pre-trail confinement is also used to reduce risks to the community, primarily in the form of further pre-trial crime by accused persons. Most everyone who examines this practice criticizes the casual ways in which such risks are assessed by the courts.[17] I am not convinced by arguments that we should never use pre-trial detention for this purpose. However, I do believe that our criteria for employing it for this purpose need to be articulated and applied much more carefully and rigorously than they currently are. Elsewhere, I have argued that pre-trial detention should be restricted to those individuals charged with crimes for which (a) confinement is a likely sentencing outcome if they are subsequently found guilty; (b) the evidence for the charges in question is found by a judge to be convincing to the "preponderance of evidence" standard; (c) there is reason to believe, independently of the current charges against accused persons, that they are likely to commit other, significant pre-trial crimes; and (d) no other means exist to reduce those risks (e.g., home confinement) short of pre-trial detention.[18]

Let me briefly elaborate these conditions. The first condition captures the intuition that it is odd, if not paradoxical, to confine persons pre-trial if the charges against them are unlikely, in the event of conviction, to result in their being assigned custodial sentences. If persons' alleged crimes are so minor as to not merit custodial sentences, then it is hard to see how society's stake in convicting them warrants the kind and degree of imposition of which pre-trial detention consists. Granted, there might be some cases in which the authorities believe that persons accused of minor offenses pose some threat to others in the community. Yet if their detention is not to be for what some scholars refer to disparagingly as "mere dangerousness," the authorities ought to be required to demonstrate to a judge that such persons' dangerous proclivities have recently manifested in one or more crimes.[19] The question then is to what standard of proof the authorities should be held in their requests for the remand of such individuals. The usual "probable cause" standard with respect to the extant charges seems too weak, especially if we are concerned to rule out such things as "usual suspects" policing, racial bias, and outright error.[20] Having to satisfy a more stringent standard, in the form of showing that the accused are more likely than not guilty of the current charges against them, would help to reduce the likelihood of error and prejudice. Also, even if persons face serious charges and the evidence against them is fairly convincing, it does not follow, of necessity, that they are a danger to others. Some serious crimes occur due to domestic disputes that are basically one-off events. The participants in them might constitute little threat to others and it is at least debatable whether, as a result, they should be confined pre-trial. Finally, as we have already seen, other options besides pre-trial detention exist and I would require the state to show that none of them is suitable for containing the demonstrated risks that some accused persons pose to others in the community.

So, where does all of this leave us? I have not argued that all pre-trial detention should be abolished. In particular, I agree that there are some persons who have been accused of crimes who we have good reason to believe constitute substantial risks to others and so might be justifiably confined until the charges against them have been adjudicated. But there are apt to be many fewer of them than we currently detain based on not-very-demanding risk assessments. Those who are appropriately subject to pre-trial detention should not be confined in jails as we know them, but instead in facilities that are significantly different from them. I am less convinced that people charged with crimes should be confined simply because they are too poor to pay bail. But if a few of them are justifiably so confined, because society has a significant enough interest in seeing to it that they answer to the charges against them, then they too should be kept in facilities that are not jails or like them.

Jails and the Convicted

Urging the substantial reduction of jail populations through the curtailment of pre-trial detention is the easy case to make. Figuring out what to do with the roughly 40 per cent of jail inmates who are convicted and serving sentences is more of a challenge. The crucial premises in the argument that we ought to radically transform our jails, if not eliminate them more or less entirely, are these: First, jail inmates who are serving sentences are hardly the kinds of serious offenders that there are many more of in our prisons. Most jail inmates who are serving sentences have been convicted of one or more misdemeanors, or perhaps one or more low-level felonies. Society is unlikely to need the kind of protection from them that it needs from armed robbers, rapists, and murderers. In fact, as we have seen, jail inmates are disproportionately poor, undereducated, homeless, and struggling with mental illness or drug and alcohol addiction—individuals who are operating at the margins of society and not very effectively.[21] They are not so much dangerous as dysfunctional. Second, they will be released from their jail confinement in relatively short order—within a year and, in many cases, within months if not weeks. Perhaps many of them were not terribly responsible citizens to begin with. But their time in jail will not have helped them become more so and will probably make them less so. What they need is help, not confinement under harsh, debilitating, and degrading conditions. The absence of help, much like the absence of prisoner re-entry programs, will almost guarantee that they will recidivate and return to jail, or in some cases, prison. Yet this cycle is one that on both humanitarian and cost-effectiveness grounds it makes sense to try to break. Jails perpetuate it.

How and why do they do so? In ways that are familiar to those who study prisons, but with a few twists. Some of the persons who are convicted and sent to jails actually had jobs before being arrested and charged with crimes, with the responsibility and normality that accompanies gainful employment. Most will lose their jobs either because they cannot pay bail and are kept in pre-trial detention or because they are ultimately convicted and jailed. Their lost jobs will diminish the quality of their lives and the lives of others who depend on them. More to the point, any criminal conviction, even for a misdemeanor, will erode their future job prospects by making employers leery of hiring them.[22] This combined with the paucity of education of the average jail inmate will make it hard for many of them to earn honest, decent livings. We know that those who have served time in prison are consigned, in the words of Bruce Western, to "secondary labor markets and informal economies."[23] Those who have served time in jails are not apt to fare much better. Also, time in jail will strain and attenuate inmates' relationships with family members, with attendant increases in the risks for recidivism. We know that offenders who can maintain ties with supportive families do better at avoiding further entanglement with the law.[24] Yet jails are usually less inviting places for family members to visit than prisons, which are hardly known for their friendliness toward visitors.[25] Lack of visitation and contact will weaken crucial pro-social ties of jail inmates.

Further, jails are not known for their provision of health care, drug and alcohol abuse treatment, or education and job training programs.[26] These are considered luxuries by cash-strapped municipal and regional governments. In short, jails are short-term confinement facilities and little more. But this means that mental health problems are likely to fester in jails. Inmates who are addicted to drugs or alcohol might have to go "cold turkey," but they will probably not learn from this experience how to more constructively cope with their addictions. Inmates without high school degrees or job skills will not be helped to gain them.

To the preceding must be added the further acculturation of jail inmates to deviant lives.[27] We must be careful to not exaggerate this point. Many of the persons convicted and sent to jails will not have been living responsible, respectable lives prior to their entanglement with the law. They will not have been legally employed, though many will have earned income in illicit ways by being hustlers, petty thieves, or involved in the drug or sex trades. More than a few will have been scrounging out livings by some combination of begging, collecting recyclables, going through dumpsters, and the like. A criminal record will not hurt the "employment" prospects of such individuals much. Indeed, time spent in jail might enhance the abilities of some offenders to earn income illicitly by introducing them to others like them among their fellow inmates. But what time spent in jail will do is ensure that inmates are around other people who, like many of them, are hardly models of responsible citizenship. Those who have observed jails report that inmates often develop a sense of camaraderie in the face of the many sleights and humiliations visited upon them by the police, courts, and jail officials. They might be scum in the eyes of the officials who have to deal with them, and in the eyes of the public who would rather not think about them, but while in jail, they are among their kind. Yet all of this seems likely to strengthen jail inmates' internalization of norms that are personally and socially destructive. As John Irwin puts it succinctly, the jail "supports and maintains the rabble class."[28]

The solution, it would seem, is to look for ways to deal more constructively with the mostly minor offenders who populate our jails. Those who study the so-called intermediate sanctions—forms of legal punishment in-between probation and imprisonment—strongly urge their use for some offenders who might otherwise be given custodial sentences.[29] If we want to reduce our use of confinement—both because it is costly and destructive—then we need to develop forms of noncustodial sanctions that address the criminogenic needs of offenders. Most jail inmates have many such needs, as we have seen. As such, they would seem to be ideal candidates for drug, mental health, or veterans courts, all of which emphasize some combination of treatment and responsibility-enforcement, along with the promotion of life skills. These diversionary courts are set up to encourage, and, if necessary, pressure offenders to take steps to become more responsible, law-abiding citizens.[30] Most operate pre-conviction; successful completion of the court-imposed requirements results in charges being dropped. Some operate post-conviction, in which case completion of the court-imposed requirements results in reduced sentences or probation for offenders. Further, some offenders who might otherwise be sent to jail might be candidates for intensive forms of probation, which closely monitor their conduct while they remain free in the community.

Importantly, offenders who would otherwise be sent to jail might be viewed as more viable and deserving candidates for intermediate sanctions than offenders who would otherwise be sent to prisons, simply because the crimes of the former are usually less serious. Moreover, those offenders whose crimes are less serious will, more or less inevitably, be returning to society sooner than those whose crimes are more so. It therefore seems sensible to give priority to addressing the educational and mental health deficits of minor offenders, along with their dysfunctional behaviors and ways of thinking. Such offenders might also be given more help in finding gainful employment so that they will not resort to offending to eke out livings. Yet they need not be confined in order to be given these kinds of help.

Also, some minor offenders who might otherwise be given jail sentences could be diverted to restorative justice programs.[31] Such programs aim at bringing offenders together with those they have victimized, in the presence of a mediator and support members for both offenders and victims, in an effort to reach an agreement on how victims might be acknowledged and made whole again by those who committed crimes against them. Often, restorative justice conferences result in apologies by offenders, promises to refrain from future harmful acts toward victims, and the payment of restitution to victims. Minor property offenders, as well as perpetrators of simple assaults, could be suitable candidates for diversion to restorative justice conferences. Drunk driving, drug, and public disorder offenders are less suitable candidates, mainly because their crimes do not have direct victims whose interests have been harmed.[32] At least with certain kinds of minor offenders, restorative justice approaches reduce recidivism as much if not more than jail sentences. It is also apparent that such approaches are cheaper and less corrosive to offenders than time spent in jail.[33]

Objections and Replies

It might be objected that seeking in various ways to aid the mostly minor offenders who populate our jails, rather than confining them, tacitly condones their behavior instead of punishing it. How can the use of intermediate sanctions, however they are devised and structured, amount to censure and hard treatment, the two distinguishing features of legal punishment?[34] Similar questions might be asked about restorative justice conferences and their outcomes. In response, a number of points might be made. First, minor offenders are just that—minor offenders. We do not need to resort to onerous or destructive criminal sanctions to punish them. Those who are convicted and sentenced, as opposed to being diverted to restorative justice programs, will, at the very least, suffer the ignominy of having criminal records.[35] Second, intermediate sanctions are not all sweetness and light; they require offenders to show up and participate in programs that they might otherwise avoid. The same is true for restorative justice programs, which typically require offenders to engage in acts of contrition and pay restitution to their victims. Third, the "dosage" of intermediate sanctions can be adjusted to give them some "punitive bite." As those who study intermediate sanctions have shown, there is evidence that offenders perceive sentences of intermediate sanctions as equivalent to short custodial sentences when the former are made sufficiently lengthy and burdensome.[36]

A more telling objection to the use of alternatives to jail confinement for minor offenders is this: Intermediate sanctions require offenders to show up sober, submit to drug tests, and participate in meaningful ways in educational programs or cognitive-behavioral therapy. Yet many offenders are not used to meeting such requirements and will refuse or fail to do so. The more or less inevitable result will be technical violations that render them ineligible for continued participation in such programs.[37] Custody then seems the only recourse and a likely one given the deeply dysfunctional habits and ways of thinking of many minor offenders. Similarly, some minor offenders who are diverted to restorative justice programs will not live up to the terms of the agreements that such programs encourage them to enter into with their victims. It might be suggested that those who fail could be rearrested and required, once again, to meet with their victims and confirm their earlier commitments to apologize or pay restitution. But at some point, continued failures to live up to those commitments will force us to respond with back-up sanctions of more formal kinds.

It is tempting to resist these disheartening predictions about the willingness of many minor offenders to take advantage of the opportunities that might be offered by noncustodial dispositions of their cases. However, I suspect that it would be naïve to do so. Some minor offenders appear to have little interest in "normal" lives, by which I mean lives of responsibility, productive labor, and sobriety. But what follows? Not that jails, as we know them, are our only recourse. For we could provide forms of custody—I will not call them "jails"—that offer many of the same forms of therapy, drug and alcohol treatment, mental health care, and educational and job training that intermediate sanctions incorporate. Those held in custody could then be required to participate in such programs, depending on their needs. More than this, we could make such facilities more "open" than our jails currently are, so that the inhabitants would have greater access to family members and the broader community. Visitation could be made easier and inmates could be provided private rooms for conjugal visitation or to have time alone with family members out of the scrutiny of others. We could even experiment with the kinds of fully "open" facilities that are common in Scandinavian countries, at least for minor offenders who demonstrate their willingness and ability to come and go from such facilities as instructed.[38] Of course, some offenders would not be reliable in this way and would have to be held in closed facilities that nonetheless provided rich programming options and relaxed visitation. But we should strive to make and keep such facilities normalcy-reinforcing ones, by which I mean facilities that encourage work, sobriety, and responsibility.

Still, there will probably be some minor offenders who will be unwilling to participate in any meaningful way in programs designed to "straighten them out." Some are too firmly committed to or sunk into what Irwin terms the "rabble life." And there seems no denying Irwin's contention that such people annoy us and excite our punitive instincts.[39] Will not jails of the kinds we currently have be our only recourse with them? Jails might seem needed to deter the recalcitrant or to punish those individuals to whom we have offered help, only to have them refuse it and continue with their offending.

I doubt that the preceding, deterrence-based argument has much merit, especially in relation to individuals of the kinds we are contemplating who seem determined to carry on with deviant lifestyles. The evidence that longer sentences enhance marginal deterrence is, to put it mildly, unimpressive.[40] Perhaps harsher forms of punishment deter better than longer sentences, but I doubt it given that sanctions like the death sentence, LWOP sentences, and supermax confinement—all of which are exceedingly harsh—seem to do little to discourage offending. We might do better to soldier on with intractable minor offenders, offering even the most difficult among them help rather than harsh treatment. We will never know when the rigors of the "rabble life" will become too much for some of them, such that they might finally be willing to take steps to turn away from it.[41]

There is also a larger background story that I have so far ignored that is relevant to our thinking about dissolute minor offenders and what they deserve. It begins with what some term "poor policing," the tendency of the authorities to focus on the erratic or disorderly behavior of the homeless, mentally ill, drunken, and addicted—especially when the "offenders" are black or Hispanic—and to subject it to more scrutiny and, arguably, more policing than it needs, in part because such behavior occurs in public places.[42] In more progressive societies than our own, if the police have to deal with the conduct of the disturbed, drunk, or addicted, instead of arresting them and charging them with crimes, they might simply take them to mental health facilities or centers for the treatment of drug and alcohol abuse. Perhaps because our welfare state is so stingy, repeatedly arresting poor minor offenders seems our only option. Add to this the role of the war on drugs—a dubious war if there ever was one—in filling up our jails with persons who are mostly harming only themselves, or when they harm others, usually do so with those others' willing participation. This is not the place to put forward alternatives to our continued harsh punishment of persons who break laws that are based on what appear to be forms of strong legal paternalism and legal moralism.[43] Yet societal complicity in producing the "rabble" by over-criminalizing their conduct should not be ignored. Neither should society's role in declining to provide decent housing, education, and healthcare for the poor, or in leaving them vulnerable to the vicissitudes of the labor market. Perhaps the poor will always be with us. The United States is not alone in having a more or less permanent group of minor offenders who cycle in and out of the criminal justice system. But our social policies might play some role in determining the size of that group and its level of dissolution and desperation. Other societies seem more willing to recognize their own complicity in producing the poor and, as a result, respond to them in more helpful and hopeful ways.[44] We send our wayward poor to facilities the implicit if not explicit message of which seems to be that they are useless creatures who are entirely to blame for their own predicaments.

This background story is also relevant to a further objection to my claims that we should substitute intermediate sanctions, or normalcy-promoting confinement facilities, for our current jails. The evidence suggests that our efforts to reduce recidivism without resorting to custodial sanctions are less than robustly successful. The most rigorous evaluations of drug courts and other intermediate sanctions show that such approaches produce modest reductions in reoffending.[45] If we abolish jails and yet lots of minor offenders continue to commit crimes, then what? I am not convinced that we should try to sell more humane and less debilitating forms of criminal justice intervention solely on the basis that they will reduce offending. A stronger case for less damaging and demeaning forms of criminal sanctions is that having them is a requirement of treating offenders with dignity and decency. Also, societies that neglect and marginalize their poor, and that criminalize their efforts to eke out livings in ways that do not involve force or fraud, should not expect even the most enlightened forms of criminal sanctions to fix the problems that pervasive and systemic deprivation yield. A willingness to try to understand and help the poor denizens of our jails is better than heaping blame and harsh treatment upon them. But such understanding and help might not make much difference because they come, as it is sometimes said, "too little, too late."

Concluding Remarks

How far have we come toward establishing that our jails ought to be abolished? Quite a ways, it seems, especially if we fudge things a bit and refer not simply to "our jails," but "our jails as we know them to be." The use of pre-trial detention should be significantly scaled back. Also, there seems little justification for confining pre-trial detainees in jails insofar as these are conceived and structured as punishment facilities. Minor criminal offenders, all of whom will soon be returning to civil society, should be helped not sent to facilities that stigmatize, damage, and marginalize them further. Those who refuse the help society proffers might have to be confined for brief periods. But our complicity in their feckless and wayward lives should not be denied, and decent and helpful treatment of them ought to remain the norm even if they exasperate us. Jails utterly fail to provide such treatment and so should be abolished.

Still, jails house other individuals besides those convicted of crimes or held in pre-trial detention. These include individuals who have been re-arrested for probation or parole violations and are awaiting the dispositions of their cases. They also include individuals being held at the request of Immigration and Customs Enforcement (ICE). The complexities raised by immigration enforcement are best left for another time. With respect to the individuals held for parole or probation violations, some might reasonably be offered help while they are detained. Many will have been rearrested because they failed a drug test or resorted to further offending in the face of bleak job prospects. For the reasons discussed earlier, it behooves us to try to address the criminogenic needs of such detainees on both humanitarian and cost-savings grounds. Even if some held in jails seem unsuitable candidates for rehabilitative programming because they soon will be deported or transferred to prisons, there seems little excuse for confining them in the kinds of squalid facilities that are currently the norm.

Notes

1. Minton, Todd, and Zhen Zang. 2015. *Jail Inmates at Midyear 2014. Bureau of Justice Statistics*. Washington, DC: U. S. Department of Justice. https://www.bjs.gov/content/pub/pdf/jim14.pdf.
2. Subramanian, Ram, et al. 2015. *Incarceration's Front Door: The Misuse of Jails in America*. New York: Vera Institute of Justice, 5. It should

be noted that 2–3% of persons held in jails are being detained for U.S. Immigration and Customs Enforcement. On that, see Minton and Zang. 2015, 9.

3. Subramanian, et al., report the average length of stay in jails was 23 days in 2013. See Subramaniam, et al. 2015, 10.
4. See Irwin, John. 1986. *The Jail: Managing the Underclass in American Society*. Berkeley, CA: University of California Press. Beyond Irwin's book, there are mostly scattered articles in academic journals on the jails and reports from such organizations as the Vera Institute for Justice and the American Civil Liberties Union.
5. Subramanian, et al. 2015, 4–5.
6. Subramanian, et al. 2015, 11–12; Irwin. 1986, 18–41.
7. For a sampling of the abolitionist literature, see Mathiesen, Thomas. 2000. *Prison on Trial, 2nd Edition*. Winchester, U.K.: Waterside Press; Bianchi, H. 1994. *Justice as Sanctuary: Towards a New System of Crime Control*. Bloomington, IN: Indiana University Press; Bianchi, H., and R. van Swaanigen (eds.). 1986. *Towards a Non-Repressive Approach to Crime*. Amsterdam: Free University Press. In the United States, abolitionism has been advocated by Davis, Angela. 2003. *Are Prisons Obsolete?* New York: Seven Stories Press.
8. See, for instance, Petersilia, Joan. 2003. *When Prisoners Come Home: Parole and Prisoner Reentry*. New York: Oxford University Press.
9. See Miller, Marc, and Martin Guggenheim. 1990. Pretrial Detention and Punishment. *Minnesota Law Review* 75: 335–426; Alschuler, Albert W. 1986. Preventive Pretrial Detention and the Failure of Interest-Balancing Approaches to Due Process. *Michigan Law Review* 85: 510–69; and, Duff, R. A. 2013. Pre-Trial Detention and the Presumption of Innocence. In *Prevention and the Limits of the Criminal Law*, eds. A. Ashworth, L. Zedner, and P. Tomlin. Oxford: Oxford University Press, 115–32.
10. Miller and Guggenheim. 1990, 377–88.
11. See Bowers, Josh. 2008. Punishing the Innocent. *University of Pennsylvania Law Review* 156: 1117–79, at 1136.
12. These reforms in the conditions of pre-trial detention are discussed more fully in Chapter 7 of Lippke, Richard. 2016. *Taming the Presumption of Innocence*. New York: Oxford University Press.
13. For doubts about a pre-trial presumption of innocence, see Lippke. 2016, Chapter 6. In its place I urge a pre-trial non-presumption of guilt, along with a robust commitment to full and fair due process.
14. Duff. 2013, 126. Duff argues that the bail requirement is justified since enough evidence that a formally accused person has committed a crime has been amassed that the accused must assure us that she will appear to answer to the charges. Bail provides that assurance.

15. See Roberts, Jenny. 2011. Why Misdemeanors Matter: Defining Effective Advocacy in the Lower Criminal Courts. *University of California-Davis Law Review* 45: 277–372, at 281.
16. Estimates on bail skipping are hard to come by, but it appears that between 5 and 10% of defendants skip bail. For some discussion of this, see Romano, Jay. 1991. Defendants Increasingly Skip Bail. *New York Times*, December 22. http://www.nytimes.com/1991/12/22/nyregion/defendants-increasingly-skip-bail.html?pagewanted=all. Accessed January 22, 2016.
17. See Miller and Guggenheim. 1990, 373–88, and Alschuler. 1986, 537–48.
18. Lippke. 2016, 162–65.
19. See Tribe, Lawrence H. 1970. Preventive Justice in the World of John Mitchell. *Virginia Law Review* 56: 371–407, at 415.
20. On "usual suspects" policing, see Lempert, Richard O., Samuel R. Gross, and James S. Leibman. 2000. *A Modern Approach to Evidence, 3rd Edition*. St. Paul, MN: West, 327–28. For a sobering account of error in investigating and adjudicating crimes, see Findlay, Keith A, and Michael S. Scott. 2006. The Multiple Dimensions of Tunnel Vision in Criminal Cases. *Wisconsin Law Review* 2: 291–397.
21. See Subramanian, et al. 2015, 11–12.
22. Subramanian, et al. 2015, 16. Moreover, as the authors point out (pp. 15–16), many jails charge inmates for services of various kinds, which means that jail inmates wrack up debts that few of them are in a position to pay.
23. Western, Bruce. 2006. *Punishment and Inequality in America*. New York: Basic Books, 122.
24. See Berg, Mark T., and Beth M. Huebner. 2011. Reentry and the Ties that Bind: An Examinations of Social Ties, Employment, and Recidivism. *Justice Quarterly* 28: 382–410; Nasser, Rebecca L., and Nancy G. La Vigne. 2006. Family Support in the Prisoner Reentry Process: Expectations and Realities. *Journal of Offender Rehabilitation* 43: 93–106.
25. Irwin. 1986, 49.
26. Irwin. 1986, 71–2; Subramanian, et al. 2015, 12.
27. Irwin. 1986, 85–98.
28. Irwin. 1986, 85.
29. See Tonry, Michael, and Mary Lynch. 1996. Intermediate Sanctions. *Crime and Justice: A Review of Research* 20: 99–144, at 100–101.
30. On drug courts and their effectiveness, see Mitchell, Ojmarrh, David B. Wilson, Amy Eggers, and Doris L. Mackenzie. 2012. Assessing the Effectiveness of Drug Courts on Recidivism: A Meta-analytic Review

of Traditional and Non-traditional Drug Courts. *Journal of Criminal Justice* 40: 60–71; on mental health courts, see Redlich, Alison D., Henry J. Steadman, John Monahan, John Petrila, and Patricia A. Griffin. 2005. The Second Generation of Mental Health Courts. *Psychology, Public Policy, and Law* 11: 527–38; on veterans courts, see Hawkins, Judge Michael Daly. 2010. Coming Home: Accommodating the Special Needs of Military Veterans to the Criminal Justice System. *Ohio State Journal of Criminal Law* 7: 563–72.

31. For a useful overview of restorative justice programs and their impact on reducing recidivism, see Sherman, Lawrence W., and Heather Strang. 2007. *Restorative Justice: The Evidence*. London: The Smith Institute.
32. The evidence suggests that restorative justice approaches do not work well to reduce the recidivism of such offenders. See Sherman and Strang. 2007, 71.
33. Sherman and Strang. 2007, 86.
34. See von Hirsch, Andrew. 1993. *Censure and Sanctions.* Oxford: Clarendon Press, 9–14.
35. Nonetheless, the case for permitting minor offenders to have their criminal records expunged at some point, so that such records do not dog them indefinitely into the future, seems a strong one. For more on this, see Jacobs, James B. 2015. *The Eternal Criminal Record* Cambridge, MA: Harvard University Press.
36. See Petersilia, Joan, and Elizabeth Piper Deschenes. 1994. Perceptions of Punishment: Inmates and Staff Rank the Severity of Prison Versus Intermediate Sanctions. *The Prison Journal* 74: 306–28.
37. See Tonry and Lynch. 1996, 105.
38. For a description of Scandinavian open prisons, see Pratt, John. 2008. Scandinavian Exceptionalism in an Era of Penal Excess: Part I: The Nature and Roots of Scandinavian Exceptionalism. *British Journal of Criminology* 48: 119–37, at 122–24.
39. A point made forcefully by Irwin. 1986, 23–25.
40. See, for instance, Doob, Antony N., and Cheryl Marie Webster. 2003. Sentence Severity and Crime: Accepting the Null Hypothesis. *Crime and Justice: A Review of Research* 30: 143–95.
41. The age-crime curve is one of the best-documented findings of criminology. See Nagin, Daniel S. 1998. Deterrence and Incapacitation. In *The Handbook of Crime and Punishment*, ed. Michael Tonry, 345–68, at 364. New York: Oxford University Press.
42. See Websdale, Neil. 2001. *Policing the Poor: From Slave Plantation to Public Housing*. Boston: Northeastern University Press; Stuntz, William J. 1998. Race, Class, and Drugs. *Columbia Law Review* 98: 1795–1842; Gelman, Andrew, Jeffrey Fagan, and Alex Kiss. 2007. An Analysis of

the New York City Police Department's 'Stop and Frisk' Policy in the Context of Claims of Racial Bias. *Journal of the American Statistical Association* 102: 813–23.

43. See Husak, Douglas. 1992. *Drugs and Rights*. Cambridge: Cambridge University Press; Husak, Douglas, and Peter de Marneffe. 2005. *The Legalization of Drugs*. Cambridge: Cambridge University Press.
44. See Pratt. 2008, 126–29.
45. See Tonry and Lynch. 1996, 104. For a summary of the evidence about drug courts and recidivism, see Mitchell, Ojmarrh et al. 2012, 63–4.

Restorative Justice and Punitive Restoration

Thom Brooks

The Challenge

Penal theorists rarely confront a key challenge facing attempts to justify a theory of punishment for policy-makers: how can the criminal justice system deliver *less* reoffending with *greater* public confidence? This chapter will try to answer this challenge.

Perhaps the primary reason why this is the case is because these aims appear opposed to each other. For example, what works at reducing reoffending does not always satisfy the general public demands for tougher sentences. Increasing prison sentences may be popular, but they rarely make reoffending less likely. Furthermore, the kinds of penal options the public can support can make reoffending rates even higher. California's "Three Strikes and You're Out" might have been born from a popular referendum, but it had virtually no effect on reducing crime and dramatically increased spending on prisons with little, if any, benefits.[1] Studies have indicated that the public's willingness to support more punitive

T. Brooks (✉)
Durham University, Durham, UK
e-mail: thom.brooks@durham.ac.uk

M. Gardner and M. Weber (eds.), *The Ethics of Policing and Imprisonment*, Palgrave Studies in Ethics and Public Policy,
https://doi.org/10.1007/978-3-319-97770-6_8

penal policies rests on a mistaken belief that they will lead to crime reduction and at less cost—neither of which are true.[2]

While much of the academic literature has moved in a rehabilitative turn, public denunciations of allegedly overly lenient prison sentences are all too common.[3] It is as if we must somehow not only make a choice between following the evidence that might yield better results but also an increased lack of confidence in the criminal justice overall or appeasing the crowds and failing to make further progress in tackling reoffending. Neither is appealing and there is an alternative.

In what proceeds, I will argue that restorative justice approaches provide us with a promising first step in the right direction in addressing this challenge. I will next explain what restorative justice is, what it is not, and the problems it confronts. I will conclude by offering a distinctive view of restorative justice I call *punitive restoration* that can address the shortcomings plaguing other restorative approaches while providing a new model for how we can deliver less reoffending while improving public confidence by increasing the available options for restoration to include more punitive elements, but no less restorative. I will conclude that a more punitive approach to restorative justice could help reduce the punitiveness in the criminal justice system.

This is a key challenge worth confronting for any legal philosopher concerned with bridging the perceived—and too often real—gap between the development of new penal theories and their applications in practice.[4] As I have argued before, the justification of any view of punishment should not be considered in isolation from other factors, like the justification of their corresponding crimes that can give rise to punishment as a response.[5] A further issue is the importance of public confidence in the criminal justice system which seems at an all-time low in many jurisdictions. The question of how to build such popular confidence without supporting a popularist view of punishment is one it seems few see valuable enough to ask or too difficult to answer. I deny both views and attempt to show how bringing the public back into the fold is attractive and compelling.

A First Step

How might we find a bridge between an approach to punishment that delivers less reoffending with greater public confidence when it appears each goal is contrary to the other? A promising first step is restorative justice approaches. I speak of a plurality of approaches because restorative justice encompasses multiple practices and "a definitive definition has proven elusive."[6] These extend to usages in schools,[7] prison interventions,[8] and South Africa's Truth and Reconciliation Commission.[9]

My focus on restorative justice will be on approaches used as an alternative to the criminal trial and traditional sentencing by the court. These approaches provide victims and offenders alike a voice in an informal setting away from the judge's bench. The golden thread uniting these diverse approaches is their aim at enabling closure to a conflict through informal, but not unstructured, deliberation that creates understanding and healing. This setting is fundamentally a choice—victims and offenders can choose whether or not to take part and no one is coerced into doing so. The alternative to taking part in a restorative justice meeting is to proceed as normal to the courtroom.

How restorative justice happens can take different forms. The most common are victim–offender mediation where victims meet with offenders in an informal session chaired by a trained facilitator. These meetings are predicated on the offender's agreement to admit his or her crime and make some apology to victims. Victims gain an opportunity to face offenders and explain the impact of their crimes upon them. This two-way dialogue is meant to help victims confront offenders and bring closure while offenders can gain closure too by understanding better the consequences of their criminal actions and apologise for them.

A second popular, but less common, form of restorative justice is the restorative conference. This brings victims and offenders together in a similarly structured meeting, but with additional people including any source of positive support like a spouse, family member or friend. Some members of the community might also take part with a facilitator chairing these meetings. The same kinds of interaction take place as with victim–offender mediation with the added benefits of gaining insights from friends, family members, and the local community about how a crime affected them. This is best summed up by T. F. Marshall's well-known definition of restorative justice as "a process whereby all parties with a stake in a particular offence come together to resolve collectively how to deal with the aftermath of the offence and its implications for the future."[10]

These two forms of restorative justice are the primary ways that these approaches have been used as an alternative to the criminal trial. Instead of entering a courtroom represented by a lawyer who speaks for the offender, the offender meets in an informal setting without the pomp and circumstance of the trial—and speaks for himself or herself. Victims rarely have any opportunity to give voice to how a crime impacted on them as most criminal cases never go to trial, ranging from 94% in the United States to as high as 98% in Scotland.[11] Yet in restorative justice, the victim can always have such an option.

Restorative justice has been shown to make progress on the challenge of reducing crime while improving confidence. Studies have found these approaches—as an alternative to trial and sentencing—can bring up to 25% less reoffending.[12] This is made possible due to the contracts agreed for offenders at these meetings that better target individual offender need and will be explored later. Restorative justice can also deliver greater participant satisfaction among victims, community members, and even the offender over alternatives. This is higher in uses of restorative conferences than victim–offender mediation where more can express their voices. Finally, restorative justice can be delivered at less cost saving up to £9 for every £1 spent. This is partly due to lower non-trial administrative costs, less future reoffending, and avoidance of custodial sentencing.

My aim is not to consider further studies that replicate these findings, but to explore the wider importance of these results for addressing our primary challenge. If restorative justice approaches can bring about significant reductions in reoffending while improving the confidence of victims, offenders and communities—at least for restorative conferencing—then they are an important first step at meeting this challenge. But there are a number of key problems that these approaches face that greatly restrict the progress made to a relatively small number of cases. I will explore these restrictions in the next section followed by how—and why—they should be overcome.

What Restorative Justice Is Not

As a diverse range of approaches, restorative justice is perhaps best understood by what it is not about. This can be found across four areas.

The first is that it is not victim displacement. With over 90% of convictions in common law jurisdictions made without a trial by way of an early guilty plea or some form of plea bargaining, victims rarely have an opportunity to give their voice in public to the wrong inflicted on them or their property. Nor are victims able to have any meaningful role in a process focused almost exclusively on the offender.

Restorative justice is a way to bring the victim back and end his or her displacement in the oft-times alienating criminal justice system. Nils Christie argues:

> The victim is a particularly heavy loser in this situation. Not only has he suffered, lost materially or become hurt, physically or otherwise. And not only does the state take the compensation. But above all he has lost participation in his own case. It is the [state] that describes the losses, not the victim.[13]

Part of restorative justice's appeal to those victims that have wanted it is because it returns their voices to them by permitting their participation in the process. While the normal trial process would keep victims quiet on the sidelines, restorative justice brings victims to the table.

A second area is that restorative justice is not formal. This inclusive, participatory setting helps yield high satisfaction rates for all who take part.[14] Victims regularly report feelings of anxiety when taking a rare part in courtroom trials. The less intimidating atmosphere of the restorative meeting provides a more relaxed context where all participants can more readily engage directly.

A third area is that restorative justice is not inflexible. There is a general order for most meetings where the victim speaks first, the offender offers an apology, and a contract is agreed for what the offender must do in order to escape further punishment for the crime. These contracts are tailored to fit the specific needs and circumstances of individual offenders. There is generally some combination of community service, reparation to victims, and treatment for any underlining issues relating to alcohol or drug abuse and/or mental health. This flexibility of outcomes—that must be agreed by offenders or the restorative meeting is ended and the case transferred to the courts in the usual way—allows better targeting of individual needs with minimal disruption. Factors associated with offending are varied, including a criminal history, housing insecurity, lack of education, training/employability skills, financial insecurity, poor positive networks, lifestyle, drug and alcohol abuse, and psychological factors. Restorative contracts individually tailored can help ensure that those who require specific support can find it—which is often impossible otherwise.

Finally, a fourth area is that restorative justice is not "punishment" where this is conceived of as some form of hard treatment. This is a crucial near article of faith among restorative justice proponents: that all forms of hard treatment, including prison, are forbidden as possibilities for restorative contracts.[15] The reason is that prison is thought to undermine, not enable, restoration. The problem of prisons making offenders more likely to reoffend—some argue even "criminogenic"—is addressed by advocating for much less use of prisons.[16] This is also part of the wider appeal of restorative justice as a non-punitive alternative. It provides a possibility for lowering reoffending without raising punitiveness.

Problems

Restorative justice approaches face some potentially serious challenges. The first is that the diversity of approaches—in criminal and non-criminal contexts—can render it difficult to discuss "restorative justice" as a particular practice or single entity. The effect is that there are many studies of restorative practices but with each exploring different kinds of restorative approaches in various contexts that can make comparability difficult.

The second serious challenge is the limited application of restorative justice. By and large, restorative justice is the province of minor offences by minors.[17] Most jurisdictions sanction restorative justice as an alternative to criminal trials for juvenile offenders relating to relatively minor property offences only. Thus, the promising benefits of restorative justice are promoted almost exclusively to mid- to late-teens for shoplifting, small-scale vandalism and other less serious offences. It is rarely used for young adults or older citizens and virtually never—as an alternative to trial—for any serious violent crimes.

The third serious challenge is the limited public confidence, or its perception, by policy-makers. While there is strong support for greater use of restorative justice for minor offences by juveniles in the United States, United Kingdom, Australia and elsewhere, there is no push to embed restorative justice more deeply into the criminal justice system. Restorative justice is not the default approach, but a relatively rare exception. This perspective may be because it is assumed that the public would view restorative justice's rejection of any hard treatment as being too soft on crime.

A fourth, and critical, problem for restorative justice is its outcomes are too limited in constraining the use of hard treatment. While it may be right to assume that as practiced many forms of hard treatment are counterproductive or worse for offender rehabilitation and recovery, it is perhaps too far—as I will argue in the next section—to assume that hard treatment must always inhibit or damage "restoration"—and this takes to some fundamental questions lying at the heart of restorative justice.

One such question is "who is 'restoring'?" This is a point raised by Andrew Ashworth:

> If the broad aim is to restore the "communities affected by the crime," as well as the victim and the victim's family, this will usually mean a geographical community; but where an offence targets a victim because of race, religion, sexual orientation, etc., that will point to a different community that needs to be restored.[18]

Restorative justice is about providing healing and closure through this restorative process. The issue raised by Ashworth is that it is unclear to what—or by who—someone is to be restored for a crime. If it is to the community affected, is it some or all—and how might we know? For example, criminal damage like scraping a key against my car damaging its paint can obviously affect me by decreasing the value of my car and damaging its appearance. But it can also have a knock-on effect on others by raising concerns among neighbours that their cars might be next or prospective homebuyers in the area might be dissuaded from purchasing a home in the area when seeing a car was damaged like that in the neighbourhood. There might also be psychological effects on the car owner who may feel anxious about leaving the house or unnecessarily worry about being a victim again.

But we need not identify *everyone* so potentially affected, from all neighbours to all car owners, to bring together a productive setting featuring the victim and offender in conversation about the crime and its negative effects and agree upon a restorative contract for the offender. Likewise, juries can function as a group of twelve providing an approximate representation of the public without requiring expansion to all of the public. Indeed, we may be rightly sceptical of "the public" as a single entity to channel in the way Ashworth describes.[19]

A second, related fundamental question is about the idea of "restoration" itself. One of the biggest challenges for restorative justice approaches is providing a definitive view about what they will "restore" through their individual approach. It is commonly noted that "there is no agreement on the actual nature of the transformation sought by the restorative justice movement."[20] Restorative justice aims at a restoration of an offender with the wider community. This is built on a view that there is a wrong to be made right and an injustice between affected persons requiring closure. If this is the case, then it is unclear why restorative justice requires a criminal offence where there may be injustices requiring repair.

For example, restoration may bring benefits to individuals and communities, despite no crime having taken place. There may be a need for providing support to overcome addictions or enable greater financial independence—yet this support might only be available to "restore" those affected should there have been a crime. Short of offending, individuals may lack access to support they need benefiting themselves and their community. Another example is the case of restorative approaches used in schools for children to resolve conflicts and promote healing. If this is our goal, then crimes can be incidental to whether restoration is required.

Restorative justice approaches bring several potential benefits that include higher victim satisfaction and more effective crime reduction at lower costs. These benefits are not without their own costs. Restorative justice approaches are difficult to pinpoint and provide anything but broad comparisons given their diversity. They have limited applicability and limited public confidence, operate with limited options by excluding prison, and are subject to a serious problem concerning what is "restored" and by which community.

Restorative justice approaches may be worth defending, but we require a new approach to yield the potential benefits while avoiding these obstacles. Otherwise, restorative justice approaches might remain an underutilised resource at the margins of mainstream criminal justice policy. This situation might change if there is a new formulation of restorative justice that could address these challenges.

Restorative Justice as Punitive Restoration

This section presents and defends a particular approach to achieving restorative justice in a novel way: the idea of *punitive restoration*.[21] Punitive restoration offers a distinctive view about restorative justice. It is a single practice taking the form of a conference setting where the victim, the offender, their support networks, and some local community members are represented. Punitive restoration is *restorative* insofar as it aims to achieve the restoration of rights infringed or threatened by criminal offences.[22] This is accomplished through recognition of the crime as a public wrong leading to a contractual arrangement agreed by stakeholders. Punitive restoration is *punitive* because it extends the available options for a restorative contract to achieve restoration, and this may include forms of hard treatment, such as drug and alcohol treatment in custody, suspended sentences or brief imprisonment. These claims will now be defended.

Restorative justice approaches lack clarity about what is to be restored and how it should be achieved. Andrew von Hirsch and Andrew Ashworth argue that restorative justice "suffers from unduly sweeping definition of aims and insufficient specifications of limits" with a conceptually incoherent model.[23] In fact, its claim to bring restoration to a community may be criticised because restorative approaches do not insist on community involvement and the overwhelming majority of restorative meetings are victim–offender mediations where the community is excluded.

Punitive restoration operates with a more specific understanding about restoration.[24] The model of punitive restoration is a conference meeting, not unlike restorative conferencing. This is justified on grounds of an important principle of stakeholding: *that those who have a stake in penal outcomes should have a say in decisions about them*.[25] Stakeholding has direct relevance for sentencing policy. Stakeholders are those individuals with a stake in penal outcomes. These persons include victims, if any, their support networks and the local community. Each marks himself or herself out as a potential stakeholder in virtue of his or her relative stake.

This view of restoration endorses the primary working definition from Marshall that is used by most proponents of restorative justice considered above and restated here: "Restorative justice is a process whereby all parties *with a stake* in a particular offence come together *to resolve collectively* how to deal with the aftermath of the offence and its implications for the future."[26] Restorative justice has often been understood as a process that brings "stakeholders" together.[27] Its distinctive form as punitive restoration better guarantees this understanding by promoting the conference meeting and not victim–offender mediation.

Relevant stakeholders become more easily identifiable as persons immediately involved or connected with a criminal offence. This does not require *all* such persons to participate, but rather that opportunities exist for persons beyond the victim and offender to take part. Similarly, there must be opportunities for members of the general public to take part. This working idea of a conference setting is without any specific recommendation on capping the number of persons included although feasibility may render groups of ten or more impractical.

The key idea is that if restoration is worth achieving, then it should not be a private affair between only the victim and offender: crimes are public wrongs that affect all members of the community, including the support networks of victims and offenders whose voices are regularly left out.[28] These individuals have a stake in the outcome that should not be silenced. Restorative conferencing demonstrates this model is achievable and successful: participant satisfaction is higher in this setting than in mediation. We should take the idea of stakeholding central to restorative justice approaches more seriously and ensure that any restoration of offenders with their community is enabled through including the community—as this is too often not the case.

So one benefit of punitive restoration is its specifying the restorative process. Restoration is aimed at stakeholders through a conference setting. Furthermore, we should recall that our focus is on alternatives to sentencing: punitive restoration is conceived of as an alternative to the formal procedures of the criminal trial and sentencing guidelines. Punitive restoration can then overcome an important obstacle—the diversity of restorative approaches. It can do this because our speaking of "punitive restoration" is linked with a particular, informal use of restorative justice. We can then better compare the dynamics and outcomes from punitive restoration given the more specified content. When referring to "punitive restoration," we know which restorative practice we are talking about.

Another benefit is that punitive restoration can better address the issue of community than alternative restorative approaches. This is because punitive restoration endorses the principle of stakeholding where those who have a stake should have a say.[29] There is no need to consider the more difficult task of discerning which type of community is most relevant for "restoration," but rather focus on identifying the primary stakeholders and engage them.

It should be noted that orthodox restorative justice approaches typically require both victims and offenders to participate. An additional benefit of punitive restoration over these approaches is that only punitive restoration can address situations of the so-called "victimless" crimes or where a victim is either unable, or unwilling, to participate. Those offences most often considered "victimless," such as possession of illegal drugs, might normally be unavailable to a restorative approach and the potential benefits it can offer. While there may be no specific victim, crimes are public wrongs where the public have a stake in how criminal offences are managed no matter their degree of seriousness. Punitive restoration's principle of stakeholding better helps us identify persons to participate in conference meetings and expand their applicability to a wider range of offences than alternative restorative approaches.

The public's having a say on penal outcomes is subject to several safeguards as found in current restorative justice practices that punitive restoration builds upon. Offenders have a right to legal representation throughout. Participation by everyone from offender to victim and community members is voluntary. The public can contribute already to penal outcomes through serving on a jury or submitting a victim impact statement so having a voice on sentencing is not unknown. Flexibility is constrained by national guidelines providing necessary discretion, but all outcomes must be overseen by a trained facilitator and agreed to by the offender to be confirmed.

Further problems for restorative justice approaches concern their limited applicability to less serious offences, the limited confidence the public may have in restorative approaches because they may be viewed as too soft an option, and their limited available options by excluding any use of hard treatment. Punitive restoration takes these obstacles together. It enables *wider* applicability by *increasing* the kind and range of available options. Punitive restoration does not assume that restoration must never require the use of hard treatment. While incarceration may often make successful crime reduction efforts more difficult, it is also clear that prisons can, and should, be transformed to improve their disappointing results.

For example, restorative contracts regularly include an obligation on offenders to undertake treatment for any drug or alcohol abuse and to participate in programmes designed to develop their employability and life skills.[30] There is no reason to accept these activities could never be delivered successfully within a prison or some other secure facility for particular offenders. Perhaps hard treatment should be used sparingly because its use can be counterproductive: this is still not grounds for avoiding custodial sentences altogether. It is a realistic possibility that prisons may prove the best environment for some offenders in specific cases.[31]

Prisons can and should be transformed so incarceration does not undermine offender rehabilitation. Short-term imprisonment is associated with high rates of reoffending. This is a significant problem because most offenders receive short-term sentences of less than 12 months and about 60% will reoffend within weeks of their release.[32] Most offenders receiving short-term imprisonment do not receive any rehabilitative treatment. This is a major contributing factor to the likelihood these offenders will reoffend when released from prison.

This problem may be overcome through providing effective treatment. Brief intensive interventions employed to address problems associated with drugs and offending were found to benefit from "significant gains in knowledge, attitudes and psychosocial functioning."[33] These sessions were corrections-based treatment of moderate (30 outpatient group sessions three days per week) or high intensity (six-month residential treatment) and were found to yield cost savings of 1.8–5.7 the cost of their implementation.[34] These policies suggest prisons can be reformed to better support offender rehabilitation and improve post-release crime reduction efforts without sacrificing cost-effectiveness.

Reforms like these have important relevance for punitive restoration. This is because offenders who have committed more serious, even violent, crimes may require more punitive outcomes than currently available to restorative justice approaches. For example, in England and Wales, the currently available restorative practices reject all uses of hard treatment including the imposition or its threat in contracts agreed at restorative meetings. If these contracts are not agreed or satisfied in full, the offender may have his case transferred for consideration by a magistrate where hard treatment can become a possible outcome. Despite having admitted guilt in a restorative setting and apologised to the victim, the offender is permitted to plead not guilty where his or her failure to honour a restorative contract cannot be raised at trial. This current practice fails to fully respect the integrity of the restorative process as neither apologies nor promises are supported by any available sanction.

Punitive restoration might permit the inclusion of a suspended sentence for non-compliance of a contract within the contractual agreement—this would be made clear to offenders upfront. This option would extend the flexibility of punitive restoration to more varieties of offence-types and offenders bypassing the need for a trial in cases of non-compliance and further reducing potential sentencing costs. Nor should this be problematic: offenders receiving a suspended sentence in a punitive restoration conference meeting would retain access to legal representation throughout, must confirm any guilt without coercion, and must agree to all terms presented to him or her at the conclusion of this meeting *for committing offences where the alternative—through the traditional formal procedures of the courtroom—would include options that are at least as punitive*. Note that one major difference is that only with punitive restoration would the *possibility* of hard treatment be an issue that must be agreed by the offender prior to its use.

Let us consider two further instances where punitive restoration might justify some form of hard treatment. One is the idea of prison as a form of cooling off. Recall that imprisonment is often not the beginning of an offender's socio-economic and legal difficulties, but rather their confirmation after an extended escalation. Imprisonment is characteristically *disruptive*. A consequence is that this can end already fragile support networks and render an individual's road to sustainable prosperity tenuous. This is a significant problem for most offenders—but not for all. Perhaps for only a small, yet important minority, the disruption from strongly negative support networks or difficult personal circumstances can provide an opportunity for offenders to take a break where they might become open to personal transformation possible only through a prison-like environment. And this could be readily knowable as offenders are assessed by probation officers prior to any sentencing decision anyway to ensure that any allocated prison place is suitable for any offender to be considered for hard treatment.

A second form of hard treatment that punitive restoration might incorporate is the idea of *less* time in prison with *more* intensity. This addresses the fact that most offenders serve short-term sentences without receiving any rehabilitative treatment. These treatments are costly and so prison wardens normally reserve expensive rehabilitative programmes for offenders serving more than one year in prison: this permits sufficient time for these programmes to be effective.

However, these programmes are rarely intensive and—as already noted above—such high-intensity programmes have been found to be effective at reducing drug and alcohol abuse, for example. More such programmes would increase costs, but these might be accounted for by reducing the overall time spent in prison made possible by intensive rehabilitation programmes: the savings from the reduced time spent in prison overall could contribute to the increased costs of ensuring all inmates have access to the appropriate intensive rehabilitative programmes. Further savings might accrue through less reoffending on release if the programmes are successful.

Objections

Punitive restoration might be objected to on the grounds that hard treatment, even for a few days, is a major curtailment of individual liberty which requires special safeguards only the formal procedures of the courtroom could satisfy. The problem with this objection is that only a relatively few cases are brought to trial. Thus, the vast majority of cases are never heard in court and so victims and others affected by a crime are not permitted opportunities to gain a better understanding of why crimes occurred or receive an apology from their offenders. It is hardly surprising to recall the widespread dissatisfaction many victims have with the traditional sentencing model. Punitive restoration is a concrete approach that can overcome this problem by providing greater opportunities for restorative meetings where victims express much higher satisfaction.[35]

Restoration might not be for everybody. Restorative justice—as an alternative to traditional sentencing—is typically only available to offenders with little to no past criminal record. Punitive restoration attempts to create a space whereby more offenders can be brought into a restorative approach. While more punitive options can enable restoration and expand potential applicability, it is not argued that punitive restoration is appropriate for all crimes, including the most serious violent offences. If it was used, it might undermine its goal of winning over public confidence. Social reality matters and punitive restoration must "restore"—strong public opposition to its use could damage its ability to provide some form of restoration.

Moreover, punitive restoration requires a time commitment. Not all victims or offenders will want to take part. Community members may not wish to participate. If punitive restoration is to work, then its conference format requires stakeholders to come together. It is my contention that since restorative conferences are shown to create more strongly positive experiences for victims and offenders than alternatives that their wider use could extend these experiences for more people. Over time punitive restoration might become more regularly practiced as the public becomes more supportive both through positive experiences and results.[36]

Punitive restoration might also be objected to for a lack of any stated purpose beyond its endorsing the principle of stakeholding: this may help identify relevant participants, but which penal purpose should inform their sentencing outcomes? Punitive restoration is more than an improvement over alternative approaches to restorative justice, but a concrete realisation of a compelling perspective on penal purposes in practice. Punishment is often justified in reference to a justifying aim or purpose, such as retribution, deterrence or rehabilitation. Philosophers disagree about which among these is most preferable despite general agreement that hybrid combinations of two or more purposes often suffer from inconsistency.[37] This is illustrated well in Britain by s142 of the Criminal Justice Act 2003 which states that punishment must satisfy at least one of five penal purposes. This claim is restated in more recent sentencing guidelines.[38] However, there has been no attempt to claim how two or more such purposes can be brought together in a coherent, unified account. This "penal pluralism" may be legally possible, but its practicality remains questionable.[39]

Punitive restoration is one form that a *unified theory of punishment* might take. This is because it is able to bring together multiple penal purposes within a coherent, unified framework.[40] For example, desert is satisfied because offenders must admit guilt without coercion prior to participation in a conference meeting. The penal goals of crime reduction, including the protection of the public and enabling offender rehabilitation are achieved through targeting stakeholder needs arising from the meeting. The satisfaction of these goals is confirmed through the high satisfaction all participants report which suggests a general unanimity that the appropriate set of contractual stipulations has been agreed by all and the improvements in reducing reoffending suggest success in crime reduction and treatment consistent with deterrence and rehabilitation. The argument here is not that any such unified theory is best or preferable to alternative theories. Instead, it is claimed punitive restoration is an example of how multiple penal principles might be addressed within a coherent, unified account.

Conclusion

This chapter focused on the challenge of how to support less reoffending with greater public satisfaction—when doing one appears to undermine the other. I argued that restorative justice is promising as a first step in the right direction. What evidence we have suggests it can lead to significant reductions in reoffending, improve satisfaction of all who take part and even lead to considerable savings. If such an approach were more deeply embedded in the criminal justice system, then crime rates could be lowered and public confidence improved as more took part in restorative conferencing in particular.

Yet this attractive potential is inhibited by several obstacles. There is no one "restorative justice" approach, its application is too limited, its outcomes, too circumscribed, and there are fundamental questions to answer concerning who restores and what is restored. Without revision, restorative justice's promising potential for addressing the central challenge cannot succeed.

I have argued for a distinctive approach to restorative justice called punitive restoration. This is a single type of approach taking a conferencing format that is more open in its use of possible outcomes permitting any that can legitimately enable the restoration of rights open to stakeholders. These outcomes include limited, and targeted, uses of hard treatment such as intensive drug or alcohol therapy. In short, by making available more of these punitive outcomes—designed to support, not undermine, restoration—we can further embed restorative justice more deeply in the criminal justice system and reduce its overall punitiveness.

So while this alternative may appear like heresy for many restorative justice advocates, punitive restoration may prove a kind of Trojan's horse making much further progress to less punitive criminal justice across the board. Moreover, punitive restoration provides a model for improving public participation in criminal justice outcomes that commands high satisfaction by victims and offenders alike with up to 25% less reoffending compared to alternatives. We can build public confidence without moving toward great popularism—and we can bring together different penal goals of desert, deterrence and rehabilitation within a unified framework designed to restore rights.

Acknowledgements I am enormously grateful to the Department of Philosophy at Bowling Green State University for comments on an earlier draft with special thanks to Albert Dzur, Douglas Husak and Richard Lippke.

Notes

1. Durlauf, Steven N., and Daniel S. Nagin. 2011. Imprisonment and Crime: Can Both Be Reduced? *Criminology and Public Policy* 10: 13–54.
2. Williams, Monica. 2011. Beyond the Retributive Public: Governance and Public Opinion on Penal Policy. *Journal of Crime and Justice* 35: 93–113.

3. I do not ascribe any particular view of penal justice to the public. My analysis accepts a plurality of individuals supporting retribution, deterrence, and alternatives. Public criticisms of lenient sentencing can be made from any of these perspectives. This is not to claim these criticisms have merit, but only that "the public" should be considered a composite of differing views about penal justice that may not always cohere.
4. My work on what became punitive restoration is a result of advisory meetings held with Sadiq Khan, now London Mayor but then a Member of Parliament and Shadow Lord Chancellor, into how restorative justice could become more embedded in the criminal justice system. This opened up new ways of examining restorative justice and developing models that went beyond traditional restorative approaches to create a new policy for penal reform that was as philosophically novel as it remains practically realisable.
5. Brooks, Thom. 2012. *Punishment*. London: Routledge.
6. Shapland, Joanna, Gwen Robinson, and Angela Sorsby. 2011. *Restorative Justice in Practice: Evaluating What Works for Victims and Offenders*. New York: Routledge, at 4.
7. Morrison, Brenda. 2007. Schools and Restorative Justice. In *Handbook of Restorative Justice*, eds. Gerry Johnstone and Daniel W. Van Ness, 325–350. New York: Routledge.
8. Van Ness, Daniel W. 2007. Prisons and Restorative Justice. In *Handbook of Restorative Justice*, eds. Gerry Johnstone and Daniel W. Van Ness, 312–324. New York: Routledge.
9. Llewellyn, Jennifer J., and Robert Howse. 1999. Institutions for Restorative Justice: The South African Truth and Reconciliation Commission. *The University of Toronto Law Journal* 49: 355–388.
10. Marshall, T. F. 1999. *Restorative Justice: An Overview*. Home Office Occasional Paper. London: Home Office.
11. Brooks, Thom. 2004. The Right to Trial by Jury. *Journal of Applied Philosophy* 21: 197–212.
12. See Shapland, Joanne, Anne Atkinson, Helen Atkinson, James Dignan, Lucy Edwards, Jeremy Hibbert, Marie Howes, Jennifer Johnstone, Gwen Robinson, and Angela Sorsby. 2008. *Does Restorative Justice Affect Reconviction? The Fourth Report from the Evaluation of Three Schemes*. London Ministry of Justice and Restorative Justice Council (2011). *What Does the Ministry of Justice RJ Research Tell Us?* London: Restorative Justice Council.
13. Christie, Nils. 1998. Conflicts as Property. In *Principled Sentencing: Readings on Theory and Policy*, eds. Andrew von Hirsch and Andrew Ashworth, 312–316. Oxford: Hart, at 314.
14. Shapland et al. 2008.

15. Ashworth, Andrew. 1994. Sentencing. In *The Oxford Handbook of Criminology*, eds. Mike Maguire, Rod Morgan, and Robert Reiner, 819–860. Oxford: Oxford University Press, at 822.
16. Durlauf and Nagin. 2011, 21–23.
17. Brooks, Thom. 2015. Punitive Restoration: Rehabilitating Restorative Justice. *Raisons Politiques*: 65–81, at 67–68.
18. Ashworth, Andrew. 2002. Responsibilities, Rights and Restorative Justice. *British Journal of Criminology* 42: 578–595.
19. See Parekh, Bhikhu. 2008. *A New Politics of Identity: Political Principles for an Interdependent World*. Basingstoke: Palgrave Macmillan, 21–26.
20. Johnstone, Gerry, and Daniel W. Van Ness. 2007. The Meaning of Restorative Justice. In *Handbook of Restorative Justice*, eds. Gerry Johnstone and Daniel W. Van Ness, 5–23. New York: Routledge.
21. This section develops my argument in Brooks, Thom. 2014a. Stakeholder Sentencing. In *Popular Punishment: On the Normative Significance of Public Opinion for Penal Theory*, eds. Jesper Ryberg and Julian Roberts, 183–203. Oxford: Oxford University Press.
22. Criminal offences infringe, or threaten the infringement, of rights. For example, theft is a violation of an individual's right to property. Attempted offences are instances where the violation of rights is threatened. An attempted robbery is an instance where my rights to property and self are in jeopardy. Punishment as a restoration of rights recognises offences, including attempts, as the infringements, or threatened infringements, of rights that they are and it seeks to render their maintenance and future protection more secure by acknowledging just deserts and addressing underlying causes to rehabilitate if necessary and deter where possible. Brooks, Thom. 2014b. Criminal Harms. In *Law and Legal Theory*, ed. Thom Brooks, 149–161. Boston: Brill.
23. Von Hirsch, Andrew, and Andrew Ashworth. 2005. *Proportionate Sentencing: Exploring the Principles*. Oxford: Oxford University Press, 110–111.
24. Brooks. 2015.
25. Brooks, Thom. 2016a. Justice as Stakeholding. In *Theorizing Justice: Critical Insights and Future Directions*, eds. Krushil Watene and Jay Drydyk, 111–127. New York: Rowman and Littlefield.
26. Marshall. 1999.
27. Braithwaite, John. 2002. *Restorative Justice and Responsive Regulation*. Oxford: Oxford University Press, 11, 50, 55.
28. One study found that restorative conferences often include friends and family of the victim and of the offender, respectively, in 73 and 78% of cases examined. Parents were far more likely to attend restorative conferences (50% of offenders and 23% of victims) than partners

(3% of offenders and 5% of victims). Shapland, Joanna, Anne Atkinson, Helen Atkinson, Becca Chapman, E. Colledge, James Digman, Marie Howes, Jennifer Johnstone, Gwen Robinson, and Angela Sorsby. 2006. *Restorative Justice in Practice: The Second Report from the Evaluation of Three Schemes.* Centre for Criminological Research, University of Sheffield.

29. Brooks, Thom. 2016b. Punitive Restoration: Giving the Public a Say on Sentencing. In *Democratic Theory and Mass Incarceration*, eds. Albert Dzur, Ian Loader, and Richard Sparks, 140–161. Oxford: Oxford University Press.
30. Towl, Graham J. 2006. Drug-Misuse Intervention Work. In *Psychological Research in Prisons*, ed. Graham J. Towl, 116–127. Oxford: Blackwell.
31. Perez, Deanna M., and Wesley G. Jenings. 2012. Treatment Behind Bars: The Effectiveness of Prison-Based Therapy for Sex Offenders. *Journal of Crime and Justice* 35: 435–450.
32. See Ministry of Justice website, http://open.justice.gov.uk/home/.
33. Joe, George W., Kevin Knight, D. Dwayne Simpson, Patrick M. Flynn, Janis T. Morey, Norma G. Bartholomew, Michele Staton Tindall, William M. Burdon, Elizabeth A. Hall, Steve S. Martin, and Daniel J. O'Connell. 2012. An Evaluation of Six Brief Interventions That Target Drug-Related Problems in Correctional Populations. *Journal of Offender Rehabilitation* 51: 9–33.
34. Daly, Marilyn, Craig T. Love, Donald S. Shepard, Cheryl B. Peterson, Karen L. White, and Frank B. Hall. 2004. Cost-Effectiveness of Connecticut's In-Prison Substance Abuse Treatment. *Journal of Offender Rehabilitation* 39: 69–92.
35. It might be objected that some victims may see the opportunity to confront offenders as a chance to lavish anger and hostility. This is not what happens most often in practice. Yet even if it were so, the conference setting gives victims a voice but not the only say—and any contract (punitive or otherwise) must be acceptable by the offender to have any effect. Furthermore, contracts are not constructed in some anything goes fashion. There are guidelines to ensure that flexibility is restrained to ensure some consistency.
36. This is why it is claimed that if we want to find an approach that reduces crime more and increases public confidence then punitive restoration is a possibility we should consider because of its likely results and by the positive experiences by participants. Yet this is not about grafting punitive restoration onto an already criminogenic criminal justice system—it is the aim to help launch a shift towards more, not less, restorative justice within the criminal justice system thereby reducing the system's criminogenic features.

37. Brooks. 2012, 89–100.
38. For example, see Sentencing Council, Download a guideline. http://www.sentencingcouncil.org.uk/publications/?type=publications&s=&-cat=definitive-guideline&topic=&year.
39. Brooks, Thom. 2014c. On F. H. Bradley's 'Some Remarks on Punishment'. *Ethics* 125: 223–225.
40. A unified theory of punishment may be constructed in different ways. The construction favoured here is to view crime as a harm to individual rights and punishment as "a response" to crime with the purpose of protecting and maintaining individual rights. This model rejects the view that penalties and hard treatment have different justificatory foundations, but rather they share a common justificatory source: the protection and maintenance of rights. The model of a unified theory can then better address the fact that penal outcomes are often multidimensional and include both financial and punitive elements. Brooks. 2012, 123–148.

Bibliography

Ashworth, Andrew. (1994). "Sentencing," in Mike Maguire, Rod Morgan, and Robert Reiner (eds.), *The Oxford Handbook of Criminology*. Oxford: Oxford University Press, 819–860.

Ashworth, Andrew. (2002). "Responsibilities, Rights and Restorative Justice," *British Journal of Criminology* 42: 578–595.

Braithwaite, John. (2002). *Restorative Justice and Responsive Regulation*. Oxford: Oxford University Press.

Brooks, Thom. (2004). "The Right to Trial by Jury," *Journal of Applied Philosophy* 21: 197–212.

Brooks, Thom. (2012). *Punishment*. London: Routledge.

Brooks, Thom. (2014a). "Stakeholder Sentencing," in Jesper Ryberg and Julian Roberts (eds.), *Popular Punishment: On the Normative Significance of Public Opinion for Penal Theory*. Oxford: Oxford University Press, 183–203.

Brooks, Thom. (2014b). "Criminal Harms," in Thom Brooks (ed.), *Law and Legal Theory*. Boston: Brill, 149–161.

Brooks, Thom. (2014c). "On F. H. Bradley's 'Some Remarks on Punishment'," *Ethics* 125: 223–225.

Brooks, Thom. (2015). "Punitive Restoration: Rehabilitating Restorative Justice." *Raisons Politiques*: 65–81.

Brooks, Thom. (2016a). "Justice as Stakeholding," in Krushil Watene and Jay Drydyk (eds.), *Theorizing Justice: Critical Insights and Future Directions*. New York: Rowman and Littlefield, 111–127.

Brooks, Thom. (2016b). "Punitive Restoration: Giving the Public a Say on Sentencing," in Albert Dzur, Ian Loader, and Richard Sparks (eds.),

Democratic Theory and Mass Incarceration. Oxford: Oxford University Press, 140–161.

Christie, Nils. (1998). "Conflicts as Property," in Andrew von Hirsch and Andrew Ashworth (eds.), *Principled Sentencing: Readings on Theory and Policy*. Oxford: Hart, 312–316.

Daly, Marilyn, Craig T. Love, Donald S. Shepard, Cheryl B. Peterson, Karen L. White, and Frank B. Hall. (2004). "Cost-Effectiveness of Connecticut's In-Prison Substance Abuse Treatment," *Journal of Offender Rehabilitation* 39: 69–92.

Durlauf, Steven N., and Daniel S. Nagin. (2011). "Imprisonment and Crime: Can Both Be Reduced?" *Criminology and Public Policy* 10: 13–54.

Joe, George W., Kevin Knight, D. Dwayne Simpson, Patrick M. Flynn, Janis T. Morey, Norma G. Bartholomew, Michele Staton Tindall, William M. Burdon, Elizabeth A. Hall, Steve S. Martin, and Daniel J. O'Connell. (2012). "An Evaluation of Six Brief Interventions That Target Drug-related Problems in Correctional Populations." *Journal of Offender Rehabilitation* 51: 9–33.

Johnstone, Gerry, and Daniel W. Van Ness. (2007). "The Meaning of Restorative Justice," in Gerry Johnstone and Daniel W. Van Ness (eds.), *Handbook of Restorative Justice*. New York: Routledge, 5–23.

Llewellyn, Jennifer J., and Robert Howse. (1999). "Institutions for Restorative Justice: The South African Truth and Reconciliation Commission," *The University of Toronto Law Journal* 49: 355–388.

Marshall, T. F. (1999). *Restorative Justice: An Overview*. Home Office Occasional Paper. London: Home Office.

Morrison, Brenda. (2007). "Schools and Restorative Justice," in Gerry Johnstone and Daniel W. Van Ness (eds.), *Handbook of Restorative Justice*. New York: Routledge, 325–350.

Parekh, Bhikhu. (2008). *A New Politics of Identity: Political Principles for an Interdependent World*. Basingstoke: Palgrave Macmillan.

Perez, Deanna M., and Wesley G. Jenings. (2012). "Treatment Behind Bars: The Effectiveness of Prison-Based Therapy for Sex Offenders," *Journal of Crime and Justice* 35: 435–450.

Restorative Justice Council. (2011). *What Does the Ministry of Justice RJ Research Tell Us?* London: Restorative Justice Council.

Shapland, Joanna, Anne Atkinson, Helen Atkinson, Becca Chapman, E. Colledge, James Digman, Marie Howes, Jennifer Johnstone, Gwen Robinson, and Angela Sorsby. (2006). *Restorative Justice in Practice: The Second Report from the Evaluation of Three Schemes*. Centre for Criminological Research, University of Sheffield.

Shapland, Joanne, Anne Atkinson, Helen Atkinson, James Dignan, Lucy Edwards, Jeremy Hibbert, Marie Howes, Jennifer Johnstone, Gwen Robinson, and Angela Sorsby. (2008). *Does Restorative Justice Affect*

Reconviction? The Fourth Report from the Evaluation of Three Schemes. London Ministry of Justice.
Shapland, Joanna, Gwen Robinson, and Angela Sorsby. (2011). *Restorative Justice in Practice: Evaluating What Works for Victims and Offenders.* New York: Routledge.
Thomas-Peter, Brian A. (2006). "The Needs of Offenders and the Process of Changing Them," in Graham T. Towl (ed.), *Psychological Research in Prisons.* Oxford: Blackwell, 24–53.
Towl, Graham J. (2006). "Drug-Misuse Intervention Work," in Graham J. Towl (ed.), *Psychological Research in Prisons.* Oxford: Blackwell, 116–127.
Van Ness, Daniel W. (2007). "Prisons and Restorative Justice," in Gerry Johnstone and Daniel W. Van Ness (eds.), *Handbook of Restorative Justice.* New York: Routledge, 312–324.
Von Hirsch, Andrew, and Andrew Ashworth. (2005). *Proportionate Sentencing: Exploring the Principles.* Oxford: Oxford University Press.
Williams, Monica. (2011). "Beyond the Retributive Public: Governance and Public Opinion on Penal Policy," *Journal of Crime and Justice* 35: 93–113.

The Racial Politics of US Gun Policy

Amanda Gailey

On a sunny early fall day in 2015 in Lincoln, Nebraska, a shooting took place that is so mundane as far as gun violence incidents go that it got little press outside of the state. But its very mundanity makes it an instructive case study in the racial imbalance of the criminal, civil, health, and financial consequences of gun violence in the United States.

In the afternoon of September 22, a Lincoln police officer saw Tareik Artis, an 18-year-old black man, get into the back seat of a car at a downtown convenience store. The officer says he identified Artis as someone who had fled a traffic stop a month earlier, so he followed the car and pulled it over. When the officer directed Artis to get out of the car, Artis took off running, and the officer saw a handgun tucked into the waistband of his pants.

Artis ran several blocks, at some point picking up the handgun when it fell, and ended up in front of the state capitol building, gun in hand, surrounded by law enforcement. When Artis did not drop the gun as commanded, a sheriff's deputy and a US Marshall each fired two shots at him, striking him three times. Two bullets hit his right thigh, and the

A. Gailey (✉)
Department of English, University of Nebraska-Lincoln, Lincoln, NE, USA
e-mail: gailey@unl.edu

M. Gardner and M. Weber (eds.), *The Ethics of Policing and Imprisonment*, Palgrave Studies in Ethics and Public Policy,
https://doi.org/10.1007/978-3-319-97770-6_9

third entered through his buttocks, shattered his hip, damaged his liver, and collapsed his diaphragm and right lung.

By our national standards, this was an unproblematic police shooting. There were dozens of witnesses. Artis had a gun—a stolen gun, no less—in his hand. He did not listen to orders to drop the gun, and the officers on the scene reasonably feared for the safety of themselves and the public. And unlike the 986 people fatally shot by police in 2015,[1] Artis even survived the shooting. Within six months, he took a plea deal and was sent to prison.

When we look closer at the case of Tareik Artis, we see a system of regulatory, civil, and criminal codes that are rigged to shield corporations and white gun owners from accountability for gun violence and instead shift that accountability onto marginalized people, particularly black men. This article is concerned with the biopolitics of these gun laws. Biopolitics refers to the way in which modern Western democracies tend to enact state and corporate power through policies that manipulate the life, quality of life, and health outcomes of their populations. Through biopolitics, state and corporate entities can foster life and health in some portions of the population while suppressing health or even killing other portions of the population. US gun laws socially, financially, and politically empower that portion of the population regarded most fully as white citizens while they disproportionately incarcerate, injure, oppress, and kill populations of color, especially black people. The biopolitics of gun laws lead to firearm manufacturers and sellers making profits, the taxpayer base shouldering much of the economic costs of gun violence, and minoritized communities suffering lower life spans, poorer quality of life, and reduced economic prospects.

The Open Spigot

Laws regulating the manufacture and importation of guns in the United States are paltry by comparison to our peer nations. Automatic weapons, which continuously fire, along with silencers, short-barrel shotguns, and some other weapons and accessories, are the most strictly regulated products, though they can still be sold through a more extensive process than other gun sales. Semiautomatic rifles and handguns, which fire bullets as fast as the trigger can be pulled, along with large capacity magazines, are legal and are not treated differently than other rifles and handguns in the law. Guns manufactured to look like toy guns are legal.

Bump stock, which allows some semiautomatic weapons to fire at a rate close to that of a machine gun, is legal.

Few laws govern the sale of these products. Individuals or companies who are in the business of selling guns to consumers must have a Federal Firearm License (FFL), which requires filing a photograph and fingerprints with the ATF and undergoing a background check and interview that ensures the applicant is in compliance with state firearm laws and zoning requirements, which are nearly nonexistent in many states. An FFL does not require that the seller limit sales to individuals, take care not to oversaturate the legal market, or refuse to sell to a person in distress. It does not prohibit marketing guns to children or angry young men. It does not require the seller to take steps to avoid theft or loss—no security cameras, alarms, locks, or other basic measures to prevent the theft of guns are required by the law.

Additionally, federal law offers a number of special shields for the firearm industry, affording gun makers and sellers protections that few other industries enjoy. The most significant is the Protection of Lawful Commerce in Arms Act (PLCAA), which passed in 2005. PLCAA shields firearm manufacturers and sellers from liability that other industries are not shielded from. Consumers can sue a gun maker for a product defect, but they cannot sue for damages wrought by the intended function of the gun, no matter how foreseeable, preventable, egregious, and common those damages are. If a man buys a gun based on an advertisement that it will help him protect his family, he can sue the gun maker if the gun has a defect that causes it *not* to fire, but he cannot sue the gun maker if his child picks up the gun and, seeing that it appears to be unloaded, accidentally shoots himself. Because firing is what the gun is intended to do, the buyer can sue the manufacturer for failure to fire, but not when a lack of warnings and safety features allow it to be accidentally fired by a child, as happens predictably many times a year with no significant industry effort to implement safety features.

Similarly, gun and ammunition sellers are not required to take basic precautions to avoid or limit sales of their product to people who mean harm. If you wish to buy Sudafed, you must show your pharmacist an ID and she will log your purchase to keep you limited to about two boxes a month because the government wants to prevent bad actors from using it to produce methamphetamine. However, you can buy unlimited quantities of ammunition, including high capacity magazines and armor-piercing bullets, with no such required scrutiny—and a retailer is shielded from a negligence suit even if they sell thousands of rounds of ammunition to a dangerous person sight unseen.

For example, in 2012, an online gun and ammunition retailer, Lucky Gunner, sold 4,000 rounds of ammunition in a single online sale to the man who used the ammunition to open fire on a theater in Aurora, Colorado. Among the twelve people who were murdered in that shooting was 24-year-old Jessica Ghawi, whose parents, Sandy and Lonnie Phillips, filed a lawsuit against Lucky Gunner seeking no financial reward, only injunctive relief. Working with the Brady Center to Prevent Gun Violence, which represented the Phillipses pro bono, they simply sought a judgment—like those that have set precedent for requiring responsibility and due diligence in other industries—that would indicate that ammunition sellers have some responsibility to take basic, reasonable care that their products are not being sold to a person likely to cause harm. The Phillipses described the motivation for their lawsuit in an opinion piece:

> One of the six, steel-jacketed bullets that killed her slammed through a theater seat, entered her left eye and left a five-inch hole in her face as it blew her brains out on to the theater floor. The other five specially designed bullets tumbled when they tore through her flesh and did devastating damage to both legs, arms, and intestines.
>
> Those bullets were six of 4,000 that Lucky Gunner sold to a mass murderer in one sale without even checking his driver's license.
>
> Why is there a law that says you cannot sue an ammunitions dealer that allowed 4,000 rounds of armor-piercing bullets into the wrong hands?
>
> How else are we as citizens going to get them to stop doing that?
>
> No other industry has this immunity.[2]

The Phillipses here allude to one of the arguments against PLCAA—that it deprives Americans of their right to seek civil justice through the courts. Indeed, negligence is a foundational concept in civil law—the law requires that individuals and corporations exercise reasonable care in avoiding exposing people to harm, and people who experience harm are permitted to seek the assistance of the courts. But PLCAA offers a unique carve-out for the gun industry, marking them as a special industry that does not have to exercise such care, and designating the people harmed by that industry as a special group of people who cannot seek assistance from the courts.

Even worse, PLCAA works in concert with state laws that further penalize gun violence victims. Jessica Ghawi was shot in Colorado, and the state passed a law building on PLCAA to further shield the gun industry and dissuade those harmed by the industry from having their day in court. The state law rearticulates the special protections of PLCAA, and adds a provision entitling defendants in gun industry suits—so gun and ammunition makers, importers, and sellers—to attorney and court costs resulting from any lawsuit brought against them that tried to hold them accountable for damage someone foreseeably caused with their products. Together with PLCAA, these special gun industry protections and punitive measures against victims led to the Philipses' lawsuit being dismissed in a single ruling before it got to court—as well as a ruling that the Phillipses, whose daughter was blown apart by the product Lucky Gunner sold, had to pay Lucky Gunner $203,000. So Lucky Gunner was able to sell 4,000 rounds of ammunition in one sale, sight unseen, to a man who shot up a theater, and the parents of a slaughtered young woman were punished for seeking redress by being forced to pay hundreds of thousands of dollars to the people who equipped their daughter's murderer. Lucky Gunner celebrated their win online, inviting the gun-loving public to vote on gun rights organizations who would receive a portion of the settlement money. Organizations across the country, including the Nebraska Firearm Owners Association, competed for a piece of the bankrupting settlement the Phillipses were required to pay the specially shielded company that contributed to their daughter's death, calling that company—not Jessica or her parents—a "victim."

Since the passage of PLCAA, only one negligence lawsuit against a gun dealer has resulted in an award of damages by a jury, and it was a special case that pitted one interest group implicated in racialized armed violence against another. In 2015, two Milwaukee police officers sued a local store, Badger Guns, for selling a gun that was used to shoot them in 2009. Badger Guns sold three thousand guns a year, and multiple guns from their store were used in shootings of police officers. In this case, a 21-year-old man visited Badger Guns with an 18-year-old friend who was too young to buy a handgun. The two discussed the gun purchase in a way that should have tipped off the employee that they were engaging in a straw purchase, but the store sold the 21-year-old the gun anyway. He gave it to the 18-year old, who used it to shoot the two police officers when they stopped him for riding a bike on a sidewalk. The jury awarded the officers almost six million dollars in damages.

This case clearly involves negligence, but it is unlikely that in the 13 years since the passage of PLCAA no other similarly negligent sales of guns and ammunition have taken place. Yet the Badger Guns suit, in which the injuries were to police officers, but not any of the other million gun injuries or deaths in the last decade, remains the only case of a jury settlement against gun sellers since the law's passage. This seems suggestive—insofar as courts have discretion in agreeing to hear negligence cases that rise to a level of egregiousness and legal violations allowing them to work around PLCAA, law enforcement may appear to the courts to be a special class of victim.

The lax regulations surrounding gun sales and the special shields protecting gun and ammunition manufacturers and sellers from the kinds of lawsuits that regulate other industries constitute a wide-open spigot at the top of the gun violence conduit. From this virtually unregulated and criminally and civilly unaccountable point flow approximately eleven million guns per year into American communities. One of these, at some point, was the Regent Arms handgun that would eventually make its way to the hand of Tareik Artis in Lincoln, Nebraska, in September of 2015.

The "Law Abiding Gun Owner"

From manufacturers and sellers, the next step for the majority of guns sold in America is the "law-abiding gun owner" or "responsible gun owner"—phrases that pepper the gun control debate, and which I will problematize.

The laws that govern the legal purchase of guns vary by state. At the federal level, the only requirements governing the purchase of a gun are that the following kinds of people are prohibited: felons, fugitives, people who use illegal drugs, people who have been adjudicated as mentally defective or committed to a mental institution, illegal immigrants, people with dishonorable discharges from the military, people who have renounced American citizenship, people under current domestic violence protection orders, and people who have been convicted of domestic violence. Federally licensed sellers are typically required to run a NICS (National Instant Criminal Background Check System) check on a prospective buyer. In some cases, such as Nebraska, the state runs a background check and provides the purchaser with a certificate allowing him to legally purchase a gun.

The NICS system is itself byzantine and unreliable, relying heavily on voluntary and variable participation of states to supply records. However, even assuming a background check system that works flawlessly, the classes of persons that are prohibited from legal gun ownership is one of the primary ways that legal and criminal gun ownership becomes racialized. While some of the prohibited classes are unproblematic, several have far-reaching implications for the legal and social status of gun ownership in the United States and racial justice of gun-related incarcerations.

According to the NAACP, black people endure over five times the incarceration rate of white people.[3] Many of these convictions are non-violent felonies related to the war on drugs—in fact, according to the ACLU, 74% of people imprisoned for drug possession are black, despite similar drug use rates among white and black people.[4] A 2003 Bureau of Justice Statistics report predicted that a black man had about a one out of three chance of going to prison in his lifetime.[5] These numbers are deeply implicated in American gun laws, starting with who qualifies as a "law abiding gun owner." Because black people are much likelier to belong to the prohibited class of felons, black people are disproportionately barred from the category of "law abiding gun owner," a phrase that consequently is infused with whiteness. Beyond these legal prohibitions that disproportionately affect black would-be gun owners, a farther-reaching penumbra of the whiteness of "law-abiding gun owners" extends into the social realm. If black men are visually designated as a category of person less likely to legally own guns, they carry a far greater risk in being misidentified as *illegal* gun owners when purchasing or carrying guns in public. Several prominent news stories indicate how this can happen: Tamir Rice, a 12-year-old-black boy, was fatally shot by police for holding a toy gun in Ohio, a state where the open carry of firearms is legal. John Crawford III, a black man, was fatally shot by police for carrying a BB gun in Ohio, in his case in the Walmart where he had picked up the BB gun because he was buying it there. In a suburb of St. Paul, Minnesota, Philando Castile, a black man, was killed by police when an officer became frightened at a traffic stop after Castile, a licensed conceal carrier, informed him that he had a firearm in the car. The many similar cases in which police shoot unarmed black people who are suspected of having guns indicates that for black men in particular, the mere suspicion of a gun is enough to prompt lethal force from police—lethal force that usually faces no criminal consequences.

Similarly, the prohibition against "alien[s] illegally or unlawfully in the United States" has implications for how gun ownership is performed and perceived in a racialized social context. "Illegal alien" is a category of persons related to race-based policies, and is a term racists use to label people with Mexican or Central American origins or ancestry as second-class persons, including even legal immigrants from those places. The law against gun ownership by "alien[s] illegally or unlawfully in the United States" has ramifications, then, beyond the actual individuals prohibited by law from purchasing a gun and extending to all persons who believe they run a risk of being intentionally or unintentionally confused with this class of prohibited people and incur greater odds of violence, law enforcement contact, or social opprobrium if seen with guns.

The underlying scant federal laws governing who can purchase guns do afford some minimal, important protections, but they also shape a basic legal and social landscape upon which "law-abiding gun ownership" is performed as a role inflected with whiteness. This basic context is not fundamentally changed by state laws, which, with few exceptions, fail to impose meaningful or racially neutral additional restrictions, such as waiting periods, training, or storage laws. Only one state, California, requires that gun purchasers undergo safety training. In the remaining 49 states, it is legal to purchase a gun with no education about safe handling. Only one state, Massachusetts, requires that all firearms be locked when not in use. And only three states—California, New York, and Connecticut—even require legal gun owners to lock their guns if a prohibited person resides in the home. In such a racially skewed, lax legal context that puts almost no responsibility on the shoulders of the gun purchaser, calling oneself a "law-abiding gun owner" amounts to little more than preening oneself for one's racial privilege.

The Right to Negligence

At the top of the gun pipeline is the open spigot of lax federal gun laws governing what kinds of firearms and how much are legal for import and sale in the United States. The spigot is locked wide open by PLCAA, which guards gun manufacturers from the kinds of lawsuits that have reined in the excesses of other harmful industries. From that open spigot, the guns flow into a consumer market that has very few slowing mechanisms in regulatory or criminal statutes, and some of the few that are in place notably work to create a class of "law-abiding gun owner" that is functionally predominantly white, while other adults carry an increased burden of being identified or misidentified as members of a racially skewed class of illegal or criminal gun owners.

The wide latitude afforded to the racially inflected category of "law-abiding gun owners" is amplified by how the criminal justice system and civil courts address harm resulting from legally owned guns. The most notorious example of this disparity is through "stand your ground" laws (SYG), which vary somewhat state to state, but in general remove the duty to avoid conflict or escalation from someone who actually is or merely believes himself, another person, or even another person's property to be under threat. Traditionally, a person has a legal duty to leave a situation in which violence is likely to result, but SYG laws statutorily empower people to meet the threat of violence—or the mere perception of a threat of violence or of harm to property—with force. For people who carry handguns, who arguably are looking for such encounters or are psychologically primed for them, SYG laws can be a get-out-of-jail card for shooting or menacing others. Given the influence of race on who can comfortably carry guns in public and who is more likely to seem "threatening" due to implicit or explicit bias—bias shared by police and juries—SYG laws function to empower white gun owners to kill black people. The empirical evidence bears this out. In 2015, the American Bar Association published a comprehensive report on the effects of SYG laws and concluded that they were instruments of racial disparity that should be repealed. Among their findings: "a white shooter who kills a black victim is 350 percent more likely to be found to be justified than if the same shooter killed a white victim."[6]

The negligent use of firearms is not well-documented—more on that in a moment—but is another area of the law in which a racially defined class of people is largely immunized against accountability for the damage they cause. In criminal law, it is rare for people who unintentionally shoot others or allow access to children who shoot others to face criminal consequences. Prosecutors tend to find many of these cases unwinnable—lacking specific state statutes that define negligent shootings or negligent access as a crime, most prosecutors must gamble on whether they can convince a jury that such shootings are worth incarcerating someone over.[7] Given that gun ownership has been normalized in our society, most of these shootings are within the home, and the negligent party is often also both white and grieving, prosecutors believe it will be difficult to convince the jurors that the person acted so aberrantly that they deserve criminal consequences. In one case, as when a young white man named Kasey Wilson shot a four-year-old girl in head when he decided to practice shooting while children played in his yard, the prosecutor in Missouri went so far as to redact his name from all documents in an effort to protect him even from public opprobrium. When we do hear of parents facing criminal consequences, the parents are often black. For example, the attorney for Douglas County, Nebraska, explained to me in a 2015 interview that prosecutors find it difficult to charge parents with gun negligence without a specific statute from the legislature defining negligent storage or use of a firearm as a crime. However, as I was researching the present article, his office won a conviction for an African American father, 22-year-old Marquell Buie, who was charged with negligent child abuse resulting in serious bodily injury when a toddler in his home accessed a gun and shot another child. These comparisons are anecdotal because no systematic study in racial disparity in gun negligence conviction exists, but it stands to reason that when "law-abiding gun ownership" occupies a mostly white social and legal space in our culture, prosecutors will find it easier to charge and convict people of negligent crimes who fall outside those boundaries.

Even in civil cases, the law, in practice, holds a special exception for people who are negligent with their guns. Andrew Jay McClurg, professor of law at the University of Memphis, calls this a "right to be negligent" with the "only legal product designed to inflict what the tort system is intended to prevent: death and injury to human beings."[8] McClurg has looked at a number of cases in which a gun owner failed to take reasonable precautions to deter theft of a firearm, which resulted in harm to another person. For example, a Montana man left a loaded handgun, along with several visible high-value items, in an unlocked pickup truck parked on a public street. A group of boys entered the truck and found the handgun, and one of them unintentionally fired it and killed another boy. The courts found the gun owner, who took no precautions to prevent the theft of a lethal product, blameless for the damages that resulted. In another case, parents left a gun unlocked in their home, and a friend of their 16-year-old daughter either stole or was given it. He used the gun to murder a man, and the parents who left the gun accessible were found to not be responsible for damages. In these cases we again see how the racially inflected category of "law-abiding gun owner" or "responsible gun owner" actually implies little to no responsibility for the consequences of gun violence, and instead designates a racialized category of individuals who (a) operate freely within lax regulations, and (b) benefit from racialized social norms that hold white people who seek out and negligently keep firearms blameless for the ills that result from those decisions.

It was within exactly such a context that Tareik Artis came to possess that stolen handgun in Lincoln, Nebraska, in 2015. Umarex, a German company that owns Regent Arms, was legally allowed to import a product designed to kill people into the United States, with no fear of being held legally or financially responsible for its harm. Nebraska Gun, located in downtown Lincoln, was allowed to legally sell the handgun with no legal requirements other than some minor paperwork and asking to see the state handgun purchase permit that certifies the buyer had passed a NICS background check. The buyer, Christian Biggerstaff, a 23-year-old white man, was able to legally purchase the handgun despite minor criminal offenses in his background and showing no evidence of training or knowledge of firearm laws or best practices. He claims he put this gun and another he bought from Nebraska Gun in his mother's car for safe keeping, and his mother drove the car to different locations and left it unlocked with the guns inside. The police theorized the guns were stolen from the car—they were not reported stolen, and there is no way to know if they were actually straw purchases or resold. In any case, the 23-year-old buyer and his mother incurred no charges for buying lethal weapons and acting at best negligently with them. Up to this point in the handgun's travels to a crime scene, the manufacturer, retailer, buyer, and car owner have all been white and "law abiding," legally exchanging money and guns with virtually no requirements to behave in ways that significantly mitigate the foreseeable damages the product could cause. But from this point forward in the story, the attitude of the law toward guns radically changes.

The War on Drugs Is Fought with Guns

Scholars of racial justice call attention to what Reva B. Siegel terms "preservation through transformation": society maintains unjust social hierarchies even as the laws and customs that enforce them collapse under ethical scrutiny because new laws and customs—sufficiently disguised to appear different from the old, arise to enforce the same hierarchies through different means.[9] Michelle Alexander cites Siegel's "preservation through transformation" in her persuasive argument that Jim Crow took the place of slavery, and that mass incarceration from the war on drugs has taken the place of Jim Crow—each a successive paradigm for enforcing the subjugation of black and brown bodies for state and corporate profit.[10]

In a nutshell, Alexander argues that a false color-blindness conceals a system of municipal, state, and federal laws that define crime and focus punishment in ways that so disproportionately target black people as to effectively replace older, supposedly delegitimized paradigms of racial subjugation, and leading to similar outcomes: a deprivation of personal freedom through mass incarceration and disenfranchisement through laws that purport to target behavior—felony status—but are functionally targeting race.

I want to add to Alexander's argument that US gun law is one of the ways through which the New Jim Crow operates. The law shows a shocking lack of concern for gun violence in policy areas that would have the most impact on reducing gun violence but would impact corporate profit and white legal accountability, but becomes invested in identifying and punishing gun violence when that legal involvement disproportionately impacts people of color. The bodies of black and brown people are where the consequences of firearm law are disproportionately inflicted, starting with lax laws that allow a glut of firearms to plague with violence structurally impoverished communities, police militarization that enriches firearm manufacturers, police shootings that disproportionately kill people of color and are widely excused based on the justification of fear of guns, and enhanced criminal sentencing and prolonged incarceration for nonviolent offenses committed in the presence of a gun—a presence that the law treats as wholly unproblematic almost everywhere else in society.

According to a study that looked at a decade of data from the Center for Disease Control and Prevention, black Americans are more than twice as likely to die by gun injury than white Americans. In some locations, this disparity is startling: in Washington, DC, black residents are thirteen times as likely to die from gunshot as white residents. These numbers include suicide by gun, which involves significant racial disparity: five out of six white people who died by gunshot were suicides, and for black people that number is flipped—for every black person who commits suicide by gun, five black people die by gun homicide.[11]

For white America, then, the majority of gun deaths are the kind of deaths our society treats as private concerns that rarely get media attention and are widely dismissed as irrelevant to gun control because of persistent cultural myths about suicide as an inevitability for people who make the choice to do it. For black America, the majority of gun deaths are homicides—and it seems reasonable to assume this disparity influences how racially segregated America views gun violence in disparate ways. Among white people, only one-sixth of gun deaths, which are experienced at only half the rate they occur among black people, are homicides—among black people, five-sixths of that double gun death rate are homicides.

Black people bear the biopolitical burden of our gun policy not only through a higher gun death and astronomically higher gun homicide rate, but also through the terror of hyperpolicing and reduced quality of life, economic outcomes, and citizenship rights that result from racially targeted criminal codes. The militarization of American police departments in recent years has been well-documented—around the country, police departments equipped for war are using military equipment and methods to perform basic policing. For example, the ACLU found that nearly 80% of SWAT raids, originally intended to be rare responses to extreme situations such as hostage-taking, were used to serve search warrants, typically for low-level drug cases.[12] Little public oversight or transparent decision-making led to the escalation of police equipment and methods, but the implicit argument for this militarization is that the potential threat of guns to police in such situations warrants any level of equipped aggression by the state. To the extent that guns are present in raided homes (about 35% of the time), they are either legal or made their way there due to a wide-open regulatory spigot and lax consumer laws. Rather than addressing the source of the problem, which would impact corporate profit and the conspicuous display of white citizenship, we instead allow our police departments to engage in an arms race with the civilian population that results in increased gun sales—police in a single county in Arizona received 1,034 guns from the military[13]—and brutalized black people.

Similarly, American police shoot civilians at a rate unthinkable in other developed countries. In 2015, police killed over a thousand people in the United States.[14] Although black people were less likely to be armed than white people when encountered by police, they were three times as likely to be killed. And a vanishingly small number of police are ever found guilty of a crime for these killings—about 1%.[15] The only rationale for this state of affairs is that the general public agrees that police justifiably feel threatened because of the likelihood a person they stop will have a gun in a country awash in guns, and that a proper response to this threat is the use of a gun. This rationale accepts that the disproportionate killing of black people by the state is more tolerable than strictly regulating the manufacture, sale, purchase, and possession of firearms by corporate and white America.

From even a purely financial perspective, the cost of gun violence is not paid by the people who profit most from it. When Tareik Artis was shot after running from police that fall day in Lincoln, Nebraska, he was taken to the emergency room with horrific bodily trauma. A recent Johns Hopkins study concluded that firearm injuries cost US hospitals about $2.8 billion a year in initial emergency and inpatient care, with those patients who were admitted for inpatient care after an ER visit incurring, on average, $95,887 in hospital bills.[16] It seems likely that Tareik Artis's astronomic hospital bill was, like so many others, passed on not to the gun industry but to other patients in the form of increased rates. Even though guns result in billions of dollars of predictable damage every year, we do not collect those costs from the industry that profits from the gun sales. Instead we force even people who want nothing to do with the industry to pay for the mutilation it causes. Regent Arms, Nebraska Gun, Christian Biggerstaff, and his mother did not necessarily pay any more for Tareik Artis's shattered pelvis and collapsed lung than I did.

When Artis was released from the hospital a week after the shooting, he pled no contest to possession of cocaine and a stolen firearm and was sentenced to 17–22 years in prison. His prior criminal record included only infractions for marijuana possession. The Offices of the US Attorneys, part of the Department of Justice, offers guidance in the US Attorneys Manual to adding enhanced weapons charges to drug charges. The section titled "Firearms Charges" begins with a paragraph describing the availability of guns to "gang members":

> A recent study of gang members showed that nine in ten members said their gang possessed a stash of guns members could use "whenever they wanted to," and an equal proportion described guns as plentiful "whenever the gang got together." Joseph F. Sheley and James D. Wright, *Youth, Guns and Violence in Urban America* Tulane University (April 1992).

> Nearly half described gun thefts as a regular gang activity, and two-thirds said their gang regularly bought and sold guns.[17]

Nothing in the section addresses how guns became so plentiful and easy to steal and how that source of the problem might be dealt with through prosecution. Instead, it details how gun charges can be tacked on to a number of other charges, for example: "possession of firearms by convicted felons or *drug users* can provide punishments of up to ten years imprisonment" (emphasis mine). One passage notes that the use of a silencer—currently one of the few tightly regulated firearm accessories—in a violent crime adds 30 years onto sentencing. Silencers are bad enough to warrant an additional 30 years of incarceration for violent offenses, but Congress is currently considering the "Hearing Protection Act," which out of concern for "law-abiding" gun owners'[18] hearing will legalize silencers and make them easier to acquire. The section on Firearms Charges concludes with: "The mandatory and enhanced punishments for many firearms violations can be used as leverage to gain plea bargaining and cooperation from offenders." Here, finally, after no such concern in the law for reducing the number of guns in circulation, requiring harm mitigation from manufacturers or sellers, or requiring responsible behavior from "responsible gun owners," the law finally kicks in to aggressively address gun violence, directed at the most marginalized and disproportionately prosecuted members of society, who are also the ones most likely to be shot. Whether it is in the grave or behind bars, black bodies are overwhelming where the crime and punishment of gun violence are enacted.

Notes

1. Somashekhar, Sandhya, and Steven Rich. 2016. Final Tally: Police Shot and Killed 986 People in 2015. *The Washington Post*, January 6.
2. Phillips, Lonnie, and Sandy Phillips. 2015. We Lost Our Daughter to a Mass Shooter and Now Owe $203,000 to His Ammo Dealer. *Huffington Post*, September 2.
3. National Association for the Advancement of Colored People (NAACP). 2016. Criminal Justice Fact Sheet. http://www.naacp.org/criminal-justice-fact-sheet/. Accessed March 2018.

4. American Civil Liberties Union (ACLU). 2003. Race & the War on Drugs. https://www.aclu.org/other/race-war-drugs. Accessed March 2018.
5. Bonczar, Thomas P. 2003. Prevalence of Imprisonment in the U.S. Population, 1974–2001. U.S. Department of Justice, Office of Justice Programs. https://www.bjs.gov/content/pub/pdf/piusp01.pdf. Accessed March 2018. Incarceration rates for black men have dropped somewhat since that prediction, but an updated figure for lifetime likelihood of imprisonment does not yet exist.
6. American Bar Association. 2015. National Task Force on Stand Your Ground Laws Report and Recommendations. https://www.americanbar.org/content/dam/aba/images/diversity/SYG_Report_Book.pdf. Accessed March 2018.
7. Gailey, Amanda. 2015. Why Americans Don't Treat Fatal Gun Negligence as a Crime. *The New Republic*, April 26.
8. McClurg, Andrew Jay. 2016. The Second Amendment Right to Be Negligent. *Florida Law Review* 68.1: 1–47.
9. Siegal, Reva B. 1997. Why Equal Protection No Longer Protects: The Evolving Forms of Status-Enforcing State Action. *Faculty Scholarship Series*, Paper 1091. http://digitalcommons.law.yale.edu/fss_papers/1091.
10. Alexander, Michelle. 2010. *The New Jim Crow: Mass Incarceration in the Age of Colorblindness*. Revised Edition, The New Press, 2012, 21.
11. Keating, Dan. 2013. U.S. Gun Deaths Shaped by Race. *Washington Post*, March 23.
12. American Civil Liberties Union (ACLU). 2003, 31.
13. American Civil Liberties Union (ACLU). 2003, 13.
14. Swaine, Jon, Oliver Laughland, Jamiles Lartey, and Ciara McCarthy. 2015. Young Black Men Killed by US Police at Highest Rate in Year of 1134 Deaths. *The Guardian*, December 31.
15. Mapping Police Violence. 2018. https://mappingpoliceviolence.org/. Accessed April 13, 2018.
16. Gani, Faiz, Joseph V. Sakran, and Joseph K. Canner. 2017. Emergency Department Visits for Firearm-Related Injuries in the United States, 2006–14. *Health Affairs* 36.10: 1729–1738.
17. United States Department of Justice, Office of the U.S. Attorneys. U.S. Attorneys Manual, Criminal Resource Manual, Section 112. https://www.justice.gov/usam/criminal-resource-manual-112-firearms-charges. Accessed April 13, 2018.
18. The American Suppressor Association. 2018. https://americansuppressorassociation.com/hearing-protection-act/. Accessed April 13, 2018. The American Suppressor Association claims their product is "one of

the most misunderstood tools in existence" and that the act will ensure "*law-abiding citizens* will remain free to purchase suppressors, while prohibited persons will continue to be barred from purchasing or possessing these accessories" (emphasis mine).

Destabilizing Conceptions of Violence

Lori Gruen, Clyde Meikle and Andre Pierce

Introduction

"Non-violent" crimes tend to be met with less punitive responses because the "non-violent" modification seems to soften or at least mitigate the fact that a law was violated. Prison reform policies in recent years have tended to emphasize "non-violent" offenders as more worthy of sentence reconsideration and alternatives to incarceration. This reinforces the distinction between violent and non-violent crime and strengthens negative attitudes and state sanctions against so-called violent offenders. In this chapter we want to explore the variety of ways

Gruen will be referred to in this chapter as P.L.G, Pierce as D.R.E., and Meikle as C.M. P.L.G. has been teaching philosophy to and learning from D.R.E. and C.M. since 2010 in a maximum security prison. The three of them decided to take on this project given their shared interest in and experiences of violence as well as their philosophical interest in dignity.

L. Gruen (✉)
Wesleyan University, Middletown, CT, USA
e-mail: lgruen@wesleyan.edu

C. Meikle · A. Pierce
Cheshire, CT, USA

M. Gardner and M. Weber (eds.), *The Ethics of Policing and Imprisonment*, Palgrave Studies in Ethics and Public Policy,
https://doi.org/10.1007/978-3-319-97770-6_10

that violence operates in an effort to destabilize the distinction. Common conceptions of "Black-on-Black" violence in marginalized communities of color, both inside and outside of prison, for example, can be seen through different lenses. One overlooked use of violence is as an alternative way of promoting dignity. While being denied democratic resources that typically allow for the promotion of dignity in many contexts, people from poor Black communities, often while immersed in violence, can nonetheless protect and promote their dignity. In the first section below, we show how violence and dignity are not mutually exclusive. There is a fairly widely held belief among many white people, as well as middle class people of color, that to act violently is to both violate the dignity of the victim as well as to prove oneself unable to control one's impulses and thus to lack self-respect and dignity. We will suggest that the violence common in some poor, predominantly Black communities can be understood as an expression of dignity in the state of emergency that obtains in the interstices that are generated and undermined by dominant (and violent) social institutions.[1] We describe the ways that excluded communities are engaged in an inner struggle to define for themselves what it means to live with dignity in an anti-black racist world and how to best promote their dignity while being denied all of the dignity promoting resources available to whites. In the second section, we analyze particular types of violence that occur in these interstices. We identify three types of violence: retributive, pre-emptive, and destructive violence. We argue that the first two types are often deployed to protect dignity. In the last section we imagine what it would take to reach a non-violent state in Black interstices, one that allows for the promotion and protection of dignity. We discuss how a critical assessment of the damaging effects of white values and norms on Black knowledge can contribute to violence and how empathy building may correct the negative effects.

One

Dignity and violence are often thought to be at odds. It seems that it is impossible to live with dignity in the midst of constant threats of bodily harm. Conversely, causing someone bodily harm is not typically viewed as a dignified act. While these views are widely shared in communities where a range of state resources and democratic protections are available, in the Black interstices, where individuals are attempting to live meaningful and honorable lives against the odds, certain situations demand action to protect both life and the various relationships and things that give life meaning. In addition, given that dignity itself is best understood within particular relations, any generalization is prone to be inapt.

P.L.G. has argued for a relational understanding of dignity, one that upholds social demands for recognition and respect. This conception of dignity brings into focus the relations between the dignified and the person or community being judged to be dignified in the appropriate context (Gruen 2014). The relational conception of dignity is compatible with a recognition of a range of values often connected to autonomy including: (1) being free from internal barriers to form a conceptions of a good life; (2) being free from external barriers to pursue one's conception of the good life; and (3) having both one's conception and one's action in pursuit of that life respected by one's community. Given the unpredictability of life, as well as good and bad luck, and the various ways people act from implicit and explicit biases, it makes sense to think of dignity in particular social contexts, rather than as an intrinsic attribute that persists across time and space.

There is another important social tendency with respect to dignity that we should note. Generally speaking, those who are members of dominant social groups, primarily white people, tend to have their dignity promoted at an institutional level. Dominant institutions authorize particular ways of being and protect their realization. This social tendency creates various opportunities for members of dominant groups to conceive of the good life and to pursue it, instantly earning the respect of those similarly situated, without internal struggle. Often, these opportunities for dignity promotion and maintenance remain invisible as they are so readily assumed to be available, and the lack of availability for people on the margins is thus very hard to notice.

Because those in the interstices do not see themselves reflected in the dominant social institutions and are often precluded from the path to dignity that members of dominant groups take more or less for granted. Their lack of dignity promoting opportunities, as well as other opportunities and resources, is much more apparent to them. When this exclusion is explicit, it is often in the form of stigmatization that delegitimizes alternative ways of being. In the worst-case scenario, the dominant institutions prescribe a dehumanizing existence for those on the margins. These social institutions thus generate an internal struggle within marginalized Black bodies, making the achievement of meaning, comfort, and dignity all the more difficult. We (C.M. and D.R.E.) have lived in these interstices our entire lives. We, and those similarly situated, have struggled to live with dignity without democratic protections and resources, while fully recognizing that our way of being is stigmatized by the dominant group.[2]

The quest to live with dignity in a precarious, deprived, and undermined space involves a double stunt of appropriation and rejection. There is a struggle between, on the one hand, incorporating the mainstream values that appear conducive to enhancing one's life and dignity in the margins, while on the other hand, rejecting those stigmatizing values that render marginal bodies forever undignified. For example, mainstream values designed to help dominant individuals achieve economic security are largely capitalist. Many individuals on the margins have adopted these values to establish what is commonly known as the underground economy. This marginal capitalist market bares the hallmarks of the dominant one. Top drug dealers, like CEOs, conceive of creative ways to successfully run their businesses, seek out new markets to increase demand for their products, hire managers to oversee the daily operations of the business, empower these managers to hire people to manufacture, sell, and advertise the product. And just as with dominant markets, there are individuals attempting to go into business for themselves, to compete with the success of those already established. The underground economy also resembles the mainstream economy in that hard work and ingenuity are rewarded both financially and in terms of respect. While this is clearly an instance of appropriation of capitalist values, resistance is also in play, in that the product being bought, sold, advertised, and distributed is illegal.

We (C.M. and D.R.E.) intimately understand that our Black being is devalued by the dominant group. Evidence abounds in a society that places premium value on whiteness and a discount price on Blackness. It was evident in the large photo on my (D.R.E.) grandmother's bible of a blue-eyed, blond haired, white Jesus. It was evident in an education system that chose the shortest month of the year to teach me about my long rich history. It was evident in that all my heroic G.I. Joe's were white and my younger sister's pretty Barbie dolls were too. It was evident when, as a child, I watched as the police station in the middle of the projects where I lived went dark, the lights turned off, as soon as gunshots rang out.

For generations, individuals on the margins have been attempting to construct uniquely dignified Black identities in contrast to the otherizing white ones of dominant culture. Sometimes it was in the literary world, such as the Black protest novels written during the Harlem Renaissance. Or it was through slogans such as "I'm Black and Proud!" There were times when it was through style, such as allowing one's naturally Black curly hair to grow out into an Afro rather than "conk" or straighten it.

Many individuals on the margins are creating oppositional Black identities by attempting as much as possible to abandon white culture and openly rebel against white institutions. D.R.E. calls this "reversing butterflies to caterpillars"—to beautify those which were stigmatized. Pejorative terms—dope, stupid, bad, dumb, and crazy became positive aesthetic adjectives; ill fitting clothes became stylish; broken English becomes poetic expression. Black existentialist, Lewis Gordon, notes this particularly empowering re-appropriation in hip-hop music, writing "the orthography of Hip-Hop stands as a refusal to seek recognition in a system of rules in relation to which black, brown, and beige youth have often been politically and pedagogically constructed as illiterate"[3] (Gordon 2005).

The open rebellion against white institutions is also manifest in the "no snitching" rule. This rule expresses a refusal to cooperate with a system that arrests, prosecutes, sentences, and incarcerates Black people unfairly. The high school drop-out rate is another instance of opposition. Many individuals in the interstices conceptualize the American educational system as a white institution, in which white values and texts about white people are taught primarily by white people. Black people who participate in the white institution are being "white washed."

These few instances, and there are others, of reverting butterflies to caterpillars are attempts to reject the otherizing identity of the powerful and carve out an alternative, dignified way of being. Yet, as many people can attest, this opposition often proves counterproductive and represents a very modest challenge to the oppressive system.[4] Nonetheless, these meager acts of resistance can feel empowering to people who otherwise feel too disempowered to affect radical social transformations, and in these acts the seeds of dignity can be sown.

The dignity that marginalized Black people formulate in the interstices is a peculiar one and presents a bit of a conundrum. The process of dignity reclamation demands that social recognition and resources are available to those in the margins, but it also involves a critical, sometimes violent, response to the denial of these protections and resources. The stigmatization that emanates from the center causes many to turn to an alternative space or way of being in search of self-worth. The tendency for marginalized Black people to assert their dignity, particularly in the form of violence, against other Black bodies, is due, in part, to a process of internalizing the dominant view that Black bodies must be subdued. It is also due, in part, to the lack of resources and external force absent in Black communities, leaving these spaces akin to a Hobbesian state of nature.

For Hobbes, when in a state of nature it is natural for human beings to function to preserve their lives. "Each person" Hobbes says, "has the liberty to use his own power…for the preservation of his own nature" (Somerville and Santoni 1963, 13). In a state of nature, human beings are motivated by fear and desire, rather than inherent viciousness. Self-preservation then compels individuals to develop bonds that will quell their fears and appease their desires. In the interstices, these bonds coalesce into socioeconomic bonds with implicit and explicit rules developed to establish order. The bonds that are formed and the roles established are often maintained through indirect violence as well as occasional direct violence. The way that violence operates to protect interests is not formed in a vacuum.

Force is what keeps whites out of these spaces but also contains Blacks within them. This forceful exclusion has caused young Black men to see themselves as a sign of not only pollution but potential taint that cannot be cleansed. When a Black youth looks out at the center of society, he feels unwanted while simultaneously looked upon as threatening, tainted, a cause of pollution. This suggests two conflicting possibilities: first, if he would change his ways and become like the imagined white body of purity, then he may be included. Second, this figure should be eliminated because he cannot adapt to the image of the ideal. This veiled racist conundrum produces the Black body while simultaneously condoning it negation.

Ian Hacking, citing Mary Douglas, has described how external boundaries are furnished by human activity circumscribed by particular groups: "Rules of pollution define who one is not, and hence provide a sense of self-identity and self-worth: we who are not polluted" (Hacking 2005, 114). Just as white communities form their identities by these rules, young Black males, excluded by and from the activities established by these rules, eschew them and work to form their own rules to establish an identity and a reflective, intersubjective community for self-worth.

These bonds are often formed by violence. This violence is a fact of life. Young Black males designated as problems are uprooted from the place that is supposed to ground them. The reality for these young men is a world permeated by violence. They are objectified in violence and therefore become the subjects of violence. These spaces that were violent before their birth come to inform them, but also a priori designate their very existence as problematic.

Under these conditions, the family members and community members understand that the young must be capable of defending themselves against violence. Unwittingly, these communities teach the young that violence is instrumental to their survival. Indeed, a Hobbesian logic of survival reverberates in these spaces. Self-preservation then in a violent space depends on one's ability to defend their person. Here the state of nature is produced by conditions elaborated by fear of violence. In these communities, the rule one must adhere to is the will to stand up for themselves. Yet even if these conditions of violence are imposed and emerge from destructive notions of blackness, they operate as a background that defines self-worth and social capital in black communities. This capital—violence—becomes not only a means of exchange, but also informs others that one has the will to defend one self. One is a self worth defending. Violence under certain conditions becomes a means to feel a sense of worth when their dignity is degraded.[5]

This violence becomes not only a means of exchange but also a vehicle for forming bonds between youth who feel excluded from the center. These ties become the foundation of groups with the potential to form political commonwealth. Paradoxically, many young people who have formed bonds in these permutations of violence become even more marginalized in their communities—not necessarily by their families but by the community, they become like free-floating elements that communicate the condition for communities. For instance, one member of the lifers' group (a group of men who are serving long sentences in a maximum security prison) described two distinct events that illustrate how a community and the individuals within it are conditioned by violence. What he described was an interaction he had with a gang member and then one he had with a detective:

> One time when I was on the street a car rolled up with a bunch of Spanish guys. One of them had his hand out with a gun in it. I jumped in a car to get out of the way. He ran up on the car and asked me "Why you run?" then shot me. On another occasion I was on that same block, selling weed. A cop jumped out of an unmarked car, and I ran. He caught me in a hallway of a building and asked me, "Why you run?" then bust me in the lip. To me he was no different than the gang member.

Young people experiencing this violence feel trapped within a violent space. They realize there is nowhere to run from violence. These acts of violence are part of the narrative of pollution that has designated particular people, Black people, and coded Black spaces, as tainted.

Since many young people living in communities plagued by violence develop bonds through violence, making friends and surrounding oneself with a group of young men you know will defend each other provides a feeling of security. Violence then transforms fear into security, and over time, the rhythms of violence become a form of social capital that helps one to develop a sense of self-worth. Violence is a way of connecting with others under a guise of fearlessness, and each day surviving the dangers that these friends cultivated deepens their connections and self-worth.

Growing up amidst other Black bodies living the rhythm, one becomes afraid that there is no escape from violence. On the streets, fear leads to violence which leads to more fears and more violence and this, oddly, cultivates a space of safety. These young bodies are acting out their fears. The cultivation of dangers presupposes a ground or field of violence. An act of violence calls for one to respond with violence. Cultivation of danger is an embodiment of one's hypersensitivity to threat. Internalizing one's fears and becoming that which you fear equips one with a sense of security.

But when violence provides a sense of worth, then violence will increase and become normalized. The desensitization of violence begins with an awareness of violence, which appears to the young person as threatening. In understanding the role of child development, many scholars have recognized that:

> children are at risk for joining a gang from an early age if they are hyper sensitive to threat because they regularly see shootings in the

> neighborhood, have fallen behind in school because they can't read, or live in neighborhoods where gangs and 'easy money' seem to go hand-in-hand.[6]

What these authors fail to recognize, however, is that young life in these spaces is organized around fear rather than innate dangerousness. The violence that preconditions the response was not a product of inherently dangerous individuals; rather, it is fear that conditions the individual to respond by becoming the danger.

Two

The violence we are discussing requires more nuanced elaboration, as not all violent acts have the same meaning or the same force. We distinguish three types of violence: retributive, preemptive, and destructive. Retributive violence, as the name suggests, is carried out to punish someone for a perceived offense. Preemptive violence is a deterrent for a perceived imminent threat of violence. Destructive violence, in contrast to the other two forms of violence, has less immediate triggers and can be seen as disproportional to the situation. Much state violence is destructive violence; police shootings of unarmed Black men are acts of destructive violence. The mass shootings in movie theaters, schools, workplaces, and nightclubs are destructive violence. The bombing of civilians is destructive violence. Most violence in the Black interstices is not destructive violence, but rather one of the other forms. We (C.M. and D.R.E.) were raised in communities with a high rate of violent crime. What we experience, as both victims and perpetrators of violence, was strategic use of retributive and preemptive violence, quite distinct from destructive violence.

Many people living in poor communities of color have developed strategies for surviving in conditions of extreme needs, while surrounded by extreme abundance. In their precarious and uncertain existence, cultivating social respect has become one way to organize confusion. Various codes-of-ethics and written charters geared toward establishing boundaries and defining acts of transgression often develop. As an example, one code may define major acts of transgression to include: (1) conducting economic activity, or drug dealing, in a geographical location that someone informally privatized; (2) having or attempting to have sex with a person who is in a committed relationship with someone else;

(3) violating the person or property of another; (4) involving the police in the internal affairs of the interstices; or (5) disrespecting someone else's family members, particularly their mother or committed partner. These rules are generally adhered to, based on mutual respect, thus creating an orderly state in interstices. However, there nonetheless exist a variety of factors that would cause someone to transgress. Some of the common factors include someone whose rational capacity has been compromised either by substance abuse and/or environmental factors or when someone believes they have been previously transgressed. In such instances, violence becomes the means to restore social order by way of punishing the transgressor so as to demand respect for the "rule of law" in these spaces.

Anyone unwilling to exert the force necessary to either demand a denied social good, or punish those who have violated it, essentially forfeits their entitlements to such goods. This loss of entitlement usually plays out as other individuals in these marginal spaces transgressing on the other person's property, body, or interests. Obviously, such a person finds it difficult if not impossible to survive, dare we say flourish, in these spaces. Marginal individuals attempt to successfully navigate the interstices by predicating their dignity on violence.

Violence can also foster bonding. I (C.M.) lived in a community where we felt either wholly unprotected by law enforcement, or had deep distrust of it, and thus used violence as a means to protect our bodily integrity, property, and interests. Given this state of diffidence, I tended to form bonds with other members of my community who exhibited a willingness to mete out force in order to protect each others' bodily integrity, property, and interests. I existed in such a state of uncertainty that a protective force had become a primary social good. As we assembled around this good, it allowed for bonding and kinship. Deep trust is fostered when individuals have certainty that they each will sacrifice their own lives and safety in order to protect the other. To know that another individual or individuals were willing to make the ultimate sacrifice to ensure my safety, instilled in me a deep fondness and respect for these persons.

I (D.R.E.) also come from a community that experienced a rift with the police and we did not feel they were committed to our protection. When I was 13 years old, I witnessed white police officers physically assaulting a Black man who they had handcuffed to a pole. Members of our (D.R.E. and C.M.) communities are often stopped and frisked without just cause. We never felt safe when driving 4-deep (four Black men in one car) in our communities, for fear of being pulled over. We learned in our adolescence that we could not venture into a white community without being stopped and questioned, or worse, by the police. This is now widely known, given the publicity garnered by recent shootings of unarmed Black bodies. This rift and distrust between our communities and the police departments have caused many members in marginal spaces to repurpose violence as protection, a form of community building, and a way to make sense out of chaos.

When I (D.R.E.) was 14 years old, I witnessed one young man shoot another young man to death during a heated argument. They had argued for several minutes after which the soon-to-be victim abruptly jumped in his car and attempted to drive off. The other guy then pulled out a gun, pointed inside the driver side window and began firing. While my 14-year-old mind understood that the victim's family and the larger community would have denounced this as a senseless act of Black-on-Black violence, I also understood that this use of deadly force was a strategic deployment of retributive and preemptive violence.

The violence was preemptive in that the shooter, as did anyone watching, interpreted the victim's body language as expressing deadly imminent threat. Regardless of any actual explicit threats the victim may or may not have expressed, his abrupt behavior communicated an intent to retrieve a weapon and unleash it. The shooter thus intended to thwart the perceived threat to his life.

The violence was retributive in that it was a response to a commonly understood unpardonable offense: a threat made to one's life. Anyone familiar with the street code knows that it is the ultimate sign of disrespect to threaten someone's life. Anyone who tolerates blatant disrespect risks losing social standing. To suffer such a loss would often make it difficult to successfully navigate the rocky terrain of the interstices. They would earn the ignoble title "sucker" and become a "patsy."

Retributive violence was not only intended to punish bad conduct, but it was also strategically employed to promote good conduct. I (D.R.E.) once belonged to a "family" or what many would call a gang, that used retributive violence on family members to encourage civil behavior, as well as to promote social order. For example, it was known that some of our family members were "stick-up kids" or thieves. They would often rob people to support their heroin habits. Stick-ups were frowned upon and discouraged for two particular reasons. First, they tended to lead to disorder in that the victim would sometimes retaliate, or report the crime to the police, thus making our local space "hot." Second, stick-ups were seen as representing a poor work ethic. That is to say, the people who robbed did so because they did not want to "hustle." The retribution for committing this offense was to "walk the line"—walk through two rows of people who punched and kicked the violator as he or she passed.

Although it is not common, destructive violence is often felt to be lurking. Parents often teach their children the language of violence for self-defense. The potential for deadly violence leads to an arms race of sorts. A street maxim cautions "it is better to get caught with one (gun), than without one." To get caught by the police with an illegal firearm means the loss of one's freedom. On the other hand, if another armed man encounters you intending to do you harm when you are unarmed, this could very well be the loss of one's life. This fear incited me (D.R.E) to purchase a firearm when I was 13 years old through a straw purchaser, in this instance a crack addict without a criminal record. I was fortunate to never have gotten caught without it, and I loaned it to a friend who got caught with it.

A middle-class white college student once told me (C.M.) that the community she was raised in considered physical violence to be the lowest form of violence. I attributed her attitude to the privilege of whiteness. White people have their dignity, liberties, and interests protected by major social institutions so have little reason to understand, let alone use, violence. That is the legitimate jurisdiction of the state that protects them, an arrangement that is silently negotiated at birth. The birth of a Black child, however, in a society founded on anti-black racism is the mark of otherness. While the white body has a considerable degree of protection in and outside the home, the Black body feels naked and when old enough, a Black child will decide to assume responsibility for his or her own protection in a dangerous world.

Part of this protection involves garnering respect from their peers, and given that Black children and young adults are steeped in a narrative about them being dangerous, it is difficult to not see each other in that light. What is the basis of this story if it isn't the empirical data about Black-on-Black crime that is so easy for white people to turn to in their attempts to not appear racist? Part of that basis is as justification for the white distribution of access and resources for the maintenance of dignity. During the early to mid-twentieth century, scholars made claims about the natural inferiority and inherent violent tendencies of Black people. Sociologists, historians, and others participated in a discourse that designated the black body dangerous.[7] The black body at the center of discourse about crime and poverty becomes a solution to a problem that haunts liberal-democratic society. Unable to foster consensus around inherent political problems, those in the center deflect self-examination and point to the black body as the problematic figure that threatens whitened spaces. So the dominant group actually has a vested interest in marginal spaces occupied by the black bodies imagined as a violent threat. So long as dehumanization of Black people coexists within compartmentalized geographical space, at times intermingling, always juxtaposed, a conceptualization of whiteness as pure can be maintained.

Perhaps, this narrative also functions to validate any violence committed against Black bodies. Black people, as we discussed above, tend to cultivate their fears into (or against) perceived and real threats in these interstices as a means to feel secure. As bodies standing out as dangerous these bodies form bonds through violence to generate a sense of dignity and belonging and also to feel secure. Normalization of violence, which precedes their being, eventually desensitizes them to conditions that breed violence. Violence then becomes legitimate. However, this activity becomes a fact that reinforces the narrative of danger and threat to the white center that must be protected.

Three

Given our analysis, the means used by those designated as threats to escape the violence of exclusionary practices hold legitimizing potential. Indeed, there are two poles maintained and fostered through this discourse about violence. In the interstices, those living under impoverished conditions are concerned with survival. The other end is concerned with maintaining their superiority by controlling goods and resources through institutions. On the one pole, rules are determined that relegate those on the other pole to the status of criminal.

As noted above the rhythms of violence condition the lives of people growing up in the interstices. Yet many lifers have not only assumed the role of violent criminal that gave them a sense of empowerment, they have also been victims of violence: bullying, child abuse, taunting, forceful peer pressure, assaults, and some have even witnessed close friends and family members murdered when they were young. Growing up under these conditions, life constantly feels under threat. The ability to enact and defend against violence was the hinge on which bonds were formed. The limited capacity to function was informed by illegitimate forms of violence which pitted them against legitimate forms of violence.

Importantly, these are learned responses rather than an innate antagonism toward authority. As one lifer mentioned:

> My experience with police was one of admiration as a youth. An officer pulled over once when I was 6 or 7 years old and helped me fix my bike. The chain had popped off and I couldn't figure out how to put it back on. Not only did the officer fix it but he showed me how to fix it if it came off again.

But as he grew up, he said, "I don't know if it was me or him or them but the relationship became adversarial."

In these conditions, one begins to question what is considered legitimate or illegitimate violence. "Watch out for the Police," one of the members of the Lifers Group's mother often warned his older brothers before they left the house to take him to the Saturday karate movie. "The idea," he notes "that as a Black man I had to watch out for the police caused interpellation: who am I in relation to others; what am I in relation to others." Law enforcement was no doubt necessary in these spaces because these spaces were prone to violence. However, the interactions between the police and the community have been, and continue to be, rooted in fear. The inhabitants of impoverished zones fear not only the criminals within their community but also the men and women who are responsible for protecting and serving the community. As a result, the criminal role is assumed for a sense of protection for the few that feel not merely excluded but dislodged from society (and victimized by avowedly "protective" institutions). The walls that are produced to keep out certain elements not only perpetuate the conditions that foster violence but they also legitimize it.

In the space above, we have illuminated how anti-black racism amounts to a lack of substantive protections that creates interstices where questions about the legitimacy of violence become linked to its instrumental use. Implicit in this discussion is that violence is situational rather than dispositional. In other words, violence is a response to situations in which marginalized individuals are attempting to live with dignity in spaces that lack political representation, trustworthy protections, and legal economic opportunities. By arguing that the violence occurring in poor Black communities is not dispositional but situational, we are challenging views about inherent Black criminality. At the same time we are not suggesting that violence is an automatic or necessary by-product of exclusion. That the high rate of Black-on-Black violence is a result of the exclusion and dispossession that are pillars of anti-black racism, does not preclude imagining less violent spaces.

Of course such imagining cannot rest on ignoring the fundamental ways that the idea of inherent Black criminality is central to anti-black racism and serves to reinforce it. As we have noted, the exclusions are not simply geographic, economic, and political barriers that can be readily dismantled; they are structural, conceptual, and libidinal barriers. Some have suggested that given their depth in the "ontology" of the world as we know it, there is really no place for imagining otherwise, even non-ideal imagining (see Wilderson 2010; Warren 2015). But given that the lived experience of often violent relationality in the interstices is both misperceived and criminalized, we think imagining dignity is a way to reclaim these relations on new terms, within marginalized communities.

The position of Black people is maintained by the fiction of inherent criminality and this is a view, as we have indicated, that some Black people have internalized as well. Might there be a way to imagine alternative possibilities for our non-ideal conditions, recognizing, of course, that in an ideal scenario, anti-black racism would be destroyed and possibilities currently unimaginable would emerge? One possibility is what we call a Black epistemology project (BEP) to promote dignity beyond violence.

Black epistemology reveals the way that less well off or marginalized groups are dominated by the knowledge practices of white society. BEP would be a tool to undo the distorting effects of colonizing epistemologies. Drawing on Kristie Dotson's work on epistemic oppression, BEP would address epistemic exclusions resulting not just from insufficiently shared hermeneutical resources that result from social, political, and historical oppression, but also critically engage the very features of epistemic systems themselves (Dotson 2014). As she writes, "fettered persons gain the ability to be aware of their larger epistemological systems, that is, what orients one's instituted social imaginaries, so as to possibly change them or shift out of them entirely" (130). Black testimony is not just distrusted, for example, when the claim of a Black person is not accepted or taken seriously until it is confirmed by a white person, but this skepticism is also internalized. So for example, I may not believe what I am saying until it is confirmed by a white person. Importantly, these standards for confirmation become the features of the epistemic system, they are normalized, much as capitalist standards become normalized in violence cultivating economic exchange in the interstices. By exploring the varieties of epistemic exclusion and working to identify the influence that Eurocentric norms, values, and practices have on Black knowledge production, an alternative epistemology can be formulated. This Black epistemology project would empower and equip marginalized Black people with the hermeneutical resources to identify destabilizing values that distort or impede dignity promotion and, importantly, help to show how different epistemological systems might emerge.

Empathetic engagement with others in the interstices can help facilitate BEP. This would involve building, developing ways of listening better, working to take the perspective of others, recognizing that arguing about different points of view is a sign of respect, not disrespect. It will involve critical discussions about "codes" and rethinking responses to transgressions. In a different context, P.L.G has described the errors that can often accompany the work of empathy, both ethical and epistemological (Gruen 2015). In addition to the distorting effects of epistemic oppression that inevitably influence attempts at understanding, epistemic empathetic inaccuracies can also involve the faulty estimations of another's attitudes and concerns or underestimating or missing altogether the significance of the others' experience. This sort of incomplete empathy, in which relevant details or experiences are inaccessible to the empathizer or when the empathizer is unable to grasp the information that is salient in a given situation, can be overcome by filling in gaps in knowledge. Ethical errors will be harder to overcome, as they often result from long-standing prejudices and distortions that are difficult to change. But altering one's perspectives, though difficult, plays an important role in BEP.

We believe those within poor Black communities themselves can allow this Black epistemological project to take shape. Looking to models from outside will not be useful. We here have just laid out tentative, initial thoughts about possibilities as those (D.R.E. and C.M.) who are not currently inside nor ever outside of these communities. This is not an exercise in wishful thinking, "political hope," or an appeal to a simple, quick fix, but rather a suggestion about what might be possible for creating the conditions of possibility for Black dignity beyond violence.

Notes

1. We use the term "interstices" in connection to a growing tradition, that includes the work of Hortense Spillers, Maria Lugones, Kristie Dotson, and many other scholars, in order to highlight the difficulty of articulating a space between dominant white social norms and the dominant construction of black communities. Black interstices are fragmented physical and conceptual spaces where categories are in flux due to the constructed impossibility of meaningful lives and contrarian efforts to generate possibilities.
2. We are aware that there are critiques of racism that suggest it isn't just difficult to achieve meaning, comfort, and dignity, it is impossible (e.g., Wilderson, Frank. 2010. *Red, White and Black*. Durham, Duke University Press). While we are sympathetic to such critiques, here we will imagine how meaning could be achieved. There are also important questions to be raised about gender differences in dignity promotion and violence in the interstices, we would rather let Black women and gender non-conforming folk speak for themselves about these matters.
3. Gordon goes on to identify hip-hop as immature, and we have some concerns about that characterization, but that is an argument for another day.
4. For a recent discussion, see Shelby, Tommie. 2016. *Dark Ghettos: Injustice, Dissent, and Reform*. Cambridge, Harvard University Press.
5. See, for example, Fanon, Frantz. 1963. *The Wretched of the Earth*. New York, Grove Press: "violence is a cleansing force. It frees the native from his inferiority complex and from his despair and inaction; it makes him fearless and restores his self-respect. Even if the armed struggle has been symbolic and the nation is demobilized through a rapid movement of decolonization, the people have the time to see that the liberation has been the business of each and all" (94).
6. Ritter, Nancy, Thomas R. Simon, and Reshma R. Mahendra. 2013. *Changing Course: Preventing Youth From Joining Gangs*. National Institute of Justice. https://nij.gov/publications/changing-course/pages/welcome.asp.
7. See particularly Muhammad, Khalil Gibran. 2010. *The Condemnation of Blackness: Race, Crime, and the Making of Modern Urban America*. Cambridge, Harvard University Press and Moten, Fred, and Stefano Harney. 2013. *The Undercommons: Fugitive Planning and Black Study*. Chicago, CA, AK Press.

Bibliography

Dotson, Kristie. 2014. "Conceptualizing Epistemic Oppression." *Social Epistemology* 28(2): 115–138.

Fanon, Frantz. 1963. *The Wretched of the Earth.* New York: Grove Press.

Gordon, Lewis. 2005. "The Problem of Maturity in Hip Hop." *The Review of Education, Pedagogy, and Cultural Studies* 27: 367–389.

Gruen, Lori. 2014. "Dignity, Captivity, and an Ethics of Sight." in *The Ethics of Captivity.* New York: Oxford University Press, 231–245.

Gruen, Lori. 2015. *Entangled Empathy.* New York: Lantern Press.

Hacking, Ian. 2005. "Why Race Still Matters." *Daedalus* 34(1): 102–116.

Moten, Fred, and Stefano Harney. 2013. *The Undercommons: Fugitive Planning & Black Study.* Wivenhoe: Minor Compositions.

Muhammad, Khalil Gibran. 2010. *The Condemnation of Blackness: Race, Crime, and the Making of Modern Urban America.* Cambridge, MA: Harvard University Press.

Shelby, Tommie. 2016. *Dark Ghettos: Injustice, Dissent, and Reform.* Cambridge, MA: Harvard University Press.

Somerville, John, and Ronald E. Santori. 1963. *Social and Political Philosophy.* New York: Anchor Books.

Warren, Calvin. 2015. "Black Nihilism and the Politics of Hope." *The New Centennial Review* 15(1): 215–248.

Wilderson, Frank. 2010. *Red, White and Black.* Durham, NC: Duke University Press.

Criminal Process as Mutual Accountability: Mass Incarceration, Carcerality, and Abolition

Stephen Darwall and William Darwall

Introduction

Elsewhere, one of us has argued that a mutual accountability framework best captures the nature of law and gestured toward an accountability conception of punishment as the holding responsible of violators of criminal codes.[1] Little was said, however, regarding what a conception of punishment as mutual accountability would require, structurally and functionally. How, in other words, might criminal process as mutual accountability actually work? Establishing two formal requirements that constrain punishment's legitimate exercise, we address this question in the specific context of contemporary American policing and penal institutions. From historical and empirical work on the development of the

S. Darwall (✉)
Yale University, New Haven, CT, USA
e-mail: stephen.darwall@yale.edu

W. Darwall
University of California, Berkeley, CA, USA

M. Gardner and M. Weber (eds.), *The Ethics of Policing and Imprisonment*, Palgrave Studies in Ethics and Public Policy,
https://doi.org/10.1007/978-3-319-97770-6_11

American carceral regime, we argue, first, that its institutions clearly fail to meet accountability conditions necessary for their legitimacy. This we expect to be uncontroversial. Second, we argue that these institutions are responsible for producing social dynamics that undermine the possibility of mutual accountability in general. In any case, American carceral institutions clearly lack the authority to make and enforce the criminal law that they purport to have. In a final section, we discuss possible responses to such a finding, and why an accountability framework for conceiving of the nature of law requires abolitionist politics opposing the institutions of mass incarceration.

Philosophical Background: Law and Accountability

"Law and the Second-Person Standpoint" argued that the framework developed in *The Second-Person Standpoint* (*SPS*) helps illuminate the fundamental character of law in terms of mutual accountability.[2] More specifically, the paper argued, the distinction between criminal law and the private law of torts and contracts can be understood, at least partly, in terms of two different forms of accountability that are distinguished in *SPS* and later work.[3]

Torts and contracts involve relational or bipolar obligations that are owed by one party to another: obligor to obligee.[4] Obligations in private law are legal obligations, of course, but frequently bipolar moral obligations are also involved. When a bipolar moral obligation is violated, not only does the obligor do wrong, other things being equal, at least; they also wrong the obligee.[5] With legal bipolar obligations, violation may neither wrong nor be wrong, but it does nonetheless *injure* and thereby provide grounds for the injured obligee to seek compensation in private law.[6]

The accountability that is implicated in bipolar obligations of torts and contracts is *personal accountability to the obligee* (equivalently, to the person holding a correlative claim right against the obligor).[7] This is shown by its being up to the victim to decide whether or not to bring suit. The victim has an *individual authority* or standing as the particular person to whom the obligor is obligated. Neither the state nor other individuals can sue for compensation for the victim unless they have some trusteeship relation that gives them standing. The obligee's individual authority can also include such rights as to release the obligor from the obligation, to forgive unexcused violations, and so on.

Bipolar obligations are contrasted with obligations *period*, or "pure and simple." When moral obligations period are violated, then wrong is done, whether or not there is a wronged victim. And even if there is, the appropriate response to the wrong differs from that to the wronging. Here, accountability is not to an individual obligee, even if there is one, nor to any other individual, for that matter. It is rather to the moral community or, equivalently, or to anyone as a representative person.[8]

This can be seen by reflecting on the conceptual connections between wrongdoing, violating moral obligation period, and *culpability*[9] (Darwall 2016). It is a conceptual truth that if an act violates a moral obligation and is therefore wrong, it is an act of a kind that it would be blameworthy knowingly to perform without excuse. Blame is a Strawsonian reactive attitude that is felt not as from any particular individual's point of view, neither victim, nor perpetrator, nor anyone else, but from an impartial standpoint anyone can attempt to occupy (Strawson 1968, Darwall 2006).[10] Resentment is felt as if from the victim's perspective, and guilt, from the perpetrator's, but blame is felt as if from a perspective that is impartial between any and all individuals. Whether wrongdoing was culpable is not an issue that is appropriately considered from any particular person's point of view.[11] Blame is felt as if from the perspective of the moral community or a representative member. Guilt is thus self-blame, an attitude through which a wrongdoer holds themselves accountable from the perspective of the moral community. Through the attitude, they represent morality's (the moral community's) demands to themselves and hold themselves responsible for complying with them.

Whereas bipolar obligations conceptually implicate obligees' *individual authority* to hold obligors personally accountability to them, moral obligations *period* entail *representative authority*. When we blame someone for unexcused wrongdoing, whether ourselves or someone else, we implicitly presuppose the authority to hold them accountable as representative members of the moral community.

This brings us to the criminal law and to criminal process. Not all moral obligations are legal obligations; neither is just anything that is legally obligatory necessarily morally obligatory. Bona fide legal obligations only presuppose the de facto authority of some body of law. Hart famously pointed out, however, that laws purport to *obligate* rather than simply to *oblige* by threat of sanctions.[12] That they obligate de facto or "legally" is tautologous. Hart's point was that they *purport* to bind *de jure* or morally. Whether or not this is true of every legal obligation, it is surely essential to our idea of criminal law. It is a presupposition of the criminal law that violating it is not just illegal, but *wrong*, and therefore, that judges and juries inescapably face questions of culpability and how to respond to it.[13]

The basic idea in Darwall 2007 was that while the private law of torts and contracts involves bipolar moral obligation, accountability to individual obligors, and individual authority, the criminal law involves moral obligation period, accountability to the moral community, and representative authority. It is a reflection of this that criminal cases are brought not on behalf of victims but on behalf of "the people" and standardly titled: "the people vs." the defendant. They are brought not on anyone's individual authority, but by the people's putative representatives.

Elements of a Mutual Accountability Approach to Criminal Punishment

Darwall 2007 said virtually nothing, however, about the specific form that practices of criminal accountability should take. We aim here to begin to address this question, with special attention to the form that criminal punishment currently takes in the United States. Two things follow fairly immediately from the framework laid out in Darwall 2006 and 2007. First, since accountability is always fundamentally mutual, presupposing a shared basic second-personal authority, criminal process should be conceived in terms of *mutual accountability*.[14] And second, because the authority that grounds any justifiable criminal process must always be some form of representative authority, practices of criminal accountability must be able to be justified from a perspective that is representative of the moral community as equal moral persons.

There is a difference, of course, between any de facto political or legal order and the moral community. The latter is an ideal construct that deontic moral concepts and propositions presuppose, whereas the former is instantiated in the actual world. In holding their citizens accountable for complying with their criminal statutes, however, political communities purport to have a *de jure* authority that, according to the argument of *SPS*, they can have only if their de facto authority can be grounded in the shared representative (moral) authority of equal persons as members of the moral community. Kant's argument in *The Doctrine of Right* suggests one way that might be done, arguing that persons in a state of nature would be morally obligated to constitute themselves as a collective political order for the purpose of establishing and safeguarding fundamental rights.

Whatever the details, justified practices of criminal accountability must be able to be justified in some such way from a fundamental standpoint of shared representative (moral) authority. The practices themselves will involve offices that are politically constituted as having representative legal authority de facto. But having this legal representative authority can be fully justified, and therefore be *de jure*, only if it can be vindicated from a standpoint of shared equal representative authority of the moral community.

Legislators, police, prosecutors, judges, and juries have representative legal authority, and their actions in making and enforcing law, and ultimately bringing and judging a criminal case, legally represent "the people" that the legal order their offices reside in is putatively constituted to be "of, by, and for."[15] However duly constituted their office may be, however, their authority can be fully justified only if their de facto legal authority can be suitably grounded from a perspective of equal representative moral authority. It follows from the framework of *SPS*, moreover, that any justifiable legal representative authority must be both justifiable *and accountable* to the citizenry it purports to represent. Fundamental rights of democratic political participation should be understood, therefore, as procedurally necessary to instantiate the accountability relations between citizenry and legal and political officials that are required to justify the latter's legal authority.

This creates a *proper representation requirement* on any justifiable criminal legal process: representative legal authority can be legitimate—can have the *de jure* authority to punish it purports to have—only if its institutions are actually accountable on an ongoing basis to the populations they purport to represent and derive authority from. A second condition follows from the fact that accountability is always fundamentally mutual. This fact has two aspects. First, when we hold someone morally accountable, we necessarily presuppose that they have the capacities of thought and will to hold themselves accountable, and we call on them to do this by exercising these very capacities.[16] Reactive attitudes like moral blame are unlike other critical attitudes in that they come with an implicit RSVP; they call upon the blamed person to take responsibility for their culpable act and hold themselves accountable.[17] Second, in holding others accountable, we are committed to the proposition that they have the same shared representative authority to hold us responsible as well.

Together, these generate a *participation requirement*. Any justifiable criminal process must enable violators, both as charged citizens, and also as those who have been found culpable by a criminal process to participate fully in the accountability process in ways that are called for as equal mutually accountable citizens. We shall argue that, especially clearly under circumstances of structural injustice, those who are directly impacted or injured by criminal violations ought to be recognized as having special moral and epistemic status, in spite of the culpable party's obligation being to the moral community in general, not to individuals in particular.

Before putting these requirements to work in critically assessing the realities of policing, courts, and incarceration in the United States, it will be useful briefly to contrast criminal process as mutual accountability with other rationales for legal punishment that might be confused with it. A mutual accountability rationale differs, first, both from any notion of retaliation and from any purely retributivist view according to which a perpetrator deserves to be harmed proportionately to the harm they have caused others. Deserved suffering plays no essential role in mutual accountability. Restrictions of freedom and mandatory activity may well be necessary, but only insofar as these are needed for the violator to be held, and to hold themselves, accountable, for example, by being brought to appreciate the full meaning and consequences of their actions for others, acknowledging this, and taking steps to repair and to give others the reasonable assurance that they will not commit similar actions again.

That requiring a wrongdoer to suffer harms or costs is inessential to accountability is well illustrated by a remark of Adam Smith's on the implicit goal of reactive attitudes, like blame and resentment, through which we hold people accountable. What "resentment is chiefly intent upon," Smith writes, "is not so much to make" the resented person "feel pain in his turn," as "to make him sensible that the person whom he injured did not deserve to be treated in that manner."[18] Holding others accountable seeks their holding themselves accountable through the (likely painful) realization of the interpersonal significance of what they have done. Criminal processes of mutual accountability seek to enact and restore mutual respect for the dignity of all persons.

An accountability approach to criminal process differs also from any view according to which punishment should express something like society's "revenge" or a humiliating defeat to the criminal that vindicates the victim's value or dignity and annuls a wrongdoer's disrespect.[19]

The accountability approach agrees with Jean Hampton that criminal process should be conceived as an expressive communal response to devaluing disrespect. However, Hampton conceives of this response in terms that seem more appropriate to a culture of honor than to one of accountability: "the most general and accurate definition of punishment is: the experience of defeat at the hands of the victim (either directly or indirectly through a legal authority)"[20] (Hampton 1998: 126).

Accountability theorists agree, of course, that what punishment should express is the moral community's commitment to victims' rights as persons not to be treated in the way they were treated. But it does this not by dishonoring or devaluing the violator in a way that restores the victim's honor or status, but through a process of mutual accountability that expresses equal respect for the enduring equal dignity of victim and violator, and all persons, alike.

It is a basic presupposition of criminal process as mutual accountability that all persons can demand respect for their equal dignity as persons. A criminal charge is always of some form of disrespect, most obviously, for the law, but also for the rights and duties of persons the law enshrines. Just treatment of charged defendants and those found criminally responsible must also be governed by mutual respect, expressing a demand for mutually accountable relations that falls on all citizens alike.

Everyone has the right to expect and trust that their dignity will be respected. When this trust is violated by criminal conduct, part of holding the convicted accountable is to demand that they take responsibility for, and do their part to repair, the breach of trust their actions have occasioned. It may be objected that conviction cannot warrant a demand that the convicted acknowledge their guilt, since they must retain the right to protest their innocence. Nevertheless, a breach of the public trust uncontroversially exists, and even innocent citizens who have been found guilty in accordance with due process can incur responsibilities to do their part in restoring trust and the mutual respect it helps constitute.

Mutual Accountability Punishment vs. American Penal Institutions

We turn now to discussing aspects of contemporary American penal practice in terms of criminal process as mutual accountability, especially as regards its representation and participation requirements. Even on a cursory view, it seems obvious that these standards go systematically unmet and that American penitentiaries are, at best, "warehouse prisons," in which inmates are kept in crowded, tightly controlled environments of humiliation and indignity, force and fear.[21] But further, any discussion here must take as a central focus the racialized character of the explosion of American institutions of policing, confinement, and punishment, discussed as the phenomenon, alternately, of hyperincarceration, (racialized) mass incarceration, and the Prison Industrial Complex.[22] We feel there are strong arguments to be levied against the formal or logical structure of carceral punishment from an accountability framework, but it is in their central role in effecting racial domination that the issues we discuss appear in starkest relief.

It has become well known that African-Americans, notably African-American males, are incarcerated at a much higher rate than other groups. According to the U.S. Department of Justice statistics, although African-Americans represent only 13% of the US male population, 37% of imprisoned males in 2014 were black, almost three times their overall representation.[23] By contrast, white males, who were 63% of the male population in 2014, represented only 32% of incarcerated males.[24] The black/white disparity is even greater among younger offenders. In 2014, black males aged eighteen or nineteen were more than *ten times* more likely to be targeted for imprisonment than similarly aged white males.[25]

It is also well known that in recent decades there has been a significant increase in the number of incarcerated citizens generally. In the last forty years, the United States has seen an approximately 500% increase in its prison population.[26] African-Americans have been disproportionately affected by this increase. According to Todd Clear and Natasha Frost, "growth in incarceration over the period concentrated among young black males from impoverished inner-city neighborhoods."[27] Highlighting continuities between mass incarceration and earlier systems of racial domination, Michelle Alexander's *The New Jim Crow* emphasizes imprisonment's broader marginalizing effects on African-Americans: "Once you're labeled a felon, the old forms of discrimination – employment discrimination, housing discrimination, denial of food stamps and other public benefits, and exclusion from jury service – are suddenly legal".[28]

So far, this just means that mass incarceration has been markedly racialized in its profile and effects. In addition, however, mass incarceration has been and continues to be racializing in more profound senses.

We take the fact that police, courts, and prisons have played a central role not only in widening and deepening racial social, political, and economic inequality and injustice, but also in helping to construct oppressive racial social categories to have been well established by generations of activists and scholars.

To begin with, it is impossible adequately to understand contemporary mass incarceration without placing it in the context of the history of slavery, resistance to what DuBois called "black reconstruction," white terror, lynchings, and Jim Crow, the "Great Migration" of black laborers to northern industrial cities, where they faced housing segregation, and the creation of what Kenneth Clark called "dark ghettos," and the "war on poverty" and its aftermath: the "war on drugs" and the "war on crime," along with the welfare "reform" of the Clinton Administration in the 1990s.[29] Against this background, the mass incarceration of the past forty years can be seen to have been not just racial statistically and by effect, but as part and parcel of forms of white supremacy in this country that continually construct and reconstruct oppressive racial social categories.

Loïc Wacquant distinguishes four "peculiar institutions" that "have successively operated to define, confine, and control African-Americans in the history of the United States."[30] Beginning with chattel slavery, which violently expropriated "unfree, fixed labor," Wacquant adds: second, the formally "free" but nonetheless "fixed labor" of the sharecropping, Jim Crow south; third, the "free mobile labor" of blacks as "menial workers" confined to the dark ghettos of the industrial north; and fourth "the fixed surplus labor" of "hyperghetto and prison" in an increasingly de-industrialized America in which the dominant racial types for African-Americans from the dark ghetto are "welfare recipient and criminal."[31] A historical line can be traced from slavery in the antebellum South, through periodic imprisonment and forced return to labor on the plantation with the Black Codes,[32] through Jim Crow, to exclusionary spatial confinement in deindustrializing northern urban centers, and ultimately, to mass incarceration, each marked and enforced by a particular regime of gratuitous terroristic violence.

Obviously, slavery is a form of social domination that is directly antithetical to mutual accountability. The enslavement of Africans kidnapped and brought to the Colonies was rationalized, indeed, by the idea that enslaved peoples were not fully human, in the European imperialist image, and thereby lacked features of persons on which equal rights, and by corollary mutual accountability, depend. Exclusion from the moral community of mutually accountable equals was thus built into the American concept of race from the start; indeed, this exclusion is precisely what racial ideologies were meant to bring about, ad hoc, and justify, post hoc. In the American context, ascriptive characteristics like complexion, African heritage, and others functioned as social markers that one was unfit for moral community. To the extent that continuities in the structure, dynamics, and effects of contemporary mass incarceration link it directly to historical forms of domination originating in the transatlantic slave trade and chattel slavery through a coherently white supremacist historical progression, then, it follows that it must be deeply incompatible with any criminal process that is modeled on mutual accountability.

Mobilizing criminal law to marginalize and exploit African-Americans has a long history. Slavery itself, of course, was the law in the antebellum south, not only in the sense that slavery was legal, but also because it was coercively upheld by criminal codes and legal authorities, for example, by the Fugitive Slave Law. It is, however, in the post-Reconstruction south that a more specific ideological attachment of blackness to criminality emerged in order to undermine racial progress and recapture black labor following emancipation. Although the unmediated racial policies of the Black Codes were made illegal by the Thirteenth Amendment and the Civil Rights Act of 1866, as an indefensible "badge of slavery,"[33] the practice of "convict leasing" exploited a loophole in the Thirteenth Amendment that allowed for the criminally incarcerated to be treated like slaves. A high demand for labor found itself satiated by effective re-enslavement through convict leasing, rationalized this time not by strictly dehumanizing racial ideologies, but by new targeted modes of surveillance, policing, and criminalization, which fed and facilitated the seamless integration of "[a]ssumptions of Black criminality … into collective common sense of what constituted 'the Negro.'"[34]

Khalil Gibran Muhammad's *The Condemnation of Blackness* draws out the history of "racial criminalization: the stigmatization of crime as 'black' and the masking of crime among whites as individual failure."[35] "The practice of linking crime to blacks, as a racial group, but not whites," he writes, "reinforced and reproduced racial inequality" in the service of producing a stable, exploitable workforce.[36] In examining the production by post-Reconstruction penal institutions of racialized crime and incarceration statistics, and their constant repetition in the press,

Muhammad emphasizes the "ideological currency of black criminality," as a political tool effecting racial subordination.[37]

While never dormant, this enduring racial ideology played a decisive role in the development of new forms of class and racial exploitation and expropriation in the second half of the Twentieth Century. As Elizabeth Hinton has shown, policy at the federal level addressing the urban unrest of the 1960s, and social and economic problems that had ignited it, shifted from a "war on poverty" to a "war on crime."[38] African-American communities found themselves the object of massive federal investment in state and local law enforcement that led to the "war on crime" effectively becoming a "war on the black community."[39] Hinton notes that even any legislative influence of the Kerner Commission's report, which actually "endorse[d] the ongoing merger of social welfare and crime control programs as the hallmark of federal urban policy," hardly proved racially progressive since the Commission "took for granted the guiding principle of domestic urban policy in the 1960s: that black community pathology caused poverty and crime."[40] And further, it was the report, not of the Kerner Commission, but of the 1965 Crime Commission, that laid the material groundwork for the "revolution in American law enforcement."[41]

The reproduction of racialized ideology enacted in the Johnson-era Safe Streets Act, moreover, further functioned to draw an imaginary line—often referred to as "thin" and "blue"—demarcating crime victims and law enforcement, and by way of ideological association, upright, law-abiding, and deserving citizens who ought to stand with them, against criminal threats to social peace and order. As Jonathan Simon argues, "the primary political legacy of the Safe Streets Act is to have shaped, in defining ways, the logic of representation that exists today across the political spectrum, at both the federal and state levels.[42] ... Simply put, to be for the people, legislators must be for victims and law enforcement, and thus they must never be for (or capable of being portrayed as being for) criminals or prisoners as individuals or as a class."[43]

Similarly, Loïc Wacquant emphasizes that the "peculiar institutions" he identifies—slavery, Jim Crow south, northern ghetto, and mass incarceration—must be understood as "race making," constructing a racialized binary opposition: a subordinate/alien/criminal threat to "law-abiding" people. These institutions "do not simply *process* an ethnoracial division that would somehow exist outside of and independently from them. Rather, each *produces* (or co-produces) this division (anew) out of inherited demarcations and disparities of group power and inscribes it at every epoch in a distinctive constellation of material and symbolic forms."[44] "The prison, and the criminal justice system more broadly," he writes, "contribute to the ongoing *reconstruction of the 'imagined community' of Americans* around the polar opposition between praiseworthy 'working families'—implicitly white, suburban, and deserving – and the despicable 'underclass' of criminals, loafers, and leeches."[45] "The line that divides them," Wacquant concludes, "is increasingly being drawn, materially and symbolically, by the prison."[46]

Contemporary mass incarceration thus both carries forward a history of racial oppression anchored in the transatlantic slave trade and chattel slavery *and* performs homologous functional processes as its legacy institutions: constructing the very lines of demarcation along which racial and other social groups are either excluded, marginalized, and oppressed, on the one hand, or, on the other, unduly benefitted and protected from structural violence. American penal institutions, then, clearly must fail to meet a proper representation requirement. State actors administering this criminal process not only fail to represent or be accountable to vast swaths of the moral community, including both alleged perpetrators and victims broadly construed; their actions actively *extend* policies and practices that explicitly exclude citizens from the possibility of representation and recognized membership or equal participation in the moral community. American carceral institutions are not merely unaccountable to the communities from which their purported authority derives; they actively undermine the conditions on which accountability to citizens rests.

To avoid a point of possible confusion, we clarify here that the *proper representation requirement* should be read with an emphasis on '*proper*'—at issue is whether institutional officials accountably discharge their rights and responsibilities as agents of legal authority. Although the requirement arguably mandates some form of representationalist politics as a necessary condition, reflecting the populations by whose authority institutions purport to act, say, by standards of proportional demographic representation, is insufficient. Mere representational parity, particularly where purely social factors like race and gender are emphasized over economic factors, is in no way guaranteed to ameliorate entrenched injustices. As Keeanga-Yamahtta Taylor and others have noted, the ascension of a black elite class into the halls of government has done little to change the lives of or deliver justice for impoverished,

African-American communities[47] (Taylor 2016). The electoralist politics of putting "black faces in high places" can serve more readily to deflect attention from issues of structural racial inequality, injustice, and state violence than to address them. Indeed, as James Forman, Jr. argues in *Locking Up Our Own*, black urban politicians and prominent community leaders may have played an important role in furthering mass incarceration themselves.[48]

By this point, we take the point to be well illustrated that, far from accountably representing the shared moral authority of a people, the institutions of police, courts, and prisons in the United States have subjected targeted populations to wanton marginalizing violence and exploitation. Moreover, increasing carcerality interacts with increasing inequality and marginalization in toxic ways. Increasing the capacity of punitive institutions to surveil, detain, confine, sanction, and punish individuals will reliably cause discriminatory punishment, especially in unequal societies. Inequalities in social power modulate the vulnerability of individuals and communities to carceral power. And where carceral regimes rub up against sensibilities of reasonable or appropriate response, these will tend to cause differential outcomes, distributed according to racialized sensibilities. Carceral regimes will always deepen inequality, since they will inevitably be leveraged against those who are seen as more readily punishable, exploitable, expropriable, expendable, and, finally, disposable. Far from being well placed to restore social trust in cases where the violation of the dignity of individuals or communities demands that violators be held responsible, institutions of criminal punishment are just those institutions that have themselves been responsible for some of the most heinous violations of universal human dignity.

Finally, if the proper representation requirement issues a clear indictment of contemporary American penal practices, it remains to ask how these practices fare with respect to the participation requirement. Here too, mutual accountability is systematically undermined, both for the individuals swept up by penal and policing institutions and for those their alleged criminal activity must directly involves. Recall that the participation requirement reflects the importance, on the one hand, of violators holding themselves to account, taking up an agential relation to their conduct and taking responsibility for it. On the other, participation requires that victims, construed broadly to include those who have incurred either direct harm or larger breaches or breakdown of social trust, take a central role in determining what course of action might actually effect accountability and whether or not appointed courses of action have realized reparative resolution.

We will discuss more substantively how such a requirement might be activated in the final section, but for now we note the role violators and victims play in the American penal system. Currently, penal institutions wield singular, unrivalled authority over criminal processes; victims and violators have opportunity to give testimony, to plead, to argue, and so on, but not to enter into relations of mutual accountability with state institutions.

It is hardly surprising that criminal process as mutual accountability demands a different kind of participation from non-institutional actors than those for which the American system currently makes room. Even theories of punishment emphasizing rehabilitation have traditionally done so in a prescriptive, paternalist way, in which treatment is meted out as a curative for the incarcerated's pathological criminal tendencies. Even if rehabilitative processes envision the incarcerated coming to regain agency over their life and decisions, it is generally assumed that, at the outset, criminal offenders lack such agency, thus denying an assumption on which mutual accountability depends.

Positive Steps Toward Criminal Process as Mutual Accountability

It is clear that American carceral institutions, both in their formal structure and in their real, brutal practice, are inimical to any justifiable criminal process. An abstract account of legitimacy conditions, however, is of little use if it can offer nothing to guide efforts to deliver transitional justice in response to the non-ideal, deeply unjust conditions we confront.

Questions of transitional justice raise complicated issues in their own right that we cannot pretend to treat properly. But we can suggest what an accountability frame might offer to attempts to address such issues. Darwall 2006, 2007, 2010, and 2013 discuss the conceptual structure of accountability relations. It is necessary now to consider what would actually be involved in realizing or practically applying these relations. How might mutual recognition of the standing to make and hold others answerable to legitimate claims and demands meaningfully inform the pursuit of criminal justice in patently unjust contemporary contexts? How can there be anything approaching criminal process as mutual accountability in the current American context?

It is clear, as Tommie Shelby and Gary Watson, among many others, have argued, that the state and institutions responsible for mass incarceration have lost any standing to hold citizens that their marginalizing policies target accountable for criminal violations, or, indeed, to expect their obedience more generally (Shelby 2016: 228–251; Watson 2015). But this does not vacate the necessity that culpable individuals be held responsible for the wrongs they commit; nor does it address the need to hold state institutions responsible for creating the structural conditions that foment subjective violence. While state institutions lack standing to punish, they are not freed of the responsibility to support the maintenance of social peace and security and for supporting mutual accountability more generally.

One proposal might be that in cases where these special considerations obtain to ensure more community control over the punitive apparatus. Where institutional actors have abused the legal authority to represent "the people" in criminal proceedings, this proposal would focus on reducing the representational gap between the institution and marginalized communities and thus move the institution toward better representation of "the people."[49]

Unlike private law, which seeks personal accountability of obligor to obligee, criminal law seeks public accountability to the moral community, as instantiated in a "people," through state institutions vested with the "people's" authority. In this case, however, state institutions and officials have lost the standing to hold citizens accountable for the relevant criminal conduct. Here members of marginalized urban communities have a better claim to stand in "the people's" shoes for purposes of public accountability. There are two reasons for this. First, members of these communities both bear, and have the best epistemic position to judge, the costs and risks of criminal conduct within these communities. And second, they have inherited the same history of racializing oppression as those they would be judging and so have not, unlike state actors, lost the representative authority to hold their fellows accountable.

Were these citizens to take "the people's" position in criminal proceedings, they would not be exercising an individual authority they might have as the victims of violations of bipolar obligations owed to them. They would be concerned rather with criminal responsibility, standing in for "the people," since they have the best claim to represent the moral community owing to their own relation to our country's racial oppression and their epistemic position to judge the risks and costs of the relevant criminal conduct

In concrete terms, this might involve policies requiring that jury selection reflect, in rigorous demographic and geographic terms, those involved in the criminal action and the community where it occurred. It should also include a high degree of community oversight over police protocols and procedures, as well as over prosecutorial discretion and judicial sentencing guidelines. This type of community control, if substantively implemented, might greatly impact justice outcomes in progressive ways. We are skeptical that merely representationalist reforms will address the systematic injustices of the American carceral system if they are not combined with a broader transformation of the structure of punitive institutions themselves.

In our discussion of the failure of proper representation, we noted that punitive institutions do not merely fail to accountably represent the interests of different populations; they actively construct the social differentiation by means of which social exclusion is itself made possible. It follows, accordingly, that in order to accountably represent the population from which its authority derives, punitive institutions must be re-envisioned so that they do not effect the kind of social differentiation that marks violators as ineligible for political participation, as excludable from social activity, as disposable, to be locked away, lost to the 'imagined community' that is supposedly secured against the threat they pose. Calling this position "abolitionist" seems, to us, both natural and appropriate. It seeks to abolish, as a matter of urgent necessity, the many aspects of contemporary American penal practice that, as we have noted, militate against mutual accountability

An abolitionist orientation declines to treat as legitimate institutional practices that are not, and makes institutions answerable for their abuses—both by organizing campaigns to reject particular cases of abuse, and developing alternatives that pose a direct challenge to ideologies of the necessity of incarceration. This orientation takes mutual accountability seriously by imagining and advocating for practices that do not require modes of surveillance, detention, and vulnerability to brutal state violence that violate human dignity, but rather treat individuals as capable of the mutual respect that dignity demands.

Institutional transformation is made practicable through the concept of the "non-reformist reform," articulated by Ruth Gilmore as that which "does not extend the life or the scope of the prison industrial complex."[50] Insofar as policies reforming, say, jury selection do not mandate the preservation of existing institutional structures, which would merely offer mass incarceration a new veneer of legitimacy, but begin to empower local communities to guide more fundamental transformations to criminal codes, sentencing guidelines, and the like, such reforms would clearly qualify as those that move criminal process toward achieving accountability and real legitimacy.[51] What is essential, in any case, is that the commitment to realizing accountability effect practical movements toward justice while refusing to accept the putative legitimacy of unaccountable institutions.

It should not be surprising that the functions and purview of penal institutions must shift in the process. For one thing, the current structure of these institutions is both historically contingent and often ill fitted to the tasks they are assigned. Alex Vitale identifies the "mission creep" by which hyper-militarized SWAT units have come to be used in increasingly quotidian enforcement and surveillance operations—inevitably making citizens vulnerable to the violently destructive capacity of their outsized armaments.[52] In response to welfare state retrenchment, police have come to stand in as the only remaining state response to a far too broad range of social needs.[53] Similarly, Gilmore identifies "the expanding use of prisons as catchall solutions to social problems."[54] And Jackie Wang suggests that, in the demise of entitlement programs of the New Deal and Johnson's Great Society, perhaps, "the only remaining social entitlement program ... is the entitlement of *security*," delivered at whatever human cost, borne by those left behind by the welfare state's collapse.[55] "The first step" in response, Angela Davis points out, is to "let go of the desire to discover one single alternative system of punishment that would occupy the same footprint as the prison system."[56]

An alternative system that meets the participation requirement would at the very least look very different from the legal system we now employ. As discussed above, the agential participation of violators in taking responsibility, on the one hand, and victims helping to determine what actions on violators' part constitute accountability, on the other, are necessary features of a mutual accountability criminal process, along with, more to the point, facilitated by, the presence of representatives of the wider community. Note that a tripartite process of this kind does not shift the governing authority in play from representative to the individual authority of victims holding violators accountable, as is operative in private law. Rather, the parties to the violation have a special epistemic and moral relation to it, and thus are uniquely placed to determine what would restore the safety and trust the violation undermined; determining the culpability of the violation requires representative legal authority to hold the violator responsible through whatever reparative actions the victims and violators together determine.

Shifting the material realities that preclude justice and accountability will primarily be achieved, however, not through theorizing or intellectual labor, but through work on the ground. Abolitionist organizing efforts rightly focus on developing models and processes of seeking and delivering accountability in response to violence and other wrongs. A variety of related models have been developed, organized under categories of restorative practices, community accountability, and transformative justice. These practices vary relative to the particular community and purpose for which they were created. But they are consistent in addressing the root causes, wider sets of relationships, histories, and harms, and broader social and political contexts of the entrenched patterns of violence and abuse they seek proactively to uproot, rather than reinforce through reductive, punitive reaction.[57]

Some critics dismiss calls for abolition as overly idealistic, as divorced from reality and unlikely to win public support. By moving the discussion into a theoretical register, such dismissals divert attention from the actual work and material gains of abolitionist organizing. More importantly, as longtime movement leader Mariame Kaba and others argue, they "misunderstand how social change occurs." Throughout history, "our hubristic expectations of what is possible in a given temporal horizon are chastened" by real accomplishments that prove these speculative assessments wrong.[58] Indeed, this pattern of inaccurate assessments of political possibility mirrors what Kristie Dotson describes as a combination of ineffective imagination, insufficient structural options, and an inadequate lexicon of permissibility[59] that together generate the "the kind of epistemic and structural inertia that underwrites carceral logics in the first place."[60]

We follow recent work by Elizabeth Anderson and Sally Haslanger in supporting activists, organizers, and frontline community members countering this inertia and resisting the ongoing violence and marginalization effected by mass incarceration in the United States not only in practical action but also in the development of knowledge—empirical, theoretical, and moral—of these institutions and of alternatives to them.[61] To clarify what seems to be an often-misread quotation from Frederick Douglass, that "power concedes nothing without a demand," we remind readers that Douglass did not mean "demand" merely as an articulation of an intellectual position, but as the force with which such a position is made impossible to ignore. The preceding sentence of Douglass's address reads: "This struggle may be a moral one, or it may be a physical one, and it may be both moral and physical, but it must be a struggle."[62]

Notes

1. Darwall, Stephen. 2007. Law and the Second-Person Standpoint. *Loyola of Los Angeles Law Review* 40: 891–910. Reprinted in Darwall, Stephen. 2013. *Morality, Authority, and Law: Essays in Second-Personal Ethics I.* Oxford: Oxford University Press.
2. Darwall, Stephen. 2006. *The Second-Person Standpoint*: Morality, *Respect, and Accountability.* Cambridge, MA: Harvard University Press, and Darwall, Stephen. 2007.
3. Darwall, Stephen. 2010. Justice and Retaliation. *Philosophical Papers* 39: 315–341. Reprinted in Darwall, Stephen. 2013. *Morality, Authority, and Law: Essays in Second-Personal Ethics I.* Oxford: Oxford University Press.
4. Thompson, Michael. What Is It to Wrong Someone? A Puzzle About Justice. In *Reason and Value: Themes from the Philosophy of Joseph Raz*, eds., R. Jay Wallace, Philip Pettit, Samuel Scheffler, and Michael Smith. Oxford: Oxford University Press.
5. Darwall, Stephen. 2010. Justice and Retaliation. *Philosophical Papers* 39: 315–341. Reprinted in Darwall, Stephen. 2013. *Morality, Authority, and Law: Essays in Second-Personal Ethics I.* Oxford: Oxford University Press.
6. Coleman, Jules L. and Jody Kraus. 1986. Rethinking the Theory of Legal Rights. *Yale Law Journal* 95: 1335–1371. Coleman and Kraus term these cases where rights "infringed".
7. Hohfeld, Wesley Newcomb. 1923. *Fundamental Legal Conceptions*, ed. Walter Wheeler Cook. New Haven, CT: Yale University Press.
8. There is an important analytical distinction between an obligation's being owed to each and every *individual* person and an obligation period, which involves accountability to any (every) person, but not as the individual person they are, rather as representative persons.
9. Darwall, Stephen. 2016. Making the Hard Problem of Moral Normativity Easier. In *Weighing Reasons*, eds. Errol Lord and Barry Maguire, 257–278. Oxford: Oxford University Press.
10. Strawson, P. F. 1968. Freedom and Resentment. In his *Studies in the Philosophy of Thought and Action.* London: Oxford University Press; Darwall, Stephen. 2006. Blame is an instance of what Strawson called an "impersonal" attitude. (Strawson' example is 'indignation'.) 'Impartial'

is probably a preferable term, since 'impersonal' suggests an observer's third-personal perspective, whereas it is important to Strawson's argument that reactive attitudes all involve a second-personal (he says, "interpersonal") perspective of implicit address.

11. Thus Hopkins (Hopkins, Ann. 1988. *Mens Rea* and the Right to Trial by Jury. *California Law Review* 76: 391–420) argues that the Sixth Amendment "requires a jury finding of moral blameworthiness as a prerequisite to criminal punishment" (391). Clearly, for jurors to assess this question they must consider it with the same impartiality they aspire to in determining guilt or innocence.
12. Hart, H. L. A. 1961. *The Concept of Law*. Oxford: Clarendon Press, 6–8.
13. Again, it does not follow from the fact that an act violates some society's criminal law that it is morally wrong. Rather, in making something a matter of criminal law, the society is presupposing that the act would be morally wrong.
14. Darwall and Darwall (Darwall, Stephen, and Julian Darwall. 2012. Civil Recourse as Mutual Accountability. *Florida State University Law Review* 39: 17–41. Reprinted in Darwall, Stephen. 2013. *Morality, Authority, and Law: Essays in Second-Personal Ethics I*. Oxford: Oxford University Press.) makes a related claim about tort law, viz., that it should be theorized in terms of the mutual accountability of obligee and obligor and their respective *individual* authorities.
15. The reference, of course, is to Lincoln's Gettysburg Address.
16. This is an aspect of what Darwall (Darwall, Stephen. 2006) calls "Pufendorf's Point." On its application to the theory of punishment, see Yaffe, Gideon. 2011. Prevention and Imminence: Pre-punishment and Actuality. *San Diego Law Review* 48: 1205–1228.
17. Darwall, Stephen. 2006.
18. Smith, Adam. 1982. *The Theory of Moral Sentiments*. Indianapolis: Liberty Classics, 95–96.
19. Feinberg, Joel. 1970. The Expressive Theory of Punishment, in his *Doing and Deserving*. Princeton, NJ: Princeton University Press, 100–101; Hampton, Jean. 1998. The Retributive Idea. In *Forgiveness and Mercy*, eds. Jeffrie G. Murphy and Jean Hampton. Cambridge: Cambridge University Press.
20. Hampton, Jean. 1998.
21. Irwin, John. 2004. *The Warehouse Prison: Disposal of the New Dangerous Class*. Oxford: Oxford University Press.
22. Wacquant, Loïc. 2010. Class, Race, and Hyperincarceration in Revanchist America. *Daedelus* 139: 74–90; Bobo, Lawrence D. and Victor Thompson. 2010. Racializing Mass Incarceration: Poverty, Prejudice, and Punishment. In *Doing Race: 21 Essays for the 21st Century*, eds. Hazel

Markus and Paul Moya. New York, NY: W. W. Norton & Co.; Shelby, Tommie. 2016. *Dark Ghettos.* Cambridge, MA: Harvard University Press, 209–216; Davis, Angela Y. 2003. *Are Prisons Obsolete?* New York, NY: Seven Stories Press; Gilmore, Ruth Wilson. 2007. *Golden Gulag: Prisons, Surplus, Crisis, and Opposition in Globalizing California.* Berkeley, CA: University of California Press.

23. Shelby, Tommie. 2016, 209; Carson, E. Ann. 2015. Prisoners in 2014. *Bureau of Justice Statistics.* https://www.bjs.gov/content/pub/pdf/p14.pdf.
24. Shelby, Tommie. 2016, 209; Carson, E. Ann. 2015.
25. Carson, E. Ann. 2015.
26. 2017. Trends in U.S. Corrections. *The Sentencing Project.* https://sentencingproject.org/wp-content/uploads/2016/01/Trends-in-US-Corrections.pdf.
27. Clear, Todd R. and Natasha A. Frost. 2013. *The Punishment Imperative.* New York, NY: New York University Press, 26.
28. Alexander, Michelle. 2010. *Mass Incarceration in the Age of Color-Blindness.* New York, NY: The New Press, 2.
29. Dubois, W. E. B. 2014. *Black Reconstruction in America*, ed. Henry Louis Gates. New York, NY: Oxford University Press; Clark, Kenneth B. 1967. *Dark Ghetto: Dilemmas of Social Power*, 2nd ed. Middletown, CT: Wesleyan University Press; Alexander, Michelle. 2010; Hinton, Elizabeth. 2016. *From the War on Poverty to the War on Crime: The Making of Mass Incarceration in America.* Cambridge, MA: Harvard University Press; and Shelby, Tommie. 2016.
30. Wacquant, Loïc. 2002. From Slavery to Mass Incarceration: Rethinking the 'Race Question' in the United States. *New Left Review* 13, 41.
31. Wacquant, Loïc. 2002, 13, 42.
32. Davis, Angela Y. 2003.
33. This phrase comes from the Supreme Court's decisions in the 1883 *Civil Rights Cases.*
34. Taylor, Keeanga Yamahtta. 2016. *From #BlackLivesMatter to Black Liberation.* Chicago, IL: Haymarket Books, 111.
35. Muhammad, Khalil Gibran. 2010. *The Condemnation of Blackness: Race, Crime, and the Making of Urban America.* Cambridge, MA: Harvard University Press, 3.
36. Muhammad, Khalil Gibran. 2010, 3.
37. Muhammad, Khalil Gibran. 2010, 3.
38. Hinton, Elizabeth. 2016a. *From the War on Poverty to the War on Crime: The Making of Mass Incarceration in America.* Cambridge, MA: Harvard University Press.

39. Hinton, Elizabeth. 2016b. From 'War on Crime' to War on the Black Community: The Enduring Impact of President Johnson's Crime Commission. *Boston Review*, June 21, 2016. http://bostonreview.net/us/elizabeth-hinton-kerner-commission-crime-commission.
40. Hinton, Elizabeth. 2016b.
41. Hinton, Elizabeth. 2016b.
42. Simon, Jonathan. 2007. *Governing Through Crime: How the War on Crime Transformed American Democracy and Created a Culture of Fear*. New York, NY: Oxford University Press, 100.
43. Simon, Jonathan. 2007, 100.
44. Wacquant, Loïc. 2002, 13, 54.
45. Wacquant, Loïc. 2002, 58, 60.
46. Wacquant, Loïc. 2010, 60. Recent work, for example by Jackie Wang, adds subtlety to Wacquant's binary model, explaining how criminalization, predatory lending, and parasitic governance are used to mark individuals, communities, and neighborhoods as exploitable workers, expropriable populations, and lootable spaces along a carceral continuum (Wang, Jackie. 2018. *Carceral Capitalism*. South Pasadena, CA: Semiotext(e)).
47. Taylor, Keeanga Yamahtta. 2016. *From #BlackLivesMatter to Black Liberation*. Chicago, IL: Haymarket Books.
48. Forman, James Jr. 2017. *Locking Up Our Own*. New York, NY: Farrar, Straus and Giroux. But note, as Forman does, that although the black middle class and leadership did, in the cases he discusses, ask for tougher responses to crime, these requests were made as part of a broader, comprehensive plan, the rest of which was never delivered.
49. We emphasize that we are only proposing this measure of local control for the special circumstances we are concerned with here.
50. Interview at https://www.youtube.com/watch?v=39Axc3FIu9A.
51. Obviously, it would be important to assure rights of political participation, including to participate in juries, to the formerly convicted. More representative juries would not only have greater epistemic authority to judge the particulars of cases, but, through the power of jury nullification, could also help shape a shared sense of what kinds of acts ought, and ought not, to be chargeable offenses.
52. Most gruesomely so in the case of the killing of Aiyana Stanley Jones in a no-knock SWAT attempt to serve a warrant.
53. Vitale, Alex. 2017. *The End of Policing*. Brooklyn, NY: Verso Books.
54. Gilmore, Ruth Wilson, 5.
55. Wang, Jackie. 2018, 83.
56. Davis, Angela Y. Davis. 2003, 106.

57. Incite! a national organization supporting grassroots and direct action responses to violence and abuse, explains community accountability as comprising four component axes: the development of general values and practices resisting oppression and encouraging safety and accountability; implementation processes through which community members engaging in abusive behavior can take account of and transform that behavior; provision of safety and support that respects the self-determination of targeted community members; and action to transform the broader political conditions that reinforce oppression and violence (Incite! 2014).
58. Berger, Dan, Mariame Kaba, and David Stein. 2017. What Abolitionists Do. *Jacobin Magazine*. https://www.jacobinmag.com/2017/08/prison-abolition-reform-mass-incarceration.
59. "Lexicon of permissibility" is meant to refer to the range of actions that strike an agent as permissible in a given situation.
60. Dotson, Kristie. 2017. Beyond the Now: Epistemic Oppression and Carceral Common Sense. Conference presentation at *Philosophy and Mass Incarceration*, Yale University, February 2017.
61. Anderson, Elizabeth. 2016. The Social Epistemology of Morality: Learning from the Forgotten History of the Abolition of Slavery. In *The Epistemic Life of Groups: Essays in Collective Epistemology* eds. Miranda Fricker and Michael Brady; Haslanger, Sally. 2017. *Critical Theory and Practice* (The 2015 Spinoza Lectures (booklet)). Amsterdam: Koninklijke Van Gorcum.
62. Douglass. 1999, 367.

Bibliography

Alexander, Michelle. (2010). *Mass Incarceration in the Age of Color-Blindness.* New York, NY: The New Press.

Anderson, Elizabeth. (2016). "The Social Epistemology of Morality: Learning from the Forgotten History of the Abolition of Slavery," in Miranda Fricker and Michael Brady, eds., *The Epistemic Life of Groups: Essays in Collective Epistemology.* Oxford: Oxford University Press

Berger, Dan, Mariame Kaba, and David Stein. (2017). "What Abolitionists Do." *Jacobin Magazine.* https://www.jacobinmag.com/2017/08/prison-abolition-reform-mass-incarceration.

Bobo, Lawrence D, and Victor Thompson. (2010). "Racializing Mass Incarceration: Poverty, Prejudice, and Punishment," in Hazel Markus and Paul Moya, eds., *Doing Race: 21 Essays for the 21st Century.* New York, NY: W. W. Norton & Co.

Butterfield, Fox. (2002). "Study Finds Big Increase in Black Men as Inmates Since 1980," *The New York Times*, August 28, 2002. https://www.nytimes.

com/2002/08/28/us/study-finds-big-increase-in-black-men-as-inmates-since-1980.html.

Carson, E. Ann. (2015). "Prisoners in 2014," *Bureau of Justice Statistics*. https://www.bjs.gov/content/pub/pdf/p14.pdf.

Clark, Kenneth B. (1967). *Dark Ghetto: Dilemmas of Social Power*, 2nd ed., William Julius Wilson, ed. Middletown, CT: Wesleyan University Press.

Clear, Todd R., and Natasha A. Frost. (2013). *The Punishment Imperative*. New York, NY: New York University Press.

Coleman, Jules L., and Jody Kraus. (1986). "Rethinking the Theory of Legal Rights," *Yale Law Journal* 95: 1335–1371.

Darwall, Stephen. (2006). *The Second-Person Standpoint: Morality, Respect, and Accountability*. Cambridge, MA: Harvard University Press.

Darwall, Stephen. (2007). "Law and the Second-Person Standpoint," *Loyola of Los Angeles Law Review* 40: 891–910. Reprinted in Darwall 2013a.

Darwall, Stephen. (2010). "Justice and Retaliation," *Philosophical Papers* 39: 315–341. Reprinted in Darwall 2013.

Darwall, Stephen. (2012). "Bipolar Obligation," in Russ Shafer-Landau, ed., *Oxford Studies in Metaethics*. Oxford: Oxford University Press. Reprinted in Darwall 2013.

Darwall, Stephen. (2013). *Morality, Authority, and Law: Essays in Second-Personal Ethics I*. Oxford: Oxford University Press.

Darwall, Stephen. (2016). "Making the Hard Problem of Moral Normativity Easier," in Errol Lord and Barry Maguire, eds. *Weighing Reasons*, pp. 257–278. Oxford: Oxford University Press.

Darwall, Stephen, and Julian Darwall. (2012). "Civil Recourse as Mutual Accountability," *Florida State University Law Review* 39: 17–41. Reprinted in Darwall 2013.

Davis, Angela Y. Davis. (2003). *Are Prisons Obsolete?* New York, NY: Seven Stories Press.

Dotson, Kristie. (2017, February). "Beyond the Now: Epistemic Oppression and Carceral Common Sense." Conference presentation at *Philosophy and Mass Incarceration*, Yale University.

Douglass, Frederick. (1999). *Frederick Douglass: Selected Speeches and Writings*, ed. Philip S. Foner. Chicago, IL: Lawrence Hill Books.

Dubois, W. E. B. (2014). *Black Reconstruction in America*, ed. Henry Louis Gates. New York, NY: Oxford University Press.

Feinberg, Joel. (1970). "The Expressive Theory of Punishment," in *Doing and Deserving*. Princeton, NJ: Princeton University Press.

Forman, James Jr. (2017). *Locking Up Our Own*. New York, NY: Farrar, Straus and Giroux.

Gilmore, Ruth Wilson. (2007). *Golden Gulag: Prisons, Surplus, Crisis, and Opposition in Globalizing California*. Berkeley, CA: University of California Press.

Hampton, Jean. (1998). "The Retributive Idea," in Jeffrie G. Murphy and Jean Hampton. *Forgiveness and Mercy*. Cambridge: Cambridge University Press.

Hart, H. L. A. (1961). *The Concept of Law*. Oxford: Clarendon Press.

Haslanger, Sally. (2017). *Critical Theory and Practice* (The 2015 Spinoza Lectures (booklet)). Amsterdam: Koninklijke Van Gorcum.

Hinton, Elizabeth. (2016a). *From the War on Poverty to the War on Crime: The Making of Mass Incarceration in America*. Cambridge, MA: Harvard University Press.

Hinton, Elizabeth. (2016b). "From 'War on Crime' to War on the Black Community: the Enduring Impact of President Johnson's Crime Commission," *Boston Review*, June 21, 2016. http://bostonreview.net/us/elizabeth-hinton-kerner-commission-crime-commission.

Hohfeld, Wesley Newcomb. (1923). *Fundamental Legal Conceptions*, ed. Walter Wheeler Cook. New Haven, CT: Yale University Press.

Hopkins, Ann. (1988). "*Mens Rea* and the Right to Trial by Jury," *California Law Review* 76: 391–420.

Incite! Women, Gender Non-Conforming, and Trans people of Color*. (2014). "Community Accountability: How Do We Address Violence within Our Communities?" http://www.incite-national.org/page/community-accountability. Accessed 4.18.18.

Irwin, John. (2004). *The Warehouse Prison: Disposal of the New Dangerous Class*. Oxford: Oxford University Press.

Muhammad, Khalil Gibran. (2010). *The Condemnation of Blackness: Race, Crime, and the Making of Urban America*. Cambridge, MA: Harvard University Press.

Shelby, Tommie. (2016). *Dark Ghettos*. Cambridge, MA: Harvard University Press.

Simon, Jonathan. (2007). *Governing Through Crime: How the War on Crime Transformed American Democracy and Created a Culture of Fear*. New York, NY: Oxford University Press.

Smith, Adam. (1982). *The Theory of Moral Sentiments*, eds. D. D. Raphael and A. L. MacFie. Indianapolis: LibertyClassics.

Strawson, P. F. (1968). "Freedom and Resentment," in *Studies in the Philosophy of Thought and Action*. London: Oxford University Press.

Tadros, Victor. (2009). "Poverty and Criminal Responsibility," *Journal of Value Inquiry* 43: 391–413.

Taylor, Keeanga Yamahtta. (2016). *From #BlackLivesMatter to Black Liberation*. Chicago, IL: Haymarket Books.

Thompson, Michael. (2004). "What Is It To Wrong Someone?: A :Puzzle About Justice," in *Reason and Value: Themes from the Philosophy of Joseph Raz*, eds., R. Jay Wallace, Philip Pettit, Samuel Scheffler, and Michael Smith. Oxford: Oxford University Press.

Vitale, Alex. (2017). *The End of Policing*. Brooklyn, NY: Verso Books.
Wacquant, Loïc. (2002). "From Slavery to Mass Incarceration: Rethinking the 'Race Question' in the United States," *New Left Review* 13: 41–60.
Wacquant, Loïc. (2010). "Class, Race, and Hyperincarceration in Revanchist America," *Daedelus* 139: 74–90.
Wang, Jackie. (2018). *Carceral Capitalism*. South Pasadena, CA: Semiotext(e).
Watson, Gary. (2015). "A Moral Predicament in the Criminal Law," *Inquiry* 58: 168–188.
Yaffe, Gideon. (2011). "Prevention and Imminence: Pre-punishment and Actuality," *San Diego Law Review* 48: 1205–1228.

Index

M. Gardner and M. Weber (eds.), *The Ethics of Policing and Imprisonment*, Palgrave Studies in Ethics and Public Policy,
https://doi.org/10.1007/978-3-319-97770-6